BEYOND THE QUEST FOR THE HISTORICAL JESUS

BEYOND THE QUEST FOR THE HISTORICAL JESUS

MEMOIR OF A DISCOVERY

Thomas L. Brodie

SHEFFIELD PHOENIX PRESS

2012

Copyright © 2012 Sheffield Phoenix Press

Published by Sheffield Phoenix Press
Department of Biblical Studies, University of Sheffield
45 Victoria Street
Sheffield S3 7QB

www.sheffieldphoenix.com

A CIP catalogue record for this book
is available from the British Library

Typeset by Forthcoming Publications
Printed by Lightning Source

ISBN 978-1-907534-58-4

Today I am setting you
over nations and over kingdoms
to uproot and to pull down,
to destroy and to overthrow,
to build and to plant.

—from the call of Jeremiah (Jer. 1.10)

Tread softly because you tread on my dreams.

—W.B. Yeats, 'He Wishes for the Cloths of Heaven'

Fail. Fail again. Fail better.

—sign kept above his desk by Samuel Beckett

Human words spoken from the center of ourselves...
allow a deeper dimension of reality to emerge.

—M. Catherine Hilkert, *Naming Grace*, p. 33

We shall not cease from exploration,
And the end of all our exploring
Will be to return where we started
and know the place for the first time.

— T.S. Eliot, *Four Quartets* ('Little Gidding')

CONTENTS

Part V
GLIMMERS OF SHADOWED BEAUTY

ABBREVIATIONS

AB	Anchor Bible
ABD	D.N. Freedman (ed.), *Anchor Bible Dictionary* (6 vols.; New York: Doubleday, 1992)
ABRL	Anchor Bible Reference Library
AnBib	Analecta biblica
BETL	Bibliotheca ephemeridum theologicarum lovaniensium
BHT	Beiträge zur historischen Theologie
Bib	*Biblica*
BTB	*Biblical Theology Bulletin*
BZNW	Beihefte zur Zeitschrift fur die neutestamentliche Wissenschaft
CBA	Catholic Biblical Association [of America]
CBQ	*Catholic Biblical Quarterly*
CBQMS	Catholic Biblical Quarterly Monograph Series
EDB	D.N. Freedman (ed.), *Eerdmans Dictionary of the Bible* (Grand Rapids, MI: Eerdmans, 2000)
ExpTim	*Expository Times*
FAT	Forschungen zum Alten Testament
Four Gospels	F. van Segbroeck *et al.* (eds.), *The Four Gospels* (Festschrift Frans Neirynck; BETL, 100; 3 vols.; Leuven: University/Peeters, 1992)
IBS	*Irish Biblical Studies*
JB	*Jerusalem Bible*
JBC	R.E. Brown *et al.* (eds.), *The Jerome Biblical Commentary* (London: Chapman, 1968)
JSNT	*Journal for the Study of the New Testament*
JSNTSup	Journal for the Study of the New Testament, Supplement Series
JSOT	*Journal for the Study of the Old Testament*
JSOTSup	Journal for the Study of the Old Testament, Supplement Series
LCL	Loeb Classical Library
LD	Lectio divina
LNTS	Library of NT Studies
LXX	Septuagint Greek version of the Old Testament
MT	Masoretic text
NJBC	R.E. Brown *et al.* (eds.), *The New Jerome Biblical Commentary* (Englewood Cliffs, NJ: Prentice–Hall, 1990)
NT	New Testament
NTM	New Testament Monographs
NTS	*New Testament Studies*
OBO	Orbis biblicus et orientalis
OCD	*Oxford Classical Dictionary* (Oxford: Clarendon Press, 2nd edn, 1970)

OT	Old Testament
PBVM	Presentation of the Blessed Virgin Mary
PIBA	Proceedings of the Irish Biblical Association
RB	*Revue biblique*
REL	*Revue des études latines*
RSS	St Meinrad Archabbey, *Rome and the Study of Scripture: A Collection of Papal Enactments on the Study of Holy Scripture together with the Decisions of the Biblical Commission* (St Meinrad, IN: Abbey Press, 7th edn, 1964)
RSV	Revised Standard Version
SBB	Stuttgarter biblische Beiträge
SBL	Society of Biblical Literature
SBLDS	Society of Biblical Literature Dissertation Series
VTSup	Vetus Testamentum Supplements
ZAW	*Zeitschrift für die alttestamentliche Wissenschaft*

PREFATORY INTRODUCTION

When Copernicus was seventy years old he gave himself to the publishing of his theory that the earth was not the centre of the universe, and then he died. I am no Copernicus, but I am seventy and if I am ever to provide a plain account of my work I had better do it now. I hope to live many more years, but at a class reunion in 2008, we found that, out of eighty-eight, twenty one had already died, as have younger friends and dear cousins. And one never knows.

The essence of what I want to say is simple. Having joined the Dominicans because it seemed right to do so, and having been assigned to study the Bible, there came a period of my life, 1972–1975, which eventually led me to overwhelming evidence that, while God is present in creation and in daily human life, the Bible accounts of Jesus are stories rather than history. The accounts are indeed *history-like*, shaped partly like some of the histories or biographies of the ancient world, and they reflect both factual aspects of the first century and God's presence in history and in people, but they are essentially symbolic, not factual. This idea is not new, but new evidence—from recent literary studies that trace the *transformation of sources* and *methods of composition*—tips the balance decisively in its favor. Symbolism is no small thing. It helps bring reality into being. Yet it is not an individual historical event.

The initial time of discovery—1972–1975—was intense, happy, and productive. On 17 March 1975, I completed a manuscript, *The Artists: An Exploration of the Creative Methods Used in Composing the New Testament*, and soon tried to publish it. However, publishing and communicating have proved difficult. The initial 1975 manuscript is still unpublished, and though I have developed some of its content in a doctoral dissertation (1981), and have published some books, including three through Oxford University Press, I have not communicated effectively, and have not stated my central conclusion explicitly. I had thought that by laying out much of the evidence, especially in *The Birthing of the New Testament* (2004), others would sift that evidence, assess it, and draw a reasonable conclusion. But the plan did not work. So, with time running out, it seems necessary to try to speak more clearly.

To say Jesus did not exist as a historical individual does not mean he has been eliminated. Copernicus did not eliminate the earth. He simply saw it in a new way, different from that implied by the Bible. Likewise Jesus; he is not eliminated, but seen in a new way. It is true, however, that Copernicus was disturbing. He proposed 'the most stunning reversal in perception ever to have jarred intelligent thought'.[1] He seemed literally to take the ground from under people. The earth lost its central place; and lost some of its solidity, especially its biblical image of resting on unshakeable foundations (Ps. 104.5). Jesus too loses one aspect of his solidity. But he does not lose his central place. In fact, his central place as 'an image of the invisible God' (Col. 1.15) can become clearer than ever.

It may seem that the understanding of Christ was decided long ago in great Councils. But Timothy Radcliffe, when head of the Dominican Order, remembered as a student 'the dizzy excitement of discovering that the Council of Chalcedon was not the end of our search to understand the mystery of Christ but *another beginning*, exploding all the tiny coherent little solutions in which we had tried to box him'.[2] The idea of another beginning is all the more conceivable because the early Christian centuries connected the understanding of Christ with the understanding of creation,[3] and in some ways our sense of creation has changed considerably.

Beginnings are difficult. An old Irish proverb says 'Every beginning is weak', and the churches, already variously divided and shaken, are struggling as they seek a new beginning, including a new relationship to other religions and science. But it seems appropriate that part of that new beginning should be a renewed understanding of the meaning of Christ, and even if the journey ahead looks challenging, it is better not to turn back. The Iroquois people, when considering the impact of their actions and decisions, would try to think seven generations ahead. So can we.

The story in the Gospels, then, is not the story of an individual who lived two thousand years ago. It is the story of a vital life that has been at work since time began but that became dramatically clearer to many people two thousand years ago. It is a life that, when seen initially, may seem like a killjoy, but when taken in fully, gives people increased breathing space, a greater sense of the full dimensions and possibilities of life. It is a life that the Gospels put in picture form, pictures that shaped Christianity and its rituals—and like great art, these pictures are radically true.

The impetus to speak more plainly has come partly from a thoughtful younger American colleague, Tom Thatcher, who recently invited me and several other senior people who had studied John's Gospel to write articles in

---

1. Sobel 2000: 152.
2. Radcliffe 1999: 60, emphasis added.
3. Young 2000.

which we would reflect on our work as if we were talking over a cup of coffee. The resulting articles were published by Baylor Press (*What We Have Heard from the Beginning*, 2007), but since then I have been forced to accept that a more leisurely cup is necessary. Thank you, Tom Thatcher. As you suggested, the account is generally personal and informal, a form of memoir, and so I include in the present volume as much personal information as seemed appropriate to provide the context of my work. The first three parts, the three research revolutions, tell of being struck in successive decades by diverse kinds of evidence that much of the Bible is not history. This includes the Gospels, though in one way they are history-like. The fourth part, the funeral, tells of coming to realize the need to reassess various theories, including some about St Paul. The final part asks about the way ahead.

So, coffee. Or whatever you are having yourself.

Part I

THE FIRST REVOLUTION:
HISTORICAL INVESTIGATION

*Becoming aware that biblical narratives are
not necessarily reliable accounts of history*

Chapter 1

THE FIRST REVOLUTION: INITIAL CONTACT

When I was a child the village in the west of Ireland had no electricity or running water, and so Christmas stood out all the more. Christmas Eve had a ritual of cutting out the centre of some large turnips so they would hold tall stout candles, one in each front window, and this was done not just for decoration, but to provide light for Mary and Joseph as they traveled through the night on their way to Bethlehem. And great as was the magic of Santa Claus, it did not equal the stillness in the near-darkness at the 8 o'clock Mass next morning when Silent Night had been sung, and there in the crib was the baby, Jesus.

The rest of the story of Jesus, and the stories of other people from Adam and Eve to St Paul, were as much part of life as the sun and the rain. The book containing these stories was scarcely ever mentioned, but our house did in fact contain, somewhere, a Bible, large, clean, virtually unopened, and, as far as I know, never read.

In primary school we used Schuster's *Bible History*, and its vivid drawings not only left a deep sense of the strength and frequent beauty of the ancient stories; it also gave a powerful impression of history, of the stories' factual truth. The Bible was history—solid fact. You did not argue about the historical solidity. You just took it for granted.

Later, in high school, I began to realize that science had opposing views concerning the origin of things, but somehow the opposition did not constitute a crisis. Science, even when accurate, often seemed hostile, and the origins of things seemed remote. For that matter, the Bible too was remote.

Then without notice, the situation changed.

On Holy Thursday 1960 I was struck by a preacher's description of Jesus washing his disciples' feet. That night I found the account in an old translation and began to read. It was part of a long farewell speech that occupied five chapters of John's Gospel (Jn 13–17), and it captured me like nothing I had ever read before. More than legends or lyrics, soldiers or sailors, saints or scholars, Greeks or Romans, Wild West or Far East, the farewell speech gave an extraordinary experience of depth and calm and truth.

I decided to learn the beginning of it by heart. Then the entire speech. The wording was somewhat archaic, but it was easier than the wording of the Shakespearian speeches that every high school student in the country had been expected to learn, and far easier than memorizing the Epistle to the Romans in Greek—as did some students of Professor Patrick Boylan in Maynooth. By the autumn I had memorized the entire Gospel.

As time passed the words began to recede. But not completely. Years later, I read in George Steiner that the custom of learning things by heart had had a great value, that somehow the text lodged deep within a person, in the heart. And so it seemed. The old words became a kind of treasure, an underlying joy. In an earlier age that treasure might have remained essentially undisturbed until I went to my grave.

It was not to be. Three succeeding decades, the 1960s, 1970s, and 1980s, all brought revolutions to my understanding of the Bible, and in subsequent decades these revolutions deepened.

The first revolution was a creature called 'the historical-critical method'. I first encountered this phenomenon in the shape of a throwaway remark. One day an older Dominican said casually that the words in the Gospels were not necessarily the exact words of Jesus. My heart sank. It was one thing to say that there were problems between the Bible and science regarding distant origins, but the history and words of Jesus were more central to life, closer to the bone.

Later, the evidence became inescapable. In formal studies in the 1960s I was taught in the tradition of Jerusalem's Dominican-run biblical school (the *Ecole Biblique*), with its emphasis on history and archaeology—my parents' present on my 21st birthday was *La Sainte Bible*, the original French version of *The Jerusalem Bible*—and the historical-critical method showed that the Bible was not the solid building I had imagined.

* * *

'Historical Critical': History Plus its Allies

There is nothing mysterious about the historical-critical method. 'Historical' means trying to establish the facts. The process is like that of a wise courtroom where the facts of a case are in doubt, or of a calm history department in a university. The various biblical accounts of an event or life are examined individually, compared with one another, and compared also with other accounts or with other pertinent evidence.

The book of Jonah, for instance, when read as history, has a problem. It seems highly unlikely that anyone could survive being inside a whale, but, even granting that possibility, the book's account of the conversion of massive Nineveh, capital of the Assyrian Empire, is like an account of the 1950s conversion of Moscow, capital of the Soviet Union. All the available historical evidence indicates that it never happened.

Aspects of this method were used in antiquity, and it was boosted by the Renaissance desire to rediscover the ancient sources. 'Critical' is added because historical investigation needs help. Before closing the case on Jonah a wise judge or attorney may call an outside expert, or the history department may decide to consult with some other department, such as theology, literature, or archaeology. The historical method then has various allies, various helpful 'criticisms'.

* * *

Before going on it is useful to contrast how, among the historical method's allies, some faltered and others flourished. The contrast is particularly sharp between (1) literary studies and (2) archaeology.

(1) *Leonardo's da Vinci's Flying Machines: The Bible's Early Engagements with Literary Studies*
The efforts of earlier generations of biblical researchers to work closely with literature and literary studies were sometimes like Leonardo da Vinci's efforts at designing flying machines. He was a genius, and developed some concepts for flying, but he could not clarify and expand them sufficiently to complete the process. In the case of biblical studies' efforts to join up with literature in order to reach a new level of understanding, at first the prospects must have looked good. The study of literature is a natural ally of the study of scripture. Both are concerned with writing and books; Bible (Greek *biblos*) means book, and scripture (Latin *scriptura*) means writing/written, though it often indicates *sacred* writing, 'sacred scripture'.

Yet despite this natural closeness, the relationship between these two branches of study, between scripture and literature, has not always been clear, and for about two centuries (mid-eighteenth century to mid-twentieth) the history of the efforts to get the two of them to work together is like the history of aviation between Leonardo da Vinci and the Wright brothers. It never got off the ground.

In practice, biblical researchers have varied hugely in their estimates of how much they can learn from the larger study of literature ('literary criticism'), and there have been several implied declarations of independence from literary studies—from Tertullian's famous question (c. 200 CE) 'What has Jerusalem to do with Athens?' to Rudolf Bultmann's statement (1931: 7) that the material in the Synoptic Gospels is unliterary (*unliterarisch*).

So when historical study of the Bible was developing, it was not clear to what extent biblical researchers should consult their colleagues in literature. The Bible was often treated as a historical book with a theological message—a message about God and the meaning of life—and its value was measured by the standards of *historical* research, not by the standards of literary appreciation and understanding.

Despite such uncertainty, two questions about the biblical books were prominent:

(1) What were their sources?

(2) What was their art, including their form? Art meant all the skill that shaped the text and its parts; and *form* referred to the identity of the totality: was it myth, history, story, auto/biography, poetry, narrative, prophecy, wisdom, or whatever? A book's *form* was also known as its *nature, kind, or species* (French, *genre*; German, *Gattung*). Even in daily life, being able to recognize form or genre was important—like recognizing that an apparently tough statement is really a joke. Or like recognizing that an unimpressive duckling may be something else altogether?

In more detail:

(1) *Searching for sources.* The initial search for sources focused especially on one of the greatest writings of all time—the nine-book narrative, spanning about 3500 years, from creation to the fall of Jerusalem (Genesis–Kings, *nine* books if 1 and 2 Samuel count as one, and 1 and 2 Kings likewise). Sometimes the nine-book narrative has been called a history, but is it history? Or history of some kind? It certainly sounds ancient, and contains elements of great antiquity, but here it may be necessary to think twice. The presence of twelve-year-old whiskey in a whiskey-cake does not tell the age of the cake. The problem is complicated by the ancient practice of archaism—of deliberately making writings seem old. Nowadays we tend to demand what is new, but in former times people generally treasured the old, and they sometimes shaped their writings to sound archaic.

The ancient Judeans referred to the nine-book narrative (Genesis–Kings) as prophecy, so it had a dual identity. It was history of some kind, but it was also prophecy, carrying a message. Some of it (the four final books from Joshua to Kings) was called the Former Prophets, and the rest was said to be from Moses. And Moses of course was the prophet supreme. To him were attributed all five books from Genesis to Deuteronomy, and the five together, apart from bearing the Greek title Pentateuch (literally, Five-book, *pentateuchos*), were also known by the richer Hebrew name *Torah*, meaning Instruction (or Law in a broad sense), in effect a book of great wisdom. So, among the teachers of the ancient world, Moses could be seen as old and wisest, and, among books, the Torah was the ultimate.

'Nonsense' said some seventeenth-century skeptics. The book is not even coherent. It is peppered with contradictions, and how could Moses have known about events that happened centuries before he was born?

'Unless', some suggested, 'he had sources'.

Into this situation arrived a French medical doctor. Duly coiffured, he applied his sharp medical eye to the contradictions. For Jean Astruc *the contradictions in the text were a clue that it is indeed composed of diverse sources. Ah! Moses had used diverse sources, and in doing so had allowed the diversities to remain.* In a stroke Astruc had found a way that could explain the Pentateuch's contradictions, recover its sources, and salvage Moses' authorship. And Astruc published a book indicating that Genesis was based on a variety of sources that are now lost.

Astruc was no compulsive. He was a prestigious professor of medicine at the University of Paris. As such, he also provided medical care to the court of Louis XV at the palace of Versailles. And he used current historical research methods. His distant family background was Jewish, but his father was a Protestant minister, and he himself had become a Catholic. And careful. Though he was trying to save Moses, he also knew that a book that raised questions about the unity and full Mosaic authorship of all of Genesis could bring trouble. His study of Genesis did not appear until 1753, when he was essentially in his seventieth year. His name was not on it. It was ostensibly published in Brussels, safely beyond the French orbit. And the mood of the title was tentative: *Conjectures sur la Genèse.* In case the reader missed the force of the word *Conjectures* in the capital letters of the title, the subtitle began by repeating it, and ended by repeating it yet again.

The long-term effect was immense. Within biblical research, he and the year became famous—Astruc, 1753. Though the link to Moses proved difficult to maintain, the basic idea stayed: variations are a clue to diverse sources. For a while the research field became chaotic. Every variation, every tension in the text, became a clue to diversity of sources. The Pentateuch was falling into hundreds of sources, and two things were being lost: the unity of the actual books (Genesis to Deuteronomy); and the underlying history—the history of Moses and Israel.

Finally, in the 1870s—more than a century after *Conjectures*—the formidable Julius Wellhausen arrived, a man without Astruc's inhibitions. When people were walking to church on Sunday morning they would meet Wellhausen blithely walking in the opposite direction for a swim. Wellhausen did not know how to explain all the variations in the text—crucially, he was essentially a historian rather than an expert in literature—but as a historian, he used his own work and that of others to reconstruct what he believed were some key moments in the history of Israel, and around those key moments he grouped the hundreds of variations into four main bodies—four hypothetical documents or literary endeavours—each primarily associated with a different century. Overall result: the writing of the Pentateuch, once attributed to Moses, was now assigned to several centuries. In effect, in this hypothesis ('the Documentary Hypothesis') the composing of Genesis–Kings, about 500 pages, took about 500 years.

The work of Astruc, Wellhausen and their followers was a bold effort to identify sources—and it did in fact identify real features of the narrative—but it was not a reliable indicator of specific sources. It was not possible, on the basis of just one text, to subdivide that text into lost sources. The process was out of control, and proved not to be a reliable ally.

(2) *Searching for art, including form.* The value of recognizing a text's form (nature/kind/*genre*/*Gattung*) was highlighted by Hermann Gunkel, a trail-blazing German folklorist and biblical scholar, in his books on Genesis (1901) and the Psalms (1926 and 1933). And not many years later the same idea received backing from other voices, including a papal encyclical (*Divino Afflante Spiritu*, 1943):

> The ancient peoples of the East, in order to express their ideas, did not always employ those forms or kinds of speech which we use today; but rather those used by the [people] of their times and countries. What these exactly were the commentator cannot determine as it were in advance, but only after a careful examination of the ancient literature of the East.[1]

By the 1960s the need to recognize literary forms was well established in principle. In Tallaght, Dublin, our enthusiastic young teacher, Wilfrid Harrington, could say without fuss: 'We have a problem on our hands, if the book of Jonah is a historical book. This problem vanishes when the book is taken for what it really is, a work of fiction...'[2]

The account of Jonah emerged as a prophetic novella, one that combined satire of those who had a narrow sense of God with pictures of the goodness of people and of God's compassion for all creatures.

So, the principle of identifying the form/genre/nature of writings was indeed established. But it is one thing to establish a principle, and another to implement it. In identifying the form of biblical books, implementation has frequently been slow. This is particularly so in the New Testament, where the book of Revelation clearly has an apocalyptic character, but the form/genre of the other twenty-six books is often surprisingly elusive. In particular:

- Are the five narrative books (four Gospels and Acts) history, biography, fiction, or something else?

---

1. *Divino Afflante Spiritu*, 1943, paragraph 36, in *RSS*, pp. 80-111, esp. 97.
2. Harrington's teaching was published in Harrington 1965a: 356.

- Are the remaining twenty-one documents *letters*, meaning essentially spontaneous addresses to specific situations, or are they *epistles*, studied compositions, like essays? The case of Hebrews is fairly easy to recognize. While it has aspects of a letter, such as its conclusion, overall it has the studied character of an epistle, a letter-like essay. But what of the other twenty?

The difficulty in recognizing particular forms arises partly from a larger problem in recognizing their general background: do they come from *folkloric* writing, often composed through collecting scattered pieces of folklore or oral tradition? And do they come from *literary* writing, writing composed in a way that is deliberate, with awareness of a larger literary world?

Gunkel's emphasis on form constituted a major and lasting contribution to biblical research, but his experience with folklore led him to see Genesis as folkloric saga, as a collection (*Sammlung*) of sagas, strongly influenced by oral tradition. He gives his initial reason in the opening paragraph of his commentary on Genesis (1901: i):

> Are the accounts (*Erzählungen*) of Genesis history or saga (*Geschichte oder Sage*)? For the modern historian this question is no longer a question, yet it is important to make clear the grounds for this modern position. History writing (*Geschichtsschreibung*) is no innate art of the human spirit, but has emerged in the course of human history, at a particular point of development (*an einem bestimmten Punke der Entwicklung*). Uncultured peoples (*Die uncultivierten Völker*) do not write history.

Gunkel went on to say that uncultivated people had limited attention spans and dealt mostly with single episodes, in oral form.

So the various short episodes of Genesis were interpreted not as integral parts of developed literature, but as loose-fitting elements, like diverse folkloric episodes that came from diverse situations in life. And, as in folklore, he believed that if he could identify the form, *the precise kind of episode*, he would be able to trace the history behind it.

The procedure is somewhat like bird-watching. An area may have many diverse birds, but if you can identify the nature/form/genre of a particular bird you may well be able to say where it has come from. The form is a clue to the history. In biblical studies the process became known as form-history (*Formgeschichte*), often called 'form criticism'.

The identifying of the forms of specific biblical episodes did sometimes cast light on the episodes, but, far more than with birds, it was often very difficult to say where they had come from. And meanwhile the literary form of entire biblical books remained obscure.

John's Gospel was particularly difficult to judge. My gut feeling said it was deeply true, but it is seriously at odds with the sequence and content of events in the other three Gospels. So what is a gospel, what form of writing, what genre? Is it history? Or history *of some kind*? And why is John so different?

What was certain was that while the historical study of the Bible sometimes called on literary help—whether in looking for sources or for the text's art and nature/form—the initial efforts at linking up with literary studies wilted.

(2) *Archaeology*

Meanwhile archaeology was flying high. When Napoleon chose Egypt as a place to confront England's power in the East (1798), his army was accompanied by a further small army of scholars, and before his victorious battle in the shadow of the pyramids he reminded his troops that forty centuries of history were looking down on them. Suddenly, in a new way, the past was coming alive, especially the ancient Near East. The rediscovery of Pompeii (1790) and long-lost Troy (1873) fired imaginations and attracted backing to the cause of rediscovering the world of the Bible. And while Astruc in his fine city and palace had enjoyed some royal patronage, it was small compared to the resources supplied to the researchers who dug selected sites under the Middle Eastern sun. Initial backing came especially from vying powers in Paris, London and Berlin, and later from sources closer to the scene, and from other sources much further away, especially in North America. The multi-faceted backing for biblical archaeology continues to this day. In the Spring of 2010 an expedition to find Noah's Ark on Mount Ararat, in Turkey, was funded from China.

One of the many researchers who helped excavate ancient sites was Albert Lagrange, a French Dominican who, in 1890, seven years after Wellhausen proposed his five-century hypothesis, took possession of a makeshift school house in Jerusalem. The building had been the city's disused slaughterhouse, and the rings to which the animals had been attached were still in the walls, but it was the beginning of the *Ecole Biblique et Archéologique.* In subsequent decades the *Ecole* was part of the major effort, international and interdenominational, to get archaeology to talk about the Bible's historical background, and, as I said earlier, it was from the *Ecole* that we drew much of our biblical instruction in Tallaght.

* * *

Later studies in Rome, at the Pontifical University of St Thomas Aquinas, 'the Angelicum', did not lessen the sense of having undergone a revolution. In fact, they added to it. By then the Second Vatican Council had come and gone, and, far more than in Ireland, the Council had had an impact in Rome.

Around March 1967, while in Rome, I received a letter from the regional head ('The Provincial') of the Irish Dominicans directing me to specialize in scripture, and in the Summer of 1968, an extraordinarily turbulent year, he assigned me, half-baked—I had only the Baccalaureate in Sacred Scripture (BSS), a preliminary qualification, but not the normal teaching qualification, the Licenciate (LSS)—to fill a suddenly vacated job that would begin in September and would involve teaching the whole range of scripture studies, Old Testament and New, at the Seminary of St John Vianney and the Uganda Martyrs, in the West Indies, in the land of Trinidad and Tobago.

Chapter 2

TRINIDAD: THE FIRST REVOLUTION DEEPENS

I often say I grew up in Trinidad. Early in the morning of Monday, 9 September 1968, I went down the steps of a Lufthansa plane in a heavy black suit and walked into a wall of tropical heat. Suddenly life changed—rampant steaming vegetation; countless living creatures, many of them very small; mosquitoes, hundreds of them when you woke at night before learning how to cope with them; hurricane preparations; an earthquake; and people of all colours, including forty shades of chocolate. Plus, for the first time in my life, I suddenly had serious responsibility, particularly the need to teach what the Bible said and whether it was true in a literal, historical, way.

In time, various kinds of work would bring me all over the squarish country—on average about 45 miles across—from Chaguaramas in the west to Sangre Grande in the east, and from Cedros and Moruga in the south to Toco in the north-east, and across the sea to Tobago—to Scarborough, to Delaford, and, walking, to Bloody Bay. My first visit to Tobago, in late December 1968, was a six-dollar all-night trip in an open boat, mostly standing, listening easily to people singing calypso.

But from the beginning my base was the seminary, perched on the slopes of Trinidad's Northern Range. Above the seminary was the Benedictine monastery which largely ran it. Below it, winding its way southwards down to the town of Tunapuna and to Trinidad's central plain, was a medley of fields, institutions, houses, and a 'pan yard' where a steel band practiced, sending its evocative music up the hill and lightly filling my room as I worked at night.

The students, over fifty of them, ranged from nineteen to thirty-nine, all colours, from diverse parts of the southern Caribbean, Guyana and Surinam. I was in my twenties, and felt like one of them. They became my friends, and dragooned me even into playing cricket—where my hurling instincts were colourful but costly—yet, as students, they were alert and keen, and I studied fiercely to have something to say to them.

The image that kept coming to me was of having been thrown into an ocean where soon I would either drown or learn to swim. The ocean was one of swirling evidence—books ranging from the bold theories of Julius

Wellhausen, Hermann Gunkel, Rudolf Bultmann, to the meticulous historical research of scholars such as Roland de Vaux, William Foxwell Albright, John Bright, Pierre Benoit, C.H. Dodd and Raymond Brown. In those early teaching days I was particularly helped by the publication in 1968 of the *Jerome Biblical Commentary* (the *JBC*), edited by Raymond Brown, Joseph Fitzmyer and Roland Murphy.

Two Cities

Amid the complex discussions about historical facts I realized as never before that trying to say something about the interpretation of the Bible and its history has always been partly a tale of two cities, each located about 300 miles from Jerusalem: symbolic Alexandria, and literal Antioch.

Alexandria was founded by young Alexander the Great on an ideal seashore location, slightly elevated, on 7 April 331 BCE, and quickly became the capital of a new form of Egyptian empire ruled by a Greek sister-marrying dynasty, the Ptolemies—Ptolemy I, II, III...—an empire that, as an independent entity, eventually ended with Cleopatra.

Alexandria was second only to Rome and was, proportionately, like a mixture of Washington, New York and Boston (or Beijing, Shanghai, and Hong Kong). It was the port for the world's leading food-exporter; and, despite its location within Egypt, it was so Greek and eminent that it was the cultural capital of the vast Hellenistic world—largely the world 'Greeced' by Alexander. Its landmark lighthouse was one of the world's wonders. Standing on an island in Alexandria's harbour, it was more prominent than the Statue of Liberty and about fifty percent higher. And Alexandria's cultural and scholarly pre-eminence was proclaimed by its seashore library— housing Alexander's recovered body—the most famed and endowed library of the ancient world, begun around 300 BCE by Ptolemy I and II, and lasting about seven hundred years.

Alexandria's influence included the world of the Bible. It controlled Jerusalem from soon after Alexander's death until 198 BCE, had a Jewish population of hundreds of thousands, and, in the world of biblical interpretation, it was a leader twice-over:

- It had a key role in bringing the classic Hebrew writings into the common language of much of the world, into Greek—'the Septuagint' ('Seventy') translation, or LXX, because it was reputedly done by seventy translators. And more than a translation, it was often a form of interpretation.
- Alexandria was also a leader in interpreting texts allegorically—in maintaining that stories meant something other than their surface meaning; it saw the stories as 'other-speaking' (in Greek, *allos* +

agoria). The greatest exponent of this method of interpretation was Philo, a prolific writer, and also a man of action. It was he who led an Alexandrian delegation to Rome to speak to a distracted Caligula about accusations against Judeans. Philo spanned the eras, BCE to CE (he died around 50 CE). He also spanned cultures by combining in himself Judaism and Hellenism. And above all he spanned meanings: he had a facility for indicating that history-like accounts had a deeper meaning, that they were symbolic.

Symbolic language took various forms. A *simile* told you explicitly that it was linking different things: 'A is *like* B'. A *metaphor* just linked them: 'A is B'; 'This pub is hell on wheels'. An *allegory* was an extended metaphor. It told a whole story but beneath the surface of the story it was referring to something else. So all three were symbolic—simile, metaphor and allegory— but allegory carried the symbolism further.

This symbolic approach was developed in various forms by Christian interpreters for well over a thousand years. Its early exponents included Clement (c. 150–215), head of a theology school in Alexandria, and his student and successor, Origen. Their work had major influence. In Raymond Brown's words (*JBC* 71:37):

> Through men like Clement and Origen, Philo's allegorizing achieved a dominant place in the Christian exegesis of the Old Testament.

Antioch

Syrian Antioch (now in Turkey) had been founded by one of Alexander's generals, and like Alexandria, had also been the capital of an empire, a leader in culture, and a commercial hub. It traded even with the Far East, and its ruins have revealed ancient Chinese porcelain. And after 198 BCE, Antioch too in its turn controlled Jerusalem for a time.

Antioch's relationship to Jerusalem was sometimes poisonous. Among its rulers Antiochus IV stood out—*somewhat* as did Henry VIII in England. He called himself *Epiphanes*, or 'Manifest', meaning Manifestation of God, but some people referred to him as *Epimanes*, 'Mad'. In 167 BCE he looted Jerusalem's temple treasury, and he turned the temple altar into a place of Greek worship, with a statue of Zeus—'the abomination of desolation' (Dan. 11.31; 12.11). The outrage sparked the Maccabees' revolt and led to the installation of their dodgy dynasty, the Hasmoneans.

Over two hundred years later, hostility to the Judeans again erupted dramatically. Around 70 CE, when Titus, having crushed another Jewish revolt, made a triumphal entry into Antioch, a massive crowd asked him to kill their city's Judeans.

But Antioch was bigger than the whims of Antiochus IV and the blood-lust of a crowd. The city was the third largest of the empire (after Rome and Alexandria), was set on a splendid seaward site, and its Jewish population was sizable. While Jew–Gentile relations were sometimes difficult—as they were in Alexandria—the city eventually became a major center of Christianity. It was the place where Paul tells of clashing with Peter—'I withstood him to the face' (Gal. 2.11); where, according to Acts, the disciples were first called Christians (Acts 11.26); where Ignatius was bishop until he was taken to be martyred in Rome; and, above all, a place which developed a tradition of interpretation that, in comparison with Alexandria, was generally more literal. This literal tradition, which was later than that of Alexandria, was inspired especially by Lucian, head of Antioch's theology school until he was martyred in 312, and was developed by others, including Diodorus of Tarsus, Theodore of Mopsuestia, and to some degree, John Chrysostom—all of whom died around 400.

'*Islands…[that] did not survive*'

What is essential is that at the origin of Christianity there was an ambiguity as to whether interpretation should be symbolic or literal. In practice, the two approaches were sometimes interwoven. St Augustine of North Africa, for instance, who died in 430, often interpreted the Bible symbolically, but to some degree he also wanted to interpret texts literally, and from a literal point of view he found the variations between the Gospels puzzling. However, across the sea, in southern France, the much-travelled and younger John Cassian was trying to unscramble the complexity of biblical texts, and he distinguished four senses of scripture: literal, allegorical, moral and final (or eschatological). 'Jerusalem', for instance, has four meanings:

- Literal: the actual geographic city—acres of real estate
- Allegorical: the church of Christ—the corporate body of Christians
- Moral: the individual soul
- Final (or eschatological): the heavenly city

Three of the four were symbolic, and to a significant degree this fourfold meaning dominated the Middle Ages. As Raymond Brown summarized (1968b: 42):

> During the 12th, 13th, and early 14th centuries,…literal…tendencies rose to the surface like islands in the sea, but they did not survive; and the Middle Ages drew to a close with allegory once more dominant in writers like Meister Eckhart (d. 1328), John Gerson (d. 1429) and Denis the Carthusian (d. 1471).

Eckhart, Gerson, and Denis the Carthusian were not minor figures. Eckhart held major offices as a Dominican, and was also a master mystic who rethought the meaning of God and of Christ. Gerson played a key role in the Council that ended the bewildering decades when the Church was divided between two popes ('the Great Western Schism'). And even if 'Carthusian' suggests a hermitage, Denis was no shrinking shrub. Living in what now is Belgium, he developed theology into its practical spiritual implications, advocated ordaining women, and was known as Blessed by several subsequent figures including St Francis de Sales and St Alphonsus Liguori. So, given that these three leaders, along with many others, read scripture allegorically, it is not surprising, even in the late fifteenth century, to find, as Raymond Brown noted, that allegory was 'once more dominant'.

The 1500s and All That

Suddenly something shifted. Around 1500 CE interpretation of the Bible began to move, as never before, from the symbolic to the literal. I was not able, when teaching in Trinidad, to explain fully why this happened. But there were clues.

In the forty-year period surrounding the death of Denis the Carthusian (1471), Columbus was born, and so were Copernicus, Luther and Ignatius Loyola. By the time Galileo appeared, shortly after Ignatius's died, the world had moved far from Denis the Carthusian.

The view of Copernicus and Galileo—that the earth was airborne and circled the sun—was not totally new, but for most people it was not only bewildering; it also went against the literal meaning of the beginning of the Bible (Gen. 1.14-19), and so it brought the literal meaning to centre stage.

Luther's teaching had something of the same effect. While challenging one source of authority, the Pope, he elevated another authority, the Bible, and for Luther this meaning was clear, and the clearest meaning was literal. The Pope's primary concern was not with the sun and the earth, it was with the literal meaning of the Bible. He was under pressure to be just as zealous in promoting the truth of the Bible as the Reformers.

Pope Urban VIII spoke to Galileo several times, but the Pope may have been doubly under pressure because of the religion-related multi-national Thirty Years War, and he was so distracted and sleepless at one stage that he ordered the birds in the gardens outside his bedroom to be killed. The Papacy and Reformers disagreed on many specific issues, including Galileo, but in principle they both were drawn into defending the literal truth of the Bible. And the general development of historical studies which occurred around that time pushed literal meaning further towards the historical, the factual.

Years later, in 2010, I heard Ernan McMullin, a vastly experienced professor from Notre Dame University, summarize the shift of interpretation in two short sentences: 'The Reform shifted interpretation from symbolic to literal. And the Catholics said: "If you go literal, we'll outdo you"' (McMullin 2010).

Thus emphasis fell more and more *not on the Bible itself*, these pages that you can touch and absorb, but on *the events behind the Bible*, events that were far removed from the present and that increasingly needed to be historically provable.

Those on the Reform side gradually made up their own minds what to accept as literally true, but it was more difficult for Catholics, and it was only while in Trinidad, in reading Yves Congar's *Power and Poverty in the Church*, that I began to understand the difficulty more fully.

Until around 1500 the Church generally allowed a fair degree of freedom—freedom to question or challenge Church authority. The young Catherine Benincasa from Siena could write directly to the Pope and expect to be taken seriously. But the Church authorities reckoned that the Reformers had abused that freedom, and in Congar's view *the condemnation of its abuse meant the end of its use*. Freedom waned, and, as never before, the emphasis swung to obedience.

The swing was compounded by the newly arrived Jesuits. Their inspiring founder, St Ignatius Loyola, was an ex-army man, and their Pope was embattled. So, amid great dedication, they implicitly added an army-like element to the idea of obedience, and, unusually, took a special vow of obedience to the Pope. The effect was to introduce what Congar called 'a mystique of obedience', as though obedience to Church authority were the be all and end all of religion—in contrast to the biblical principle that obedience to God comes before obedience to humans (Acts 5.29). Thus, when papal authority insisted on the literal meaning of the Bible, as it generally did, Catholics had little opportunity to offer an alternative view.

More Trouble-makers

When the time came in Trinidad for dealing with the Bible's nine-book foundational narrative (Genesis–Kings), the first hurdle was the brief account from Creation and the Deluge to the Tower of Babel (Gen. 1–11). It was clear that the publications of Copernicus (1543) and Galileo (1632) seemed to contradict the Bible, but I could make a good case that Genesis' real interest was not in the relative positions of the sun and earth but in God's role as origin of all things. So, without too much fuss, it was somehow alright to let go of the literal meaning.

But Galileo was not the only problem. On the issue of dating it seemed for a long time that James Ussher, the prestigious Dublin-born Protestant Bishop, had resolved the basic problems. In the 1650s he used the biblical chronologies to place the creation of the universe in 4004 BCE, and his calculations were so meticulous that his opinion was widely respected until the nineteenth century.

However, in 1795 geologist James Hutton, addressing the *Royal Society of Edinburgh*, argued on the basis of mountain erosion and rock formation that the Earth must be much older than previously reckoned. And in 1830 Sir Charles Lyell's *Principles of Geology* indicated that the earth has been formed by slow geological changes that are still in progress. Later nineteenth-century estimates of the world's age varied from 100,000 to billions of years—a discussion that eventually left no space for Ussher's meticulous calculations.

A further body-blow to the historical value of the opening chapters of Genesis came from Charles Darwin—influenced partly by Sir Charles Lyell's *Principles of Geology*—when his *Origin of Species* (1859) produced strong evidence that the beginnings of plants and animals was not at all as Genesis described.

Thirteen years after Darwin's *Origin of Species*, again in London, the focus moved from the creation accounts to the history of Noah and the Deluge (Gen. 6.1–9.17). George Smith, a young printer's engraver from Chelsea, had taken to reading avidly about ancient Assyria and spending his lunch break in the British Museum studying cuneiform tablets from Mesopotamia, more precisely from an area now in northern Iraq. On 3 December 1872, at age thirty-two, Smith got the opportunity to deliver a lecture providing the first evidence that the biblical account of a Deluge, far from being an original narrative, is a development from a specific literary tradition that went back to one of the oldest literary narratives in the world—the Epic of Gilgamesh. Smith's observation was not new,[1] but for his hearers it was, and his lecture was not given in a corner. The audience included the British Prime Minister, William Gladstone.

These ideas, especially those of Darwin, opened the way for a question that, at the time, was unthinkable for many people: were Adam and Eve individual historical people or were they essentially symbolic?

Many Christians were alarmed at the new ideas, and in 1901, in the hope of dealing responsibly with the issues, Pope Leo XIII set up the Pontifical Biblical Commission—a commission of Cardinals aided by expert consultors—and eight years later the Commission was asked if the arguments against the literal historical sense of Genesis 1–3 were decisive.

The reply (30 June 1909) was succinct: 'In the negative'.[2]

---

1.   See especially Hugo Grotius, *On the Truth of the Christian Religion*, 1622, sections XVI and XVII, as summarized in Robinson 2010: 27-28.
    2.   *RSS*: 122.

So in effect the argument for the literal meaning of Genesis 1–3 still held sway, and in practice a teacher would still have to defend the historical exist-ence of Adam and Eve. It was understood that the decrees of the Commission did not fall under Papal infallibility, but disagreement was not tolerated.

The people of Tennessee also were alarmed, and in 1922 passed the *Butler Act* which effectively forbade the teaching of evolution or any account of human origins other than that of the Bible. Three years later, a high-school teacher, John Scopes, was accused of violating the Act, thus leading to the Scopes Trial, sometimes called 'the Monkey Trial', the first to be broadcast on US national radio. The trial had two star performers, Clarence Darrow for the defence; and, for the prosecution, a certain Bryan—William Jennings Bryan, former US Secretary of State and barn-storming presidential candidate. On the sixth day, the defence seemed to be left with no more witnesses, but on the seventh day, amid Tennessee's July heat, when the judge had moved the hearing to a stand on the court lawn, Darrow played one last card: he called prosecutor Bryan as witness for the defence—in particular to show how little the barn-storming prosecutor knew about the Bible and science—and for two hours Darrow grilled Bryan on a variety of questions, including Adam and Eve. Darrow wanted to know where Cain got his wife. Bryan answered that he would 'leave the agnostics to hunt for her'.

Bryan won the case, and, in accord with the Butler Act, Scopes was fined a hundred dollars. Five days later, still barn-storming, Bryan died in his sleep.

The Butler Act was repealed in 1967.

Meanwhile the Pontifical Biblical Commission had reached another view concerning its early decrees, such as those involving Genesis 1–3. In 1948, the Commission secretary effectively stated that 'it was no longer necessary to teach that Adam and Eve were historical figures',[3] and in 1955, the Secretary of the Commission, Athanasius Miller, a Benedictine monk, issued a clarification:

> At present the battle is considerably less fierce; not a few controversies have been peacefully settled and many problems emerge in an entirely new light so that it is easy enough for us to smile at the narrowness and constraint which prevailed fifty years ago.

And the Secretary indicated that, as long as faith and morals were safe-guarded, researchers could now treat those early decrees 'with full liberty'.[4]

---

3. The citation is a paraphrase by Wansbrough 2010: esp. p. 6. For the full text, see *RSS*: 150-53.

4. *RSS*: 175. T.A. Collins and R.E. Brown (1968: 25) note that the emphasis on full liberty ('with full liberty, *plena libertate; in aller Freiheit*'), which was contained in the original clarification, was mistakenly omitted in the *RSS* text published by St Meinrad Archabbey.

Chapter 3

'WHEN A CHILD HAVE NO FOOD...'

Not all went smoothly in Trinidad. One day, as I was in full flight, I rattled off without thinking a conclusion I had heard from an experienced Dominican teacher in Rome, Pieter Dunker: the biblical account of Abraham was a story, a powerful meaningful story, but not historical. Several hands immediately brought me to a halt. What did I mean? I said 'Ah...' a few times, and then said I would come back to it tomorrow.

After class, as I started walking directly down the scraggy hill from the monastery classroom to the seminary residence, I was relaxed in the thought that I would ask someone. There was always someone eminent to ask. Suddenly I stopped, and in an instant, as I put my left foot into a solid-looking niche of earth to ensure safe footing—the detail is imprinted on my memory—I looked up, took in the breadth of Trinidad in a glance, from the Atlantic on the east, to the Gulf of Paria, on the west, facing Venezuela.

'You're the only man on the island.'

In the circumstances, there was nobody to ask. I would have to go into the library and work it out on my own.

Next day I gave an opinion that, whereas the first part of Genesis, from creation to the fall of the tower of Babel (Gen. 1–11), did not reflect specific individuals in history, the rest of Genesis—concerning Abraham, Isaac, Jacob and Joseph—was different, and seemed to reflect something from the lives of individual people or tribes.

But as the days in Trinidad passed, I found that even in the rest of Genesis, and in the subsequent books from Exodus to Kings, establishing solid history was not easy. Abraham and Sarah have a child in their nineties; Moses and especially Joseph play huge roles in Egypt but are never mentioned in Egyptian records; Jericho's walls fall down; Solomon has a thousand wives and concubines—I wondered about the facilities needed for a thousand prestigious women—and, above all, Solomon builds a splendid temple, of which nothing has yet been found, not a stone.

Jericho was particularly intriguing. Located between the Jordan Valley and the highlands, it is by nature a strategically placed oasis in a dry plain, and about 9000 BCE it began to develop into a city—virtually the world's oldest. It has a correspondingly prestigious role in the Bible. In the pivotal account of the Israelites conquering the land, the first great clash is at Jericho, and the conquest is a seven-day ritual culminating in shouts and trumpets—'and the wall fell flat' (Josh. 6.20).

When discussing this in Trinidad at the end of the 1960s there were two issues: Did the wall really fall? And if so, when? The exodus from Egypt and the conquest of the land were generally placed around 1200 BCE, so the hope was that archaeology would clarify the events. I knew that Kathleen Kenyon of Oxford had been excavating at Jericho in the 1950s—our teachers in Tallaght often spoke of her—but I had not followed the debate closely. Previous archaeologists had identified an excavated wall which they agreed was the wall that had fallen at the time of the conquest—'the Joshua wall' as they called it. The challenge for Kathleen Kenyon had been to figure out the date of the wall, and, to see what she had unearthed, I went back to the *Jerome Biblical Commentary* (North 1968: 74:61):

> It was to resolve the dilemma of the wall's date that Miss Kenyon organized the third major excavation of Jericho during 1952–58. Her discoveries were shattering. The alleged Joshua wall contained within itself an abundance of pottery to prove beyond cavil its demolition before 2000! Moreover, nowhere on the mound [of the entire Jericho site] was there any genuine deposit firmly attesting occupation at any time between 1500 and 800.

So at the time Joshua is reckoned to have hit the walls of Jericho, the Joshua wall was long gone and there was no one home.

That was the view around 1970.

Trinidad was pushing me, as I had never been pushed before, into practicing 'the historical-critical method', into using historical evidence to try to assess the reliability of biblical accounts. What I was doing was in no way original. Thousands of others do comparable summaries every day.

The pressure to think as I never had before came not only from the classroom. When my former co-student, Micheál O'Regan, joined the seminary staff in Trinidad in 1969 my first instinct as soon as a problem arose was to go to him to solve it. He had been three years senior to me in Tallaght, and as well as being friendly, he seemed wise. But as I was walking down the seminary corridor to his room I caught myself: 'For a year you have had to rely on yourself in dealing with most problems. Now, at the first difficulty, don't fall back on running to Micheál for help.'

The Dominicans in Trinidad were also thinking afresh. They were learning through diverse sources—through their own experience in Trinidad, through the Second Vatican Council, through reports from missionary experience in Tanzania, and through the arrival of a fresh face—Damian Byrne. Some time earlier, Damian had been sent as head of a new mission in Recreo, Argentina, but he had not lasted long. According to a later report:

> In Cuernavaca [Mexico], he came under the influence of Ivan Illich whose views on the church in South America he resisted until he later found that Illich was right… Although he set to work with a will, the view from the Provincial's mission desk in Ireland was different to that found through the window in Recreo. Before 1967 was out, Damian was to find himself parish priest of Blanchisseuse on the north coast of Trinidad.[1]

Blanchisseuse was remote, a fishing village behind the mountains, but in less than a year the Dominicans in Trinidad had elected him local chief ('Vicar Provincial'). He proved both insightful and patient. He was resolute in confronting some selfish centres of church power, but he was also tolerant and good-humoured.

Trinidad too was thinking for itself. It had taken pride in gaining political independence from Britain in 1962, but by early 1970 a combination of forces—including the university, the trade unions, and the marginalized—led to a situation where people began to take to the streets of the capital, Port of Spain. The capital was busy, Trinidad was not given to crusades, and almost nobody was listening.

On Thursday 26 February 1970, as the demonstrators seemed to meander uncertainly into Independence Square, they turned towards the Catholic Cathedral, and then they marched in, took it over, and decried an economic system that was exploiting the poor.

Suddenly they had everyone's attention, including that of the predominantly black government. Many called out for peace and condemned the takeover as an act of violence and desecration. The Gospel reading for the following Sunday described Jesus cleansing the Temple, and clearly this referred to the way Jesus would expel the demonstrators. But others saw the demonstrators as fulfilling the role of Jesus—awakening the cathedral to its encrusted habits. The archbishop too called for peace. And he added, 'There can be no peace without justice'.

In the days that followed, the demonstrators' speeches had an edge—anti-multinational business, anti-colonial, anti-Shakespeare, sometimes anti-white. And there was a longing for an African kinship that had been uprooted and half-erased from memory. St Paul was cited on the side of the revolution: 'He that does not work, let him not eat' (2 Thess. 3.10). But Paul was also an example of Christian manipulation; the purpose of his charity was to heap fire on the person who received it (Rom. 12.20). The Irish priests were an extension of the British Empire.

---

1. Excerpt from the proceedings (*Acts*) of the Irish Dominican Chapter, Tallaght, Dublin, 1996, 61.

Violence seemed to hover over the country, and though no one had been killed or badly injured at that stage, violence was being condemned by many voices. 'And what is violence?' cried leader Geddes Granger, who, later changed his name to Makandal Daaga. 'What is violence? When a child have no food in de belly—*dat* is violence!'

Chapter 4

STILL REMEMBERING AFRICA

Back at the seminary the opening paragraphs of Albert Schweitzer's *The Quest of the Historical Jesus* (1906) seemed at first to be light years away from the marches on the streets:

> When, at some future day, our period of civilization shall lie, closed and completed, before the eyes of future generations, German theology will stand out as a great, a unique phenomenon in the mental and spiritual life of our time. For nowhere save in the German temperament can there be found in the same perfection the living complex of conditions and factors—of philosophical thought, critical acumen, historical insight and religious feeling—without which no deep theology is possible.
>
> And the greatest achievement of German theology is the critical investigation of the life of Jesus. What it has accomplished here has laid down the conditions and determined the course of the religious thinking of the future.
>
> In the history of doctrine its work has been negative; it has so to speak cleared the site for a new edifice of religious thought…

Having mentioned the clearing of the site, as he saw it, Schweitzer could have concentrated on building the 'new edifice', but he had many options. Apart from being a renowned scholar he was a well-known musician, and even as *The Quest* was being published he was already studying for something else. In 1913, as a fully qualified M.D., he founded a hospital at Lambaréné, in French Equatorial Africa, where he spent most of his life, and where he died and was buried in 1965.

But if Africa got to Schweitzer, it got to the archbishop also, and eventually drew members of the seminary student body and staff into a long and potentially explosive march from the capital through the cane-fields. The government issued arms to the police. The army attempted a march on the capital. Standard study was overshadowed. There were days when the country seemed to hold its breath, and by the time it relaxed it had moved to a new phase of its history.

As for the history of Jesus, the quest would still not go away. One thing seemed sure—namely, Jesus' historical existence. It was backed both by faith and by witnesses:

- Faith: Christian faith seemed to presuppose Jesus' historical existence.
- Non-biblical witnesses: unlike characters such as Joseph and Moses, the figure of Christ is mentioned in some way by outside writers—Josephus, Tacitus, Suetonius, Pliny the Younger and Lucian of Samosata.
- Biblical witnesses: this is the main evidence—Jesus' story is given not just once but by four evangelists (Matthew, Mark, Luke–Acts, John) and, partly, by Paul's epistles; altogether five distinct sources of witness.

Yet there were problems. Faith is essentially in God, and Christian faith does not require the truth of contradictory accounts of specific events—as happens sometimes between the Gospels. As regards Josephus, Tacitus and the other non-biblical witnesses to Christ, some of them were always recognized as weak.

The crunch issue concerned the biblical witnesses, especially the four Gospels. The main problem here was that whatever solid history they might contain seemed to be covered by a heavy over-layer of theology—of narrative which was an expression not of plain history but of faith. The situation is somewhat akin to the dilemma of hearing two parents give such a rosy account of their child that, while presuming they have a child, it seems impossible to know how much is reliable. A further problem concerned the role of the evangelists as witnesses. Were they really independent? Were the four of them—five including Paul—independent of one another, or were they essentially copying from one another?

We will return to this issue later. What is essential for the moment is that, even in 1906, when Schweitzer reviewed generations of research and re-examined the problem, he concluded that the history of Jesus could not be pinned down. His final paragraph (1906: 401) became classic:

> He comes to us as one unknown, without a name, as of old, by the lake-side, he came to those who knew Him not. He speaks to us the same word: 'Follow thou me!' and sets us to the tasks which he has to fulfill for our time. He commands. And to those who obey Him, whether they be wise or simple, He will reveal himself in the toils, the conflicts, the sufferings which they shall pass through in His fellowship, and as an ineffable mystery, they shall learn in their own experience Who he is.

After Schweitzer, interest diminished in reconstructing Jesus' life as a whole, and from about 1920 to 1950 attention moved especially to form-history ('form criticism'), in other words, to looking closely at specific sayings and episodes in the hope that, by identifying their form—whether for instance a saying was law, or prophecy, or wisdom—it would be possible to detect their history. Thus, Rudolf Bultmann, the towering Professor of New Testament at Marburg who was influenced by Gunkel's eighteenth-century Romantic ideas about people and writing, visualized Jesus-stories in a rather Romantic way as 'springing up' among the early Christians, and as having virtually no link to the historical Jesus but as providing clues as to how these Jesus stories developed among distinct communities. Thus, the search for history moved from Jesus to searching for the history of these distinct communities.

However, in the 1950s and 1960s researchers started sifting the various sayings and episodes in the hope that, as well as reflecting community concerns, they might also reflect traces of an earlier stage in the life of Jesus. So, by the time I got to Trinidad it was possible to mention a further endeavour to find the history of Jesus—the Second Quest as it has been called.

Then, even while the Second Quest was going on, other researchers had begun to notice that, rather than trying to find an almost irrecoverable history *behind* individual episodes, there was valuable work to be done in looking closely at how the episodes had been assembled or edited ('redacted'), how they hung together and gave meaning. These beginnings ('redaction criticism') were modest, but they were important. They started to move the focus from an elusive history *behind* the Gospels towards the Gospels themselves— *the present Gospels in their finished state*. And so, from the shadows, the Gospels would soon emerge once more as books!

Two Steps Forward...

Amid the steam and sweat of Trinidad, I found these struggles with biblical history intriguing, and for diverse reasons it seemed right to share them with the public through newspaper articles. The articles led to controversy, and so to various meetings.

As well as being intriguing, these struggles with biblical history were also extremely difficult. For instance, the task of tracking the possible dependence between the five great witnesses to Jesus—Matthew, Mark, Luke, John and Paul—was proving to be endlessly baffling. Even the relationship between the three evangelists that look closest to one another, Matthew, Mark and Luke (the 'same-view' or 'syn-optic' Gospels), often seemed hopelessly elusive—the legendary Synoptic Problem.

On the other hand, despite all the difficulty, it was clear, in the larger picture of research, that progress had been made and, inch by inch, was still continuing. It was clearest in the work of Galileo, George Smith, and Darwin, but, even in the case of the Synoptic Problem, there had been significant progress. One key aspect of the puzzle was widely regarded as solved. Contrary to a long-standing view that the earliest Gospel was Matthew, and that Mark was later or independent, most researchers had come to a firm conclusion that the sequence was the opposite: Mark's Gospel was earliest and had been expanded by Matthew. And Mark had also been used by Luke. This conclusion, the priority of Mark, was not reached overnight. It had taken decades of testing, of trial-and-error—essentially of carefully comparing Matthew and Mark, first to try to verify that one had really used the other, and then to figure out who had used whom. Detective work, but with much methodical plodding. And the same was done regarding establishing Luke's dependence on Mark.

Yet as well as progress there was resistance. Perhaps it was easy for the Secretary of the Pontifical Biblical Commission to smile in 1955 about the narrowness of earlier days, but resistance was not over. For instance, rather than absorb the evidence that the flood account is a reworking of an older literary account, some modern investigators persist with the late tradition that Noah's Ark landed in Turkey, on magnificent Mount Ararat, virtually 17,000 feet high. And so, from time to time, people set off for Mount Ararat.

John's Gospel and Raymond Brown

My original assignment to Trinidad was for just nine months, after which I was due to take a year's study leave at the *Ecole Biblique* in Jerusalem to prepare the exam that would earn me a full teaching licence ('Licentiate in Sacred Scripture'—LSS). But the Trinidad assignment had to be extended into a second year, then into a third, and then a fourth.

Trinidad was giving me a new sense of how the Bible is both valuable and vulnerable—valuable because of its sense of what is important in life; vulnerable because its hold on specific historical events is not strong. Again and again, the historical claim, the literal interpretation, seemed fragile or impossible. In some cases this was no problem. Like many people, I could let go easily of the idea that Jonah lived 'for three days and three nights…in the belly of a whale'. But in other biblical narratives the historical interpretation seemed more crucial.

Finding reliable history in John's Gospel was particularly problematic. The account was often vivid, as if it were history, yet it not only diverged from the other Gospels, it also seemed most concerned not with history but with theology, with clarifying humans' general relationship to God, so much so that traditionally St John was often called The Theologian. In fact, according to Eusebius (c. 300)—the busy bishop of the ancient seaside diocese of Caesarea, who founded a library and wrote the oldest large-scale history of the church—Clement of Alexandria had said, around 200 CE, that 'John, last of all, seeing that what referred to externals [literally, "to bodily things"] in the gospel of our Saviour was sufficiently detailed [in the other

Gospels], wrote a spiritual gospel' (*Ecclesiastical History* 6.14.7). Still, twentieth-century researchers were putting John's historicity under fresh scrutiny, so much so that commentator Westcott lamented that the historians had driven the theologians from the field. Raymond Brown often recounted how, when he was embarking on his commentary on John, his mentor, the highly regarded William Foxwell Albright, urged him to deal with history rather than with questions about theology, about God. Brown had replied to Albright that, given how the gospel begins, he would have to engage theology; which he did. But Brown also emphasized history—big time. He developed the thesis—not completely new—that John's differences from the other Gospels, when combined with the idea of oral tradition, constituted a strong case that John had an independent link to the original events. John's Gospel, after all, somehow seemed deeply historical—a striking antidote to Schweitzer. Brown's commentary appeared extraordinarily comprehensive and helpful, and also reassuring. I read it over and over.

Yet the memory of Schweitzer lingered. In December 1953, when at age 77 he came to receive the Nobel Peace Prize, the reception committee at the Oslo railway station were taken aback when it seemed that he had not arrived. Eventually, they realized that while he had not come where they expected, in First Class, he was elsewhere down the platform, at Third Class. And with the prize money, Schweitzer returned to French Equatorial Africa, to Lambaréné, and founded a home for lepers.

As for me, suddenly it was time to leave Trinidad—13 June 1972, a Tuesday, early in the morning—one of those dates you remember without trying.

Part II

THE SECOND REVOLUTION:
LITERARY SOURCES

*Becoming aware of where biblical writers
found much of their material*

Chapter 5

OUT OF THE BLUE:
THE NEW TESTAMENT SHOWS
MORE CLEARLY ITS DEPENDENCE ON THE OLD

In September 1972 a second revolution struck. To prepare for examinations in Rome (for the Licenciate in Scripture), I had gone into virtual seclusion in a hostel of the Dominican sisters in a village in Normandy. My custom was to study Old Testament (i.e. the Hebrew Scriptures plus seven other books) in the morning and New Testament in the afternoon and evening, and I had spent much of the previous day with Matthew, a Gospel I knew well from teaching it in Trinidad. Now I was focused on Deuteronomy when I suddenly said 'That is like Matthew, that is *so like* Matthew'—something about the sense of community, the discourses, the blessings and curses, the mountain setting. I wondered about it, but needed to concentrate on the exams. I quickly made a half-page of notes, and told myself not to think about it. Yet at lunchtime I could not resist talking about it.

In the following days other similar phenomena emerged. Aspects of the Elijah–Elisha narrative showed startling similarities to Luke–Acts, and the book of Wisdom's confrontation between Wisdom and the kings of the earth felt somewhat like John's account of the meeting between Jesus and Pilate.

Eventually, when the exams were unceremoniously over, and I had moved to Jerusalem for a year's study—to the *Ecole Biblique*—I faced a dilemma. Jerusalem seemed an excellent place to study biblical history and archaeology, but I was now concerned that the New Testament appeared to come not only from the land and its people but also from a book—from the Old Testament. In fact, while in Rome I had made arrangements to do a dissertation on the relationship between the Gospels and the Old Testament. So while I embraced Jerusalem's courses and excursions on history and archaeology, including unforgettable trips to Hebron, the Negev, Sinai, Galilee, Samaria, and the Holy Sepulchre, I also bought a copy of the Greek Old Testament, the LXX (Septuagint), and with Matthew in mind, started ploughing through Deuteronomy.

The ploughing was tedious. Connections with Matthew seemed few and flimsy. Then, suddenly, in Deuteronomy 15, the search came to life. The repeated emphasis on remission resonated with Matthew's emphasis on forgiveness (Mt. 18). Both use similar Greek terminology. Obviously such similarity proved nothing. But further comparison revealed more links. And the Deuteronomic word for debt, *daneion*, is unknown elsewhere in the Bible—except in Matthew 18. Gradually the pieces of the puzzle began to fall into place. Matthew 18 had used first-century materials, including Mark, but it had also absorbed Deuteronomy 15.

Once I had got inside part of the Deuteronomy–Matthew connection, the rest of it became easier to track, and then I kept going over the two texts.

The quantity and complexity of the emerging Old Testament–New Testament links became such that I failed to obtain a diploma from the *Ecole Biblique*. When I presented my initial work on Matthew and Deuteronomy to the person who had generously offered to oversee my work in Jerusalem, the assessment of what I was doing was resoundingly negative (*ni la méthode ni la logique*), and I was instructed that the way to find out how Matthew had worked was by comparing the Gospels and by taking account of the Q source. Argument proved useless, and I began to realize that to get a diploma I would have to abandon the trail that was leading to the Old Testament. The diploma was to be a first step towards the dissertation in Rome, so once the diploma fell through I cancelled the arrangements for a dissertation. Nearly twenty years passed before the work on Matthew 18 and Deuteronomy was published (Brodie 1992a). Yet the *Ecole* provided an invaluable context for initiating the exploration. Langlamet, professor of Old Testament, said Matthew's dependence on Deuteronomy made immediate sense to him ('Some form of midrash', he said). He had once thought of the idea, but had never developed it. Boismard, lecturing on John, simply asked, 'Are you learning?', and when I answered yes, he said 'Then stay with it'.

Soon the pattern of literary dependence began to emerge. Part of that pattern was surprisingly complicated:

(1) Matthew's use of Deuteronomy was twofold:

- A small kernel of the Gospel, *a series of enigmatic sayings* in Matthew 5 and 11 (five beatitudes, five antitheses, and a revelatory cry, 'I thank you, Father...') contained a dense distillation of Deuteronomy (Deuteronomy, plus a lesser use of Sirach).
- The Gospel as a whole contained a further more expansive reworking of Deuteronomy.

The kernel, the *series of sayings*, was such, so distinctive, coherent, and complete, both in itself and as a distillation of Deuteronomy, that it looked like a distinct arrangement. As a working hypothesis, I gave this arrangement the traditional name *logia*, 'Sayings'.

(2) Luke–Acts likewise contained two modes of using LXX narrative: one heavy (in about ten chapters of Luke's Gospel, plus half of Acts, as far as Acts 15.35), the other light. I did not realize then that the variation in the two halves of Acts—heavy usage of the LXX in the first, light in the second—was a commonplace among scholars. Nor did I pay sufficient attention to C.F. Evans's detection of the use of Deuteronomy in Luke's travel narrative (1955: 37-53). However, I did become aware that many researchers maintained that Luke–Acts once existed in some shorter form, a form that in some analyses contained about half of Acts and was known as Proto-Luke.

(3) Mark's links to the Old Testament seemed so complex that the investigation halted. But then, amid a fallow period of going nowhere, in the calm of a Sunday morning, the idea dawned that perhaps Mark knew an epistle. (In reality, this idea was not new.) The epistles proved to be just one component, but an important one, first for Mark and later for the other Gospels. It emerged that each Gospel had used both the Old Testament and some epistles.

(4) Each Gospel writer also used the preceding Gospels. To some degree, this is accepted; most researchers now hold that Matthew and Luke used Mark, and some maintain Luke used Matthew. But such views began to emerge as just part of a larger pattern of Gospel interdependence.

The tracing of these connections happened very rapidly, through a trial and error process that I could not articulate but that caused me, for the first time in my life, not to be able to sleep. I tried to slow things down and to put the pieces together. A Jerusalem hospital gave help, and the nurse, from Limerick, had a sense of how far I was from my native fields. By the end of the academic year (June 1973) it was possible to trace the central sequence of literary dependence:

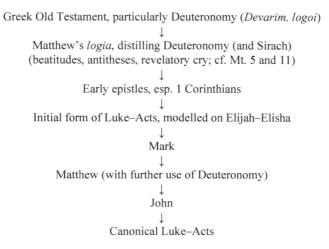

Greek Old Testament, particularly Deuteronomy (*Devarim, logoi*)
↓
Matthew's *logia*, distilling Deuteronomy (and Sirach)
(beatitudes, antitheses, revelatory cry; cf. Mt. 5 and 11)
↓
Early epistles, esp. 1 Corinthians
↓
Initial form of Luke–Acts, modelled on Elijah–Elisha
↓
Mark
↓
Matthew (with further use of Deuteronomy)
↓
John
↓
Canonical Luke–Acts

Within this sequence, each writer used all who preceded, though with vary-ing modes of dependence. This sequence of dependence was just the back-bone of a complex literary and historical process, but it had considerable implications. It gave a framework for approaching New Testament writings; it outlined a solution to the Synoptic Problem; and it provided a context for discussing John. The more pressing concern, however, was not the complex-ity or the implications, but simply whether the basic sequence was correct. This was going to take time. And I also needed time out.

The time out proved to be more than I bargained for. I felt that a brief visit to the surrounding countries, Lebanon, Syria and Jordan, would deepen my sense of the lands from which biblical and other writings emerged, and so with notebook in hand—I still sent articles to a newspaper in Trinidad—I made my way from Beirut to Damascus and on to Amman and Aqaba, but this was May 1973, in the aftermath of a deadly Israeli mission into Beirut and in the shadow of intensifying tension between Palestinian refugees near Beirut and the Lebanese government. The night journey back from Amman to Damascus and on to Beirut was punctuated by nervous military check-points until eventually, about 8 am in Beirut, a taxi I had just taken was confronted by an oncoming tank, so the taxi driver did a fast U-turn and hooshed me on to the side of the street, where, following a conversation with a soldier, I and my notebook were arrested under suspicion of spying for Israel, and, minus my notebook, I was put in jail. The jail was badly over-crowded. Most of those with me were Palestinians. When I was taken out some time in the afternoon for interrogation, the interrogators changed rooms to avoid shots from the surrounding streets. Out in the streets themselves over sixty people died that day. Less than forty-eight hours after arrest, I was deported.

Later that summer I secured more time for my work—my boss in Trinidad, Damian Byrne, was supremely generous—and thanks to the hospitality of the Dominican sisters in the village in Normandy, I was again able to go into seclusion. There, for what eventually became two and a half years, I scruti-nized the primary texts more closely, elaborating all the time, trying to some degree to articulate the criteria for establishing literary dependence, and constantly testing, testing, testing.

The biggest surprise from those years concerned the nature and role of the epistles. I had not wanted to become entangled with the epistles, but the detail of the epistles was indicating that they were part of a complex literary process of using extant writings. Many epistles had transformed the great Old Testament narratives, especially the Pentateuch, and—apart from building on one another (itself a huge phenomenon)—they in turn had been transformed into one component of the Gospels and Acts. The process was particularly decisive in 1 Corinthians. Despite its distinctive first-century content, it was pervaded by the Old Testament, especially the Pentateuch, including

Deuteronomy, and it had contributed decisively to the early shorter version of Luke–Acts, the proto-gospel modelled on Elijah–Elisha, what might be called Proto-Luke.

The overall sequence was confirmed. Like the Elijah–Elisha narrative, but more so, Proto-Luke moved from historiography towards biography (*bios*); and Mark, building on Proto-Luke, brought the process further. Unravelling Mark's use of Proto-Luke was exceptionally difficult. Matthew expanded Mark, especially with discourses. And John, building on Matthew, brought discourses to a new level. Canonical Luke–Acts retained Proto-Luke in full but expanded it with diverse distillations of the other Gospels and with an extension of the narrative to include arrival in Rome. I will not reproduce the detailed evidence here. Since then I have given it elsewhere, or at least given as much of it as was feasible.[1]

In Spring of 1975 I produced a manuscript and immediately showed it to a British publisher, and then to a second, but their responses indicated that it was not at all what publishers wanted. What ruled it out above all else was its conclusion that Jesus had not existed. As the first publisher said, 'It's not just that we won't take it. Nobody will take it.' The second publisher said no Christian publishing house would take it.

And yet the evidence was very strong. In testing the Gospels, essentially every strand concerning the life of Jesus consistently yielded clear signs of being dependent on older writings—on the epistles, and on the Old Testament, especially in its Greek version. The clincher was 1 Corinthians. I knew I had not analyzed its sources fully, but the evidence was sufficient and consistent—especially regarding its use of the Pentateuch, particularly Numbers and Deuteronomy—to know that its picture of Jesus was essentially a synthesis and adaptation of older Jewish traditions. Even Paul's list of post-resurrection appearances (1 Cor. 15.5-9) turned out to be largely a synthesis and adaptation of the diverse descents and appearances of the Lord during the crises in Numbers 11–17 (note esp. Num 11.25; 12.5; 14.10; 16.19; 17.7). So if I was convinced of the conclusion but could not get a publisher, what should I do?

I turned first to those I knew best—old friends in Trinidad, especially those experienced in scripture. If over a period of a year we could examine the manuscript closely it would be much clearer whether to scrap it or develop it. On 12 May 1975 I returned for a trial visit of six weeks—delighted to be back, regardless of the manuscript—and within an hour of landing, I was sitting with Everard Johnston, Lecturer in scripture and dogma, at his house in Picton Street, Port of Spain, discussing the manuscript. By then his young wife, June, had gone to bed, and amid the sounds of the tropical night we sipped rum and coke as I tried to explain the basic idea of rewriting.

1. See esp. Brodie 2004.

I handed him page 128 on connections between 1 Corinthians and the Old Testament.

He took his time in perusing it, then he put it down, muttering, 'In the same order...the same order apart from minor modifications'.

We turned to the gospels, discussing the extent to which they too are a product of the rewriting. Suddenly he said, 'So we're back to Bultmann. We know nothing about Jesus.'

I paused a moment.

'It's worse than that'.

There was a silence.

Then he said, 'He never existed'.

I nodded.

There was another silence, a long one, and then he nodded gently, 'It makes sense'.

For months afterwards, and even for years, in moments of basic doubt about the work and about myself, those three words could come back to me.

But during the subsequent weeks in Trinidad the plan of a team working together for a year turned out to be impractical. Despite genuine interest, people were so committed to what they were already doing that there was little prospect of giving the manuscript the amount of attention it might need.

So, plan B? We soon thought of something fairly obvious—the Dominicans. We cabled the office of the main man, the *Magister Generalis* (literally general teacher), Vincent de Couesnongle, found he was at home, arranged a meeting, and I travelled almost non-stop from Trinidad to Rome. If I could get a group of Dominican biblical scholars to examine the manuscript they would be able either to demolish it or to issue a calm and confident statement about its value and implications. And it seemed that the one person who might gather such a group was the head man.

He listened to me patiently, and looked carefully through some of the manuscript. I brought the conclusions to his attention.

'You cannot teach that', he said quietly.

I explained that I didn't want to teach the conclusions, just the method, as applied to limited areas of the New Testament. If the method was unable to stand the pressure of academic challenge, from students and other teachers, then I could quietly wave it good-bye and let the groundless conclusions evaporate in silence.

It was a Saturday afternoon. He needed time to think it over. He would see me in a few days.

On Monday morning I went to see the editors of some biblical journals. One said the journal had a two-year waiting list which could not be bypassed. To me two years seemed like eternity. Another editor said the material was outside his competence. But the third was interested, took an excerpt from the manuscript and said to call back next morning.

That evening, after supper, the Master General sent for me. The proposal of a study group was not practical. He couldn't really call up a whole lot of busy people to come and see some curious object ('*un truc*'). It would be better to work through other channels. Periodicals, for instance. Ah, I was doing that. Good. And I would be seeing the editor next morning. Good, good. And we began to talk of various other things.

Next morning I called to see the editor who had taken the excerpt. He was out but had left the excerpt, plus a letter that said 'I am not interested in this or in anything of a similar nature'.

I went out and sat for about an hour on the steps of the church, the Gesú as it is called. I was aware of people coming and going but I was seeing and hearing through a kind of daze.

'They're not going to believe it. Nobody's ever going to believe it.'

And I went on sitting there, repeating the same phrase off and on, gazing distantly at the people, realizing there was no point in just sitting on the steps, but not knowing where I would go if I got up. So it seemed best just to stay there. Or rather nothing seemed best, so I did nothing.

That afternoon and the following day I searched around Rome for various people who might help in one way or another. But it was July and most people were away.

On the way back to Etrepagny I called on the Dominicans in Paris, and having once done a minor thesis on the work of Yves Congar, decided to approach him about my project. He glanced at the manuscript and then looked at me rather sadly, 'I have neither the time nor the competence'. When I finally reached Etrepagny, the sisters were delighted to see me.

In a further search for a way forward, I checked out possibilities in France, and then in Ireland. As chances faded of finding some form of cooperation or publication, I next asked an Irish bank manager if he would loan me the money to print the manuscript so that it would have a chance either to make a contribution or to be roundly rebutted, but he just laughed at me, gently. Then, following a long family tradition, I sought permission to go to America, and my undeclared purpose was to earn as much money as was needed. A printer in Connemara agreed to produce the manuscript in book form in two years, and in September 1976 I got a job at the regional seminary in Boynton Beach, Florida, teaching Old Testament in Spanish to students from Puerto Rico, Cuba and Mexico. I chose Old Testament rather than New Testament because I wanted to protect the students from New Testament ideas that had not received any outside approval, and also because I just love the Old Testament. At that time Old Testament studies were developing quickly, especially regarding history, form criticism, and sources, including the slow-burning idea that Hebrew narrative, especially the Pentateuch, had reshaped prophetic writings—a partial precedent for the Gospels' use of the Epistles.

All was going well—I had already received the proofs of the planned book—until the summer of 1977 when I decided to tell Damian Byrne, who by now had been elected Irish Dominican provincial, what I was doing. The discussion was late at night, long and difficult, in a car parked in the rain outside my parents' new house, in Galway. He listened calmly for a long time. However, when I told him I proposed to spend £3,000 sterling on printing, he said, 'But that's daft'. Not even the head of the Dominicans in the whole country ('the Provincial') was allowed to spend that much money without consulting others, and in any case it would be better to start publishing my work slowly, for instance through articles in journals. Meanwhile he would submit the manuscript to some recognized scholar or scholars. Next morning I cancelled the printing.

Almost two weeks later I met Damian again, this time in his room in Dublin and in a lighter atmosphere. In the course of the conversation I accidentally hit his radio.

'It's all very fine to destroy my faith', said he, laughing, 'but spare my radio'.

I returned to the question of printing *The Artists*. 'I know it's daft', I said, 'but the whole affair from the beginning has been daft'.

'It is you who say it.'

As we parted he said that whatever else, he could guarantee that I would receive sympathy, but he meant emotional sympathy and, much as I valued that, I needed sympathy of mind, understanding. At one stage in the middle of an important explanation—the dramatic parallel between Gal. 3.1-5 and Jer. 5.21-25, and its implications—I had nearly cried with frustration when I realized that he was nodding agreement and opening his letters without really listening. But I stifled the frustration and he never noticed. Could I blame him for not listening when internationally known experts would not listen?

A few hours later, in Cork, I met his assistant, Micheál O'Regan, another friend both from student and Trinidadian days, a psychologist. It made literary, spiritual and psychological sense to him but he was still able to make a farce out of it. We drank, and howled with laughter. And he didn't think that printing was so daft. Then, spotting a statue of the Blessed Virgin, he paused momentarily and hurriedly crossed himself.

'She's watching us.'

Next morning, on the roundabout train back to Galway, I was struck by a passage from *Report to Greco*, the autobiographical novel by the Cretan writer Nikos Kazantzakis. He had felt the urge to confront a monk with the emptiness of his self-satisfied life:

> But I did not speak. A crest of lard, habit, and cowardice envelops the soul; no matter what it craves from the depths of its prison, the lard, habit, and cowardice carry out something entirely different. I did not speak—from cowardice. That night…I confessed this to my friend.

'You must have refrained out of courtesy, not cowardice', he said to console me, 'out of pity because you did not want to sadden such a fine fellow. Perhaps even out of the conviction that your words would have accomplished nothing.'

'No, no', I protested. 'Even if it's as you think, we must conquer the minor virtues you talk about—courtesy, pity, expediency. I am less afraid of the major vices than of the minor virtues because these have lovely faces and deceive us all too easily. For my part, I want to give the worst explanation: I say I did it from cowardice, because I want to shame my soul and keep it from doing the same thing again' (Kazantzakis 1965: 213).

What had I done? I had abandoned my bold scheme, given up my plan of printing and going for broke in 1978. Because of what? Minor virtue? Political realism? Respect for an established procedure within the Catholic community? Probably the latter…with some obscure uneasy mixture of the others. And because I trusted that the Almighty was writing straight with crooked lines. But I sometimes asked myself if the Almighty was always so finicky.

Soon afterwards I returned to Boynton Beach and then realized the annual meeting of the Catholic Biblical Association was due to begin two days later in Detroit. Did I really want to go there? So far, so much money—for what? To listen to people I didn't agree with and to talk with people to whom I didn't make sense? Exactly.

But it was still worth it. Basically because of the personal character of most of those attending, their decency, dedication and lack of pretension. As one woman put it, 'They are not a very power-hungry group'. And the prayers included one for dear old Elvis Presley who died the first day.

Though I felt I did not belong within the discussion most of the time I saw that there were some chinks in the academic armour. For instance, the century-old theory about the Pentateuch being based on four sources was in real trouble, and there were doubts here and there about the effectiveness of the method of investigation (the historical-critical method) which had been used for so long. You could hear some titters when I suggested that part of the Pentateuch might depend on the prophets, but one man encouraged me to write it up and present it in more coherent form. This was an important development. Having spoken about it fairly openly at the convention, I no longer felt that it was taboo, that I had to hide it back at the Boynton Beach seminary.

But on return to the seminary I hit the worst depression of my life, and the only one to last several days. In fact, at first, I didn't know what was happening to me, so rarely do I get depressed. Then I began to realize that intellectually the convention had been a colossal frustration, and that the array of prestigious names holding views so contrary to my own had in fact overwhelmed me, and that the depression had been building up while I was still in Detroit. Besides the stopping of the printing meant that my basic strategy was in disarray, and it was only when I settled down again in the seminary that the sense of disarray took hold more fully.

Still, I returned to the enjoyment of teaching the narratives and prophets of the Old Testament, I formally joined the Catholic Biblical Association and the Society of Biblical Literature, and the following summer, August 1978, gave a Research Report at the CBA meeting on the Pentateuch's use of the Prophets. The Report was accompanied by a 60-page home-made brochure (7 x 8½ inches) with a title in four lines:

The Hebrew Method of
C R E A T I V E   R E W R I T I N G
as the Key to Unravelling the Sources
of the Pentateuch

For me, studying the Torah was absorbing and, at some level, restorative, but I needed to get back to explaining my understanding of the origin of the New Testament, and so started trying to express my New Testament ideas in articles. But I still did not have the technical know-how. Tallaght, in its idealism, had emphasized learning theology, not exam results or the technical method of writing a research paper. For instance, when I once put considerable energy into preparing a paper on the pros and cons of capital punishment—cycling back and forth for weeks from Tallaght to the reading room in Trinity College, Dublin—the benign teacher, a Longford man, had held it up before the class and simply said several times 'There is something missing in this paper. There is something missing in this paper.' But he did not say what it was, and it was a long time before I figured it out—footnotes and bibliography, things of which I knew almost nothing, and that I was very slow to learn.

As a result, my efforts at writing articles for scholarly journals were tortuous. I was particularly keen to publish an article in the *Catholic Biblical Quarterly* (*CBQ*), a journal widely esteemed among scholars of all denominations. Ahead of submitting one particular article to the *CBQ* editor, I sent the manuscript to the eminent Raymond E. Brown in the hope that he would send me critical comments. As if he had nothing else to do. He replied promptly and helpfully, though the only two comments I remember exactly were: 'You need to tighten the grammar', and 'It has a chance'. The article did not make it, but I began another.

One of the advantages even of a rejection was that it provided a sense of what the established scholarly world would say regarding the material. This was invaluable in teaching. It gave me the freedom to give some of the material to the students, because after making a presentation, I would say something like, 'That is what I believe is true, but this is a professional assessment of what I have given you', and I would read out the rejection, along with its reasons. And then the students could wrestle with it.

Once when I had read out a rejection statement from the *CBQ*, one of the students asked, 'Is that the first rejection?'

'No, it is the fourth.'

'Four out of how many?'

'Four out of four.'

Silence.

'Well, we love you anyway.'

Outside the classroom I scarcely ever alluded to having a particular view of the way the biblical texts were composed, and when preaching at weekends in a parish, I was usually able to concentrate on the message of the text without becoming involved in problems of history. In fact, leaving history aside generally made it easier to deal with the meaning. However, when conversations developed about the Bible, it was often difficult to avoid questions of history, and one woman in the parish began to realize there was something I was not saying. She and her family became my friends, but still I hedged and hedged and hedged, dreading what I would do to her faith if I told her what I thought, and the fear of damaging her encapsulated the fear of what I would do to so many other people.

Then one night while I was visiting her home, she and I were sitting alone on the living room couch, and her husband and four children were scattered in different rooms in the house, watching TV and so forth. Our conversation was relaxed until it somehow turned to my work, and she asked what it was that most concerned me about the Bible.

Eventually I said, 'It's just about Jesus'.

Her questions were gentle, but she did want to know more. I was physically holding myself together, and looking down at the carpet. Then I looked up.

'He never really existed.'

'Oh, that's what I believed since I was a little girl.'

That night, at three different moments, I experienced a sudden forceful cascade of crying such as I did not know was possible, like a wave that rushed from somewhere deep in my body—first while sitting on the couch, later while driving home northwards on Military Trail, and again in the middle of the night when I suddenly found myself awake, sitting up.

Meanwhile, publishing articles remained important. And baffling. The four out of four became ten out of ten. I met the editor at a conference and asked him for advice. He said, 'Try another journal'.

By then, however, I was absorbing something else. The Irish Provincial, my good colleague and friend Damian Byrne, in an effort to get at the truth and to be fair to me, had submitted the entire manuscript of *The Artists* to scholarly assessment, and I understood that it was to several people—a committee of scholars with international reputations. He did not reveal their number or their identities, and I respected that as an effort to focus on the issue rather than on personalities. However, during a visit to Tallaght he told me the result of their work and allowed me to read one evaluation, that of Geza Vermes. As an Oxford-based eminent Jewish scholar who had become a Catholic priest and later returned to the Jewish faith, Vermes had huge standing. He had worked on the rewriting of Scripture and I could see how he might have seemed to be a good referee. The only details I remember from Vermes' statement, apart from his negative assessment, was that, given his personal history, his judgment was not due to any faith-based prejudice, and that I was not accurate in my comments on the Pharisees.

At the time the scholarly assessment seemed an important event, decisive. It meant that the best international opinion judged the thesis to be untrue.

I have often wondered whether the full documentation from that international committee is still in existence in some file or archive. In October 2009 I emailed Jerome Murphy-O'Connor of the *Ecole Biblique* to ask if he knew anything about it, and he replied, 'I remember vaguely the assessment you mention, but I do not think that I was involved. In any case I have no documentation relative to it. I seem to remember, however, that the MS was sent to Geza Vermes at Oxford.' I wonder now whether I misunderstood. Perhaps it was not sent to a committee, just to Geza Vermes.

Damian sometimes tried to encourage me by telling me about some Irish Dominican in earlier years, apparently in the 1920s or 30s or 40s, who had had an unusual theory—the details were never clear, and I was not sufficiently assertive to ask for them. This man had not succeeded in communicating his theory, 'but his work was kept in the archives. And so can yours.'

As I continued to work in Boynton Beach, I began to wonder about my location. Having a strange theory is bad enough, but when you are unknown and you send in a bit of the theory from an address that says a beach in Florida, then perhaps someone has had too much sun. Besides, even on paper I was not properly qualified. A Licence ('Licentiate in Sacred Scripture') was an accepted teaching qualification in Europe, but in the United States you generally required a doctorate. And most of all, I myself had an inherent need for a doctorate, not just for the degree—the piece of paper—but for the discipline of producing an extensive piece of work that, in addition to being well-argued, would be well-documented and well-presented. The idea was not far-fetched. In Rome, as a precautionary measure, I had once done all the necessary courses for a doctorate, everything except the writing of the dissertation.

Leaving Florida would not be easy. Apart from being a place of sunshine and good friends, it was close to a world to which I felt attached—Latin America. In fact, at some deep level my life was constantly torn between the academic and the practical, between the theoretical and the applied. I had once put this dilemma to a long-time colleague and friend, Michel de Verteuil.

'I find it very hard to choose between them.'

It was June 1975, and we were sitting in Trinidad's sweltering heat.

'Don't', said he, without a pause.

I looked at him.

'Keep the two of them. Keep the tension.'

And it was because of that unresolved tension that in the summer of 1979, when the news was full of the post-revolution plight of the Nicaraguans, and when the archdiocese of Miami issued an appeal for funds to help the situation, for the first time I explicitly appealed for money, and then went to Nicaragua to see if I could be of any use. There someone I met on a bus brought me to a large vivacious family, and next morning I was taken to the Archbishop of Managua, Miguel Obando y Bravo, who promptly dispatched me to the parish of Tipitapa, and he added, '*Le doy todos los poderes*' ('I give you all the powers'). I was unsure what exactly that implied, but I kept going, and I soon reached Tipitapa, where I discovered that the church and presbytery were being used to house prisoners of war—the civil war was barely over, not fully in fact—and so I was taken in by a family near the other end of the town, and I started from there. There was never a question of not returning to Florida, of quitting without notice—I simply had to stay with clarifying the sources of the New Testament—but the tension remained. And Tipitapa sharpened it.

Chapter 6

THE SECOND REVOLUTION DEEPENS:
BERKELEY, NEW HAVEN, 1981–1984

A new phase in my awareness of the ancient use of sources was sparked by a question from Joseph Fitzmyer. In the Summer of 1980, during a visit to Washington, DC, I asked him to look at some of my work—a piece on Luke's use of Chronicles that had been published in the *Journal for the Study of the New Testament* (1979)—and when he had considered it, we met again, and he asked a simple question:

'Is the process you are invoking found elsewhere in the ancient world?'

I could not answer him.

As never before I started wading through libraries, and eventually hit on the obvious—the pervasive practice of Greco-Roman literary imitation (*mimēsis*) and its sundry ancient cousins, many of them Jewish. Jewish practices included rewriting and transforming older texts; and Jewish terms included *rewritten Bible, inner-biblical exegesis,* and the processes known rather loosely as *midrash,* Hebrew for *searching*—in this case searching for meaning. What I had noticed within the Bible was the tip of an iceberg. Here was a whole world of diverse ways of deliberately reshaping diverse sources. The process I was invoking was not just *present* in the ancient world—it was *at the very centre* of ancient composition. And the New Testament use of the Old, pivotal though it is, is just part of the larger pattern whereby the Bible as a whole distils the larger world of ancient writing.

I felt like a sailor who, in the middle of what might simply have been a vast ocean, gazes at the slow emergence of a new continent. Some of this phenomenon, especially the Jewish elements, had already influenced biblical studies, especially in Old Testament, but not much. Biblical studies had developed in a world where the very concept of any form of imitation was fading, and aversion to the notion of imitation had affected even classical studies. While our high school curriculum included Virgil and Homer, no one mentioned that one had imitated the other, had used it systematically as a source. The *Oxford Classical Dictionary* gave imitation no entry of its own until its third edition (1996).

The process of identifying sources, 'source criticism', already existed as part of the traditional historical-critical method. We saw earlier that it was one of the historians' allies. But, like one of Leonardo da Vinci's flying machines, it had earned a bad name, at least in so far as it did not really fly. The essence of traditional source criticism was to take *one* finished text, such as John's Gospel and, *on the basis of that text alone, to reconstruct a second text, a hypothetical source, that no one had ever seen.* In the case of John's Gospel the favourite hypothetical source was called the Signs Source, so named because of John's striking references to signs (esp. Jn 2.11; 4.54), but this document was given such diverse shapes that the process of reconstructing it emerged as bankrupt. For instance, of the 41 verses in the account of the man born blind (Jn 9), the number of verses assigned to the Signs Source varied from 34 (Becker) or 28 (Bultmann) to 3 (Schnackenburg) or 2½ (Boismard).[1]

The essence of the other source criticism—what for me was a second revolution—was to compare *two known* texts, and *to establish that one had used the other as a source.* The basic process in fact was not new. Traditional biblical studies, the historical-critical method, included several instances of showing that one extant document depended on another, but what was new was the *quantity* of the biblical text that was so indebted, plus the *complexity* of the ways in which the source texts had been used. What was also new was that whereas the older source criticism had lost credibility, this other kind offered a prospect of verifiability that could provide progress in identifying sources. It would not be easy. It needed patience, patience, patience. But it could be done.

By patience I do not mean endurance. Most researchers have endurance— the capacity to spend long hours reading and researching. But patience means being receptive to something different, even strange, something that goes against one's established picture, that challenges the imagination.

The implications for biblical studies were radical. The notorious Synoptic Problem, for instance—the tantalizing puzzle of the relationship between the first three Gospels—was largely a problem about the use of sources, but it had made little reference to the complexity of how the rest of the world used sources. And neither did the discussion of the Fourth Gospel.

The emergence of the new continent upset my life. The situation seemed like a wake-up call for biblical studies, but above all it was a further wake-up call for myself. Without fully realizing it, I had been resting in Florida. I had indeed been working steadily—lots of hours—but not with the intensity of '72–'75. At some level within me, the pressure was off. Years later, I realized this was probably good—a needed respite in my mid-thirties for the long haul

---

1. For details, see Brodie 1993a: 48.

ahead. Even after the plan to publish *The Artists* had been scotched, I still stayed in Florida, hoping for a breakthrough, still hoping that I could write articles that would reach other researchers.

But the overall failure to publish persisted. And so in December 1980 I left the lovely job and people in Florida and set off, first to write a thesis, a dissertation, and then, with a recommendation from Brevard Childs, to take up a research fellowship in New Haven, Connecticut, at Yale Divinity School.

The dissertation was written at Berkeley, where my Rome-based supervisor happened to be living at the time, and, while writing, I taught a course on the Mosaic Torah—the Pentateuch—at the Graduate Theological Union. The students were keen, but I told them, if bored, to feel free to gaze through the massive window to their left. It looked out on the Golden Gate Bridge. Once back in my room I blocked my own small window to keep cool and concentrated, and, using materials from earlier years, wrote intensely for long hours, so intensely I developed health problems, and met an incredibly kind doctor and his family.

'Thesis' can suggest a ringing challenge—the standard image of Martin Luther nailing his theses to the door of Wittenberg cathedral—but this thesis sounded calm: *Luke the Literary Interpreter: Luke–Acts as a Systematic Rewriting and Updating of the Elijah–Elisha Narrative in 1 and 2 Kings*.

I was writing in long-hand, but with back-up from a pianist who realized her piano skills were worth more on a typewriter than on a piano. She became involved in the search for Luke's sources and enjoyed the flow of thought that was trying to track them down. 'Where's the next instalment?' she would ask, 'This is like a detective story'.

Eventually I handed my supervisor what I thought was my thesis—350 pages magnificently and expensively typed.

A week later he called me in. 'That will do fine', he said, 'as an initial, tentative, preliminary, opening first draft. You will rewrite it according to the following specifications.' And he spelled out a methodical sequence for analyzing and presenting the material.

The typist was glad of more work, but her interest plummeted. 'That's the same old kind of bull—I've been typing for that place for years'.

Later she saw it differently. 'Yes, I can see why he did it. It is better. Clearer and more convincing.'

Eventually, in December 1981, I presented the thesis in Rome. One of the requirements for obtaining the degree was to go over to the majestic Lateran complex to pay a kind of levy to the diocese of Rome. When I arrived there one bright morning I managed after a while to find a chubby genial official, in some kind of black uniform, sitting at an empty table near a door looking out on the sunny piazza, and he was open for business. I explained that I was getting a doctorate and had written a dissertation, and I placed the imposing work modestly on the corner of the table. He kept looking up at me, chatting away about where I was from, and where was I making the presentation in Rome, and where I was staying, and was I well, and said that that would be so many thousand lire. I paid, and picked up what I had left on the corner of the table, and we smiled at each other, and I went home.

Looking back, the thesis was a mixture of weak and strong. I was claiming that Luke used the Elijah–Elisha narrative as a basic model for his own work, and, while this was essentially true, I had not correctly identified the narrative's beginning, ending, or structure. For instance, I omitted the crucial opening picture of the deviant reign of Ahab and Jezebel (1 Kgs 16.29-34)—rather like omitting the scene of the witches from the opening of Macbeth, or more pertinently, like omitting the scene of the world's wrongdoing from the beginning of the story of the Deluge (Gen. 6.1-7). Also, I got one section plain wrong, concerning Luke's account of the mission to Samaria (Acts 8.1b-8); I forced the evidence. My efforts to publish the thesis failed, but the failure pushed me into rewriting parts of it as possible articles.

Meanwhile, around the end of August 1981, I had moved to New Haven. There I was delighted to find that Yale has a great phrase, 'Thinking the Unthinkable'. Yet, even in dedicated people, the reality is often far from the saying. Occasionally, while in New Haven, I took out the 1975 manuscript—the proofs—and looked at it, and wondered with whom to discuss it. I attended a seminar conducted by Luke Timothy Johnson, 'Method and Madness', in which, week-by-week, with the help of the students, he analyzed the methods used in New Testament research. His critiques were thorough and devastating. Here was a man who could think. Ultimately I was disappointed. I felt that at the crucial moment, when the time came to synthesize the conclusions of all his critiques, the seminar flinched. Maybe it seemed there was no alternative. Still, the seminar as a whole was very instructive—it spelled out my own half-formulated concerns—and above all it was encouraging.

Abraham Malherbe's seminar on history, Luke and Greco-Roman background was also instructive, and he gave me the opportunity to present to the class the evidence that part of the Stephen story (Acts 6–7) had drawn systematically on the account of the false accusing and stoning of Naboth (1 Kgs 21). At the end of the presentation, Malherbe was genial—he always seemed to be—and when I thanked him as we were coming out the door, he said to me with a smile, 'I hope, Tom, that you don't think you convinced me'.

I laughed, but afterwards I was deflated. What would it take to get someone to stop and reconsider? Or, turning it around, what would it take on my part to make the evidence sufficiently clear and strong? I discussed it with Luke Johnson, and he encouraged me to keep working on it, to keep clarifying both the content and presentation, and to submit it for publication to the *CBQ*.

I attended Childs's classes and spoke to him informally from time to time. Occasionally we had lunch together in various places, and I always learned from him. He was warm and strong and apparently always thinking. Once when we were to have lunch, I decided to go for it. I would bring my 1975 manuscript and give it to him. So I did. I brought it, we got our light lunches, and we sat down in the Divinity School cafeteria. The manuscript was on the ground beside me, resting against the leg of the table, in a large canary-coloured envelope. I would be able to take it up easily and give it to him. We finished our food, and talked on. As never before, I was still trying to get a sense of him. What if he rejected it? What if he were convinced by it? Or half-convinced? With other students I had been out to his house in Bethany, outside the city. At the Divinity School ball I had danced with his wife, Anne. Now, as I sat there, I tried to get clarity.

I grabbed another cup of lukewarm cafeteria tea.

Then after a while we parted amiably until the next time, and I put the manuscript back in my shoulder bag.

Soon afterwards, I went to the Divinity School library, asked if it had an archive section, and consigned the manuscript to the archives. I did not know whether they recorded receiving it, and sometimes wondered if it was still there.

Having spent some time trying to compose publishable articles on Luke—on Luke's imitative use of the Greek Septuagint—I turned again to John. The question was simple: Was it possible, bearing in mind the standard first-century methods of reworking texts, to establish whether John's Gospel had used known scripture texts—again the Septuagint, also the epistles, and above all the earlier Gospels, the three Synoptics? Following the lead of Louis Martyn in his search for what was happening in the Gospel and behind it, it seemed appropriate to give special attention to the account of the man born blind (Jn 9). Already in the 1970s I had worked on this account's broad link to the Naaman narrative (2 Kgs 5), but the Synoptics seemed to offer a further verifiable source, more immediate and more substantial.

For most of a year (1982–1983) I sat with a page containing two columns of Greek text: John's account of the man born blind, and the Synoptic text that seemed closest to it—a Markan sequence of episodes involving aspects of sight and insight, from the discussion about signs to the transfiguration (Mk 8.11–9.8). Some of the other students mocked me gently as they passed by or looked over my shoulder: 'You and that page'. The evidence favouring John's dependence seemed overwhelming—dozens of links, many of them substantial; but there was no clear pattern, and so the evidence as a whole was not convincing. I realized I was trying to explain how John 9 used sources without knowing John's meaning. So I started trying to trace the chapter's meaning, but then found I could not do it without examining the meaning of other chapters.

I had almost no income in New Haven, but I also had almost no expenses. In return for light duties as a chaplain, the Sisters of Mercy gave me a room and food. Sometimes I also did some work in a parish, and once, when I was giving a talk on the Pentateuch, and a debate arose about how much of it was history and how much was not, an elderly strongly built black-clad Italian woman asked, 'Why can't we just say it's a story?'

The time in New Haven, combined with the experience of writing the dissertation, enabled me, for the first time in my life, to get a handle on the proper academic way of presenting a proposal, particularly the way of patiently setting out the argument, of adding necessary qualifications, and of providing adequate supporting documentation. As I went along, I was encouraged by occasional meetings with other researchers at conferences. Once, even while still in Florida, I was attending a regional meeting of the SBL in Kentucky, at the Galt Hotel in Louisville—a hotel in which Charles Dickens had once stayed—and had given a thirty-minute paper on a small passage in the morning. Response had been as usual—some scepticism, some interest, plus a strong sense of 'So What?' In the afternoon I was sitting in the lobby when someone walked up, gave his name, which I missed at the time, and said in a gentle Southern accent, 'Tell me a little bit about yourself'. He had been present at the morning talk, but I had not noticed him. Eventually he said, 'I think you're on to something'. He would be editing a volume of papers on Luke–Acts, and if I wished I could try submitting an article. He specified what was needed, and later, while in New Haven, with time, resources and a better sense of the necessary methods, I worked carefully on a lengthy article—'Greco-Roman Imitation of Texts as a Partial Guide to Luke's Use of Sources'—and asked him if it was what he had had in mind. He replied, 'No, it's better', and he went on to include it in the volume of essays: Charles H. Talbert (ed.), *Luke–Acts: New Perspectives from the Society of Biblical Literature* (1984). When combined with the publishing of two articles in 1983—one in *Biblica*, and another in the *CBQ* (finally, the Stephen–Naboth article)—and with acceptance of a further article in *New Testament Studies*, the piece in the Talbert volume seemed to indicate that, nine years after finishing the basic manuscript in Normandy, I had recovered energy and had gained a toehold in the academic world. The former editor of the *CBQ*—the person who told me to try another journal—offered a quiet but genuine word of appreciation.

In fact, for a moment it had looked as if I was on the edge of real communication. In the summer of 1982, Wilfrid Cantwell Smith, director of Harvard's *Center for the Study of World Religions*, invited me, after he had consulted with Brevard Childs, to join a two-month post-graduate summer Seminar, funded by the National Endowment for the Humanities, on the diverse forms of scripture, Christian and otherwise. The idea was 'to forge a concept for [scripture], that may be appropriate for us to have today, as we observe its role in the life of humankind on this planet'. Housing in Harvard was hot—the windows would not open—but nearby were second-hand bookstores, green spaces and a river. Summertime!

'I commend you to one another', Smith said to us, twelve participants, on the first day that we met.

I took his commendation seriously, but the person I was really focused on was Smith. He seemed to be a man of extraordinary experience. He was a committed Christian—a Canadian Presbyterian—but he had also lived for years within Hinduism and within Islam. He seemed calm, capable and fearless. I asked him would he be interested in a manuscript, and he responded positively.

Within a short time he returned it to me.

'That is an important thesis.'

He wanted it published. I told him about some publishers' doubts, but he still thought it would be good to try again, and, on his suggestion, I sent it to Beacon Press, Boston. But eventually Beacon Press rejected it.

Chapter 7

THE SECOND REVOLUTION ILLUSTRATED: THE TRANSFORMATION OF ELIJAH'S THREE-PART CALL (1 KINGS 19) INTO JESUS' TRIPLE CHALLENGE TO DISCIPLES (LUKE 9.57-62)

Dear reader, this long chapter takes the microscope to the second revolution, or at least to one small part of it, and if you are not in the mood right now to examine a lot of detail, nor to make a judgment about it, you may prefer to read just the chapter's beginning, and perhaps a few paragraphs either from the following section, 'General Procedures of Adaptation', or from the later 'Detailed Procedures of Adaptation'.

Yet in the longer term this chapter is important. It shows that Luke depends on extant writings not only for a few aspects of his account but essentially for all its components. The older writings constitute the new. And to judge the truth of this needs prolonged attention to details. Detail is decisive. Detail can enable medicine to save and planes to fly. The Bible may seem far from modern medicine and aviation; it does not have their complexity. True, but it has its own, equally sophisticated. Bible translator André Chouraqui reckoned that a book like Genesis was 'assembled' with as much exactitude and precision as is used today in assembling a computer or missile (1975: 455). Literacy was unusual in biblical times, but people were no less intelligent. And as the pyramids show, precision in construction was already a millennia-old tradition.

So, if you want to maintain momentum in reading, skip most of this chapter, but when you have time, or when you are with friends, colleagues or students who are interested in how a literary artist might distil an old landmark episode, relax into the challenge of the detail.

* * *

Studies of how ancient writers adapted or transformed older texts, especially of how the New Testament used the Old Testament, are now becoming commonplace, but it is useful to look at an example closely because the transforming process can seem strange. As often happens in crafts, or sports, or sciences, or relationships, patience is necessary to get inside what is happening. I have already given a partial analysis of the text in question in my 2004 book, *Birthing of the New Testament*, but since *Birthing* needed to cover so much ground—to provide an overall view—its analyses were necessarily brief. This analysis, though more expansive, is still not complete. It is particularly hampered by the underdeveloped state of research into the evangelists' use of the Epistles. But it gives an example of what a fuller analysis might look like.

The example comes from the pivotal moment at the centre of Luke's Gospel when Jesus faces death and begins to walk towards Jerusalem (Lk. 9.51–10.20). The moment is deadly serious, but it does not have the sinking feeling that often accompanies the sight of someone walking to execution, the conventional movie scene that repeats 'Dead man walking'. For as Jesus walks, he also begins to talk, first in a brief rebuke to two bloody-minded disciples, James and John (9.55), then to three others—literally 'someone' and 'another' and 'another'—whom he effectively challenges or calls to true discipleship (9.57-62), and finally to seventy (or seventy-two) 'others' whom he sends on a mission that, on one level at least, is far-flung in space and time (10.1-16), a mission that entails not just talking but ultimate communal rejoicing (10.17-20). The entire text, from the initial walking to the final rejoicing (9.51–10.20) is a tight-knit literary unity.

The primary focus here is on the middle of that long text—when Jesus meets the three potential disciples and issues a three-part challenge about what will be required (Lk. 9.57-62):

- The journey is lonely—lonelier than that of wild animals
- Leave the dead and go proclaim God's kingdom
- Be like someone ploughing; no looking back

The first two of these sayings—the journey, and leaving the dead—are found also in Matthew (8.18-22), and these first two are generally said to have come from a hypothetical source that was shared by Matthew and Luke, the source named Q. The third saying also, about the plough, is sometimes attributed to Q, but scholars such as Harry Fleddermann have noticed that this saying has significant similarities to Elijah's call of the young ploughman, Elisha (1 Kgs 19.19-21). Apart from the shared references to ploughing, both Luke and the Elijah text also refer to delaying or going back (1 Kgs 19.20; Lk. 9.61), and so Fleddermann concludes that the plough saying is Luke's own composition: Luke adapted two elements of the call of Elisha, combining them with one another and with a smaller part of the Septuagint—the reference to Lot's wife looking back (Gen. 19.26)—and then adapted the phrasing in accordance with the context and with his own specific purposes and style.

Fleddermann is right, but there are other links with Elijah. The possibility of further links is suggested first by the wider context of the Elijah account with its extraordinary features, such as calling fire from heaven to destroy people, and the idea of being taken up into heaven (2 Kgs 1.1–2.2). In varying ways these two rare features occur also at the beginning of Jesus' walk towards Jerusalem (Lk. 9.51-56). There are links too with the rest of 1 Kings 19, the account of Elijah's visit to Horeb. This chapter (1 Kgs 19) is a carefully constructed unity,[1] and continued scrutiny indicates that all three sayings in Lk. 9.57-62 are based 1 Kings 19, on the three combined episodes that challenged and changed Elijah: first, his lonely journey through the wilderness (1 Kgs 19.4-8); then, the dramatic encounter at Horeb that called on him to leave his preoccupation with death (those already dead, and his own impending death) and to set forth on God's mission (1 Kgs 19.9-18); and finally, his call of Elisha as he was ploughing (1 Kgs 19.19-21). The similarity between the texts may be outlined as follows:

1 Kings 19	*Luke 9.57-62*
Elijah, fearing death, receives divine instruction:	Jesus, facing death, instructs would-be followers:
1. Wilderness journey; cannot stay lying; food at head.	1. Lonely wandering; cannot lay down his head.
2. Elijah: 'Death! Death!' God: 'Go, anoint prophet, kings'.	2. 'Leave the dead…Go, announce God's kingdom'.
3. Elisha ploughing; 'I will follow after you'; turns.	3. 'I will follow'; Do not turn/look back from the plough.

Like a patient shipbuilder who draws on models of older craft, and who shapes details with the patience and precision of a watch-maker, or like a literary Michelangelo who combines mastery on a grand scale with equal mastery of detail, Luke has made several adaptations. These adaptations are of two main kinds: general and detailed. This division is not watertight; some general features involve details. The general adaptations involve five features: repetitive structure, content, plot, interweaving, and context.

---

1. The unity of 1 Kgs 19 has sometimes been contested, but once allowance is made for a progression—from deathly discouragement to purposeful running, from a form of death to new life—the variations in the text fall into place as forming a carefully woven unity. The opening setting of a barren wilderness is replaced by the closing picture of (fruitful) ploughing, full of energy (19.4-8, 19-21, twelve yoke of oxen). The leaving of a servant at the beginning (19.3) gives way at the end to gaining a new and vigorous attendant (19.21). The deathly orientation towards one's dead fathers is replaced by a departure from one's father in a way that is full of purpose (19.4, 20). The dim hint of heat in the meagre baked cake is replaced by the sense of an extravagant fire and meal (19.6, 21). The faint suggestion of the coming of God's word, first in the shadowy 'someone' and then in the unnamed 'messenger of the Lord' (19.5, 7), gradually gives way to increasing clarity and strength in the Lord's presence and voice (19.9-14), and then turns into a mission that brings the working out of God's word into decisive action (19.15-21). And the flat word-for word repetitions of the beginning (19.4-8) and the middle (19.9-18) give way to a final scene in which nothing is repeated word-for-word and in which each phrase seems to break new ground.

General Procedures of Adaptation

Adaptation of Repetitive Structure

(a) *Adaptation of the repetitiveness of John's replies to would-be doers (Luke 3.10-14).* The initial model for the repetitiveness of Jesus' brief exchanges with would-be disciples comes from the repetitiveness of the account of John's pithy replies to would-be doers (Lk. 3.10-14), a text found only in Luke. Both exchanges (Lk. 3.10-14; 9.57-62) occur just after key moments— after the beginning of the ministry of John and Jesus, and after the central turning point in the ministry of Jesus.

(b) *Adaptation of the broad pattern of repetitiveness in 1 Kings 19.* Repetition occurs also in the account of Elijah (1 Kgs 19). *Two-part* repetition occurs, for instance, in Elijah's objection to God, a long complaint (19.10, 14), in the two references to 'my father(s)' (19.4, 20), and in the Lord's pointed question, something like 'What you here!?' (19.9, 13). And *three-part* repetition occurs when the Lord passes (19.11-12) and again when the Lord gives instructions (19.15-16). Luke takes this general phenomenon of repetition and adapts it to his own text, particularly to the form of a triple pithy exchange. To some degree Luke's procedure has already been indicated by Fleddermann; he mentions that a feature of the Elijah text, the delay motif—the request for a little time (19.20)—has been duplicated in Luke (9.59, 61).[2] A somewhat fuller account is as follows.

Introductions. Luke's repetitiveness begins with the introductions to the exchanges. Apart from the initial 'As they were journeying on the road', these introductions all include 'he said', εἶπέν:

v. 57 εἶπέν **τις** πρὸς αὐτόν·	'**Someone** said to him'.
v. 58 καὶ εἶπεν αὐτῷ ὁ Ἰησοῦς·	'And Jesus said to him'.
v. 59 Εἶπεν δὲ πρὸς **ἕτερον**·	'But he said to **another**'.
ὁ δὲ εἶπεν· (κύριε,)	'But he said [Lord]'.
v. 60 εἶπεν δὲ αὐτῷ·	'But he said to him'.
v. 61 Εἶπεν δὲ καὶ **ἕτερος**·	'But **another** said'.
v. 62 εἶπεν δὲ (πρὸς αὐτὸν) ὁ Ἰησοῦς·	'But Jesus said [to him]'.

In these introductions, most of the words (he said, to him, Lord) are so common that they cannot help in establishing any literary link between Luke and 1 Kgs 19.4-21. And the occurrence of δέ, a form of 'but', especially εἶπεν δέ, 'but he said' (59 times in Luke's Gospel), is typically Lukan. However, links with 1 Kings 19 also emerge. Some general patterns:

---

2. Harry Fleddermann, 'The Influence of Q on the Formation of the Third Gospel', a paper presented at the SBL Annual Meeting, San Francisco, 19 November 2011 (p. 20).

Luke sometimes *expands* or *contracts* the number of references to particular features. *Expansions* (or dispersals) include:

- The indefinite 'someone', τις, at the *beginning* ('someone touched him and said to him', 1 Kgs 19.4), is dispersed by Luke. He uses it to refer to *three* indefinite speakers: first the τις, 'someone' at the beginning ('someone said to him', 9.57), and then, again, in variant form, the indefinite 'another' and 'another' at the middle and end ('He said to another', 9.59; 'And another said', 9.61). The '(an)other' continues in 10.1.
- The declaration 'I will follow after you', which occurs once, at the *end* of 1 Kings 19 (v. 20), is also used three times, in variant form, at the beginning, middle and end: 'I will follow you wherever you go' (v. 57); 'Follow me' (v. 59); 'I will follow you' (v. 61).
- The decisive action of departing or going away (ἀπέρχομαι), which—apart from its use in 19.3—occurs once at the end (Elijah finally goes away, 19.19), is mentioned three times in Luke, once in the initial declaration '(I will follow you wherever you go away, ἀπέρχομαι, and twice in the central dialogue, when the man who wants to 'go away' to bury his father is told in decisive language to 'go away' and proclaim the kingdom of God (9.59-60).
- The request for time to settle matters at home before following, which occurs once at the end (1 Kgs 19.20), occurs in variant form at both the middle and end ('permit me first…', Lk. 9.59, 61).

On other occasions, Luke *contracts* elements: he uses just once elements that occur twice in 1 Kings 19:

- The *framing references* to 'my father(s)', instead of being used at the beginning and end (19.4, 20), is used in the *middle* (9.59).
- The Lord's repeated pointed use of 'you' to Elijah concerning his location (literally, 'What you here, Elijah?', 19.9, 13), which is followed later by a clear command to move and by Elijah's departure (he 'goes away', 1 Kgs 19.19)—provides a close background to Luke's emphatic 'But *you*, going away…' (9.60).
- The sharpest instance of contraction occurs in replacing repeated emphasis on various forms of deaths (esp. 1 Kgs 19.10, 14, 'they have killed', 'they have killed') with the dense 'let the dead bury their dead' (Lk. 9.60).

The elaborate repetitive account of the Lord's appearance and commissioning (1 Kgs 19.11-12, 15-18) is distilled into the repeated reference to focusing on 'the kingdom of God' (Lk. 9.60, 62).

Adaptation of Content: Prophetic Call
Luke maintains the essence of 1 Kings 19—a form of prophetic call. At first sight it may seem that, unlike other great prophets, Elijah never had a formal prophetic call. But now, in his time of crisis, the account of Elijah's journey to and from Horeb has all the marks of a conventional call (as outlined by Norman Habel),[3] though as frequently happens with conventions, its elements have been adapted.[4] And Jesus' call, especially the fractionally more elaborate central call, where Jesus takes the initiative in speaking and issuing imperatives ('Go, proclaim…', Lk. 9.59-60), is 'like God's prophetic call to Jeremiah and Ezekiel' (Fleddermann 2005: 403); and, as detailed comparison shows, it is particularly like the call of Elijah at Horeb.

Adaptation of Plot into Metaphor
The account of Elijah's journey to and from Horeb is packed with vivid elements of plot—striking actions involving either Elijah, or his enemies, or the Lord, or finally, the vivid account of the energetic young man with twelve yoke of oxen—and so Luke's brief verbal exchanges may seem far away from anything so action-packed. However Luke's text maintains a persistent thread of continuity with the older text. He has turned leading actions from 1 Kings 19 into metaphors. In the opening part (1 Kgs 19.4-8; Lk. 9.57-58) Elijah is literally alone in the wilderness, and is literally unable to lay down his head (he tries but cannot because he is told to eat the food at his head), but in Luke the allusion to the wild (the contrast with foxes and birds) and the inability to lay down his head is a metaphor for something within—for a lonely restlessness. Again, in the major central scene at Horeb (1 Kgs 19.9-18; cf. Lk. 9.59-60), Elijah is preoccupied with being literally dead—with those who have already been killed and with his own approaching death—but Luke, while first retaining the sense of someone literally dead, the dead father who needs burial, then switches to being dead in a metaphorical sense: 'Let the dead bury…', a much-debated text which most interpreters take as referring to something within, to those who are spiritually dead (Fitzmyer 1981: 836). Likewise, instead of a command to appoint Hazael and Jehu, both divinely designated but both literally kings (1 Kgs 19.15-16), Luke tells of a command to proclaim the kingdom of God, a metaphor that lays the emphasis not on territory but on something with a clearer spiritual dimension.

---

3. Habel (1965) indicates that the conventional prophetic call has six motifs: divine confrontation, introductory word, commission, objection, reassurance, sign. Part of the sign motif in Elijah's call seems to be the concluding picture of the apparent total ease with which he immediately finds a younger kindred spirit, Elisha (1 Kgs 19.19). Moses' call concluded with the surprising announcement of the approach of his brother Aaron (Exod. 4.14-16).
4. Alter 1981: 47-62.

And in the third part of the texts (1 Kgs 19.19-21; Lk. 9.61-62), Elisha is literally ploughing, ploughing even with twelve yoke of oxen, but in Luke concentration on the plough is a metaphor for something within—for maintaining focus on the kingdom of God. Likewise the action of throwing or putting, which in 1 Kings 19 is that of literally throwing or putting the prophetic mantle on ploughing Elisha, becomes in Luke an action with greater emphasis on what is within—that of putting one's hand to the plough by proclaiming the kingdom.

Interweaving of Main Source (1 Kings 19) with Other Sources
The triple challenge (Lk. 9.57-62) reflects not only 1 Kings 19, but also some other texts, especially some other parts of the LXX, and apparently some New Testament Epistles. Thus while the basic image of ploughing is from the description of Elisha (1 Kgs 19.19-21), the phrase 'looking back' is from the description of Noah's wife fleeing Sodom and Gomorrah (Gen. 19.26; Fleddermann 2005: 396). Likewise, while 'I will follow you' (Lk. 9.57, 61; cf. 9.59) is essentially from young Elisha (1 Kgs 19.20), the added phrase 'wherever you go' (Lk. 9.57) is adapted from the words of Ruth to Naomi (Ruth 1.16, the details will be seen later). And while the image of the wilderness (1 Kgs 19.4-8) provides the basic background for Jesus' references to wild animals (Lk. 9.58), the specific mention of foxes may reflect Ezek. 13.4 ('like foxes in the wilderness') and the reference to birds may likewise reflect the ravens in the drama of the drought that precedes Elijah's journey to Horeb (1 Kgs 17.2-6).

As for Luke's use of some New Testament epistles, it is an obvious possibility, but one that is rarely explored, and until it is, it is better that claims in that regard remain tentative.[5]

Adaptation of Text (9.57-62) to Luke's Context and Language
Throughout Luke's process of composition he is adapting the triple challenge (9.57-62) to its context. He blends it with its immediate setting, especially that of the journeys that precede and follow it, Jesus' journey to Jerusalem (9.51-56) and the long-term missionary journey that follows it (10.1-20). There is blending also with Luke's larger narrative. For instance, the opening reference to the road (ὁδὸς, 9.57), while it reflects Elijah's journey, fits also with Luke's larger account. And the closing emphasis on persevering, on not looking back, likewise serves a larger Lukan emphasis. Furthermore, like most writers, Luke has a preferred vocabulary, and this preference colours the choice of specific words. The details of the relationship of 9.57-62 to Luke's larger narrative are quite elaborate.

---

5. For references and partial explorations, see Brodie 2004: 138-43, 545-66; Elbert 2006.

Excursus:
The Call (Luke 9.57-62) is Shaped by Luke's Context

Luke 9.57-62 has a double role: (a) within the immediate context (Lk. 9.51–10.20); and (b) within Luke's larger work.

(a) Lk. 9.57-62 within the immediate context of 9.51–10.20

From a literary point of view, the triple challenge (Lk. 9.57-62) is embedded in Luke's narrative, particularly within a 32-verse block (9.51–10.20, a unity: Borgman 2006: 79-86) which begins with the Gospel's turning point when Jesus sets his face for Jerusalem (9.51), and which then recounts how Jesus sent out two missions: first he 'sent messengers before his face', and these went into a Samaritan village (9.52); and later he designated seventy-two others and 'sent them before his face' to diverse houses and cities (10.1).

The first mission (9.52) meets rejection and they eventually go to another village, but not before two disciples suggest calling devouring fire from heaven (Greek) and Jesus turns (*strephō*) on them (9.51-56).

In the second mission, to cities and houses (10.1-20), the seventy-two are pictured as harvesting, and as lambs among wolves, but they too have to deal with rejection, and here also rejection seems to deserve fire from heaven: the city that rejects the mission is more guilty than Sodom (on which fell fire from heaven) and, in the judgment (*en tē krisei*), other cites deserve a similar fate (10.12-15). The judgment comes from the ultimate sender (10.16). Satan too falls in a form of fire from heaven (10.18).

At the end of the first mission Jesus turns (*strephō*) and rebukes the suggestion of fire from heaven (9.55). And at the end of the second mission when the seventy-two return (*hypo-strephō*), what Jesus gives is not just a rebuke but an evocation of ultimate judgment: he has seen Satan fall like fire from heaven, but the names of the seventy-two are written in heaven (10.17-20).

The two missions are separated by an 'After this' (10.1), but their literary proximity and similarities bind them together and they are both rooted in Jesus, in his life and in his acceptance of the journey towards what awaited him in Jerusalem. The 'after this' is one indicator that this picture of two missions looks to different times, one to the life of Jesus when he was facing death, and the other evokes not only the later mission to the nations, but even the ultimate judgment when Satan has been thrown down and when the names of the seventy are written in heaven (see, perhaps, 1 Cor. 15.22-28, 47-57). (On the seventy, including a possible link to the seventy nations of Gen. 10, see Fitzmyer 1985: 843, 846.) The result is a text that expands the drama surrounding Jesus not only in space, to cities named and unnamed, but also to a vast horizon of time, even to the final judgment.

Within the evocation of this vast horizon, between these two intertwined missions, stands Jesus' triple challenge to would-be followers (9.57-62). Whatever its distinctive source(s) it is now fully integrated into Luke's vision of an expanding mission.

Further details on 9.57-62 as reflecting its immediate context:

On the one hand Jesus' triple challenge *looks back* to the initial departure for Jerusalem and to his sending of messengers. In varying forms it takes up:

The frequent image of journeying (*poreuomai*, four times in six verses, Lk. 9.51-56), recurs at the start of the next verse, the start of the triple challenge (9.57).

The distinctive sense of facing difficulty and homelessness. Having set his face to towards what awaited him in Jerusalem, Jesus was then refused hospitality (9.51-53), and his first challenge to a would-be follower concerns having nowhere to lay one's head (9.58).

The shadow of death. The emphasis on death in the second challenge ('leave the dead', 9.59-60) is in continuity with the intimation of death that hovers over Jesus' departure for Jerusalem (9.51-56).

The curious reference to heaven. The refusal of hospitality is followed by the extraordinary suggestion of calling down destructive fire from heaven (9.54-56). The reference to this fire from heaven has a two-fold edge. Its destructive power intensifies the shadow of death, but it also intimates something positive: the power of heaven is not far from the rejected Jesus. Amid the initial bleakness of the triple exchange, the use of the word 'heaven' is an intimation that life has another dimension.

On the other hand, Jesus' challenges *look forward* to the second mission, that of the seventy (10.1-20):

The repeated reference to 'another' (9.59, 61) prepares for the reference to the seventy as 'others', which itself seems to pick up also on the first messengers (9.52).

The questions about leaving one's house ('Permit me first to bury my father'; 'Permit me first to say goodbye to those in my house', 9.59, 61) are a foil for the instructions to the seventy about entering a new house: 'Whatever house you enter, first say "Peace" to this house...' (10.5-7).

The repeated challenges that refer twice, with intensifying commitment, first to proclaiming the Kingdom of God (9.60) and then to holding fast to that proclamation, without looking back (9.62), prepare the way for the repeated instruction to the seventy first to *say* that the Kingdom of God is at hand (10.9) and then to *know*, like the clear-seeing plougher, that the Kingdom of God is indeed at hand, even when the message is rejected (10.11).

(b) Lk. 9.57-62 within Luke's larger work

Apart from being linked to their immediate surroundings, the three challenges reflect key Lukan themes. The first dialogue, for instance, with its picture of Jesus going the road, *hodos*, picks up the theme of an overall journey/momentum that runs through Luke's work (cf. Lk. 3.4-6). The second challenge, with its switch from death to announcing the kingdom of God, captures the central drama of that journey, that of joining in Jesus' journey through death and resurrection, and of receiving a mission to proclaim. And the third, the call for clear-eyed perseverance, summarizes the need, seen especially in Acts, to keep on the road, even in face of persecution (Fleddermann 2005: 395). Furthermore, like most writers, Luke has a preferred vocabulary, and this preference colours the choice of specific words. Overall, as in the call narrative of the prophets, the triple challenge forms a programmatic call for the future.

Detailed Procedures of Adaptation

To get a sense of the detailed nature of Luke's work, it is useful to lay out the texts both in outline and in full:

- The outlines are given on the following set of facing pages. The outline of 1 Kings 19 is a *summary*, set out beside the *full* Lukan text. The Greek version of the summary of 1 Kings 19 is slightly fuller than the English to allow closer comparison of verbal details.
- The full text is set out in the subsequent two pairs of facing pages.

These pages of outlines/texts are intended as reference points in the detailed analysis.

Elijah's belated prophetic call (1 Kgs 19.4-21)	Disciples receive a prophet-like call (Lk. 9.57-62)
1. Restless in the wilderness: Elijah can't just lie down (19.4-8)	**More restless than foxes: The Son of Man can't lay his head (9.57-58)**
(a) v. 4: He journeys… in the wilderness, a day's road…	v. 57: And as they journeyed on the road,
v. 5: Someone… said to him… [v. 20: I will follow after you] [wherever you go (Ruth 1.16)]	someone said to him, I will follow you wherever you go.
(b) v. 4: And he said [v. 4: in the wilderness] v. 4: [Mortal] Elijah asks to die; 'no better than my fathers'. vv. 5, 6: And he lay down… And behold at his head…	v. 58: And Jesus said to him, Foxes… and birds… the Son of Man [mortal] does not have where to lay his head.
2. Not death, but God/God's mission (19.9-18)	**Not the dead, but God's kingdom (9.59-60)**
(a) [v. 5: Someone… said to him…] [v. 20: I will follow after you]	v. 59: He said to another [variation on someone] Follow me
(b) [v. 4: And he said… Lord…] v. 19: And **he departed from there**… [v. 20: I will kiss my father (cf. v. 4: 'my [dead] fathers') and (**then** JB/RSV)…]	But he said [Lord] Permit me **first** to **depart** to bury my father.
Killed, killed	Dead bury dead
(c) vv. 10, 14, 17: Elijah said: They killed… killed	v. 60: But he said to him, Leave the dead to bury their dead.
God revealed: Go, anoint kings, a prophet/proclaimer	Go: Proclaim the kingdom of God
v. 9: Why you here? v. 13: Why you here? vv. 11-12, 15-18: The Lord! Go anoint kings, a prophet	But you, departing, proclaim the kingdom of God
3. Plowing; goodbye (19.19-21)	**Plowing; no looking back (9.61-62)**
(a) [v. 5: Someone… said to him…] v. 20: I will follow after you v. 20: I will kiss my father and (**then** JB/RSV)…	v. 61: Another said to him, I will follow you, Lord Permit me **first** (as in v. 59) to say goodbye to those in my house
(b) v. 4: And he said, v. 19: He was plowing and… he cast on his mantle on him [She looked back (at Sodom, Gen. 19)]	But Jesus said to him. No one throwing on his hand on the plow and looking back is worthy (εὔθετός, New Testament: here; Lk. 14.35; Heb. 6.7 (6.1-8) of the kingdom of God (as in v. 60)

Elijah's belated prophetic call (1 Kgs 19.4-21)	Disciples receive a prophet-like call (Lk. 9.57-62)
1. Restless in the wilderness: **Elijah cannot just lie down (19.4-8)**	**More restless than foxes:** **The Son of Man can't lay his head (9.57-58)**
(a) v. 4: Καὶ αὐτὸς ἐπορεύθη ἐν τῇ **ἐρήμῳ** ὁδὸν ἡμέρας τις ἥψατο αὐτοῦ καὶ εἶπεν αὐτῷ [v. 20: ἀκολουθήσω ὀπίσω σου,] [ὅπου ἐὰν πορευθῇς, Ruth 1.16]	v. 57: Καὶ πορευομένων αὐτῶν ἐν τῇ ὁδῷ εἶπέν τις πρὸς αὐτόν· ἀκολουθήσω σοι ὅπου ἐὰν **ἀπέρχῃ**.
(b) [v. 4: καὶ εἶπεν] [v. 4: ἐν τῇ ἐρήμῳ] [v. 4: ἀποθανεῖν…οὐ…ὑπὲρ τοὺς πατέρας μου] v. 5: καὶ ἰδοὺ πρὸς κεφαλῆς αὐτοῦ καὶ…ἐκοιμήθη	v. 58: καὶ εἶπεν αὐτῷ ὁ Ἰησοῦς· αἱ ἀλώπεκες φωλεοὺς ἔχουσιν καὶ τὰ πετεινὰ τοῦ οὐρανοῦ κατασκηνώσεις ὁ δὲ υἱὸς τοῦ ἀνθρώπου οὐκ ἔχει ποῦ τὴν κεφαλὴν κλίνῃ.
2. Not death, but God/God's mission (19.9-18)	**Not the dead, but God's kingdom (9.59-60)**
(a) [v. 4: τις…εἶπεν αὐτῷ] [v. 20: ἀκολουθήσω ὀπίσω σου,	v. 59: Εἶπεν δὲ πρὸς ἕτερον· [variation on indefinite τις] ἀκολούθει μοι.
(b) [v. 4: καὶ εἶπεν…κύριε] [vv. 19, 20: **ἀπῆλθεν**…καταφιλήσω τὸν πατέρα μου καὶ (then JB/RSV) [v. 4: τοὺς πατέρας μου (dead); v. 20: τὸν πατέρα μου]	ὁ δὲ εἶπεν· [κύριε,] ἐπίτρεψόν μοι **ἀπελθόντι** πρῶτον θάψαι τὸν πατέρα μου.
Killed, killed	Dead bury dead
(c) v. 15: καὶ εἶπεν κύριος πρὸς αὐτόν…ἀνάστρεφε…ἥξεις vv. 10-17: ἀπέκτειναν, ἀπέκτειναν, θανατώσει, θανατώσει	v. 60: εἶπεν δὲ αὐτῷ· ἄφες τοὺς νεκροὺς θάψαι τοὺς ἑαυτῶν νεκρούς
God revealed: Go, anoint kings, a prophet/ proclaimer	Go: Proclaim the kingdom of God
v. 9: τί σὺ ἐνταῦθα; v. 13: τί σὺ ἐνταῦθα vv. 11-12: ἰδοὺ παρελεύσεται κύριος…κἀκεῖ κύριος vv. 15-16: πορεύου…χρίσεις…βασιλέα… βασιλέα… προφήτην	σὺ δὲ **ἀπελθὼν** διάγγελλε τὴν βασιλείαν τοῦ θεου
1. Plowing, goodbye (19.19-21)	**Plowing, no looking back (9.61-62)**
(a) [v. 4: τις…εἶπεν αὐτῷ]	v. 61: Εἶπεν δὲ καὶ ἕτερος [variation on indefinite τις]
v. 20c: ἀκολουθήσω ὀπίσω σου	ἀκολουθήσω σοι, κύριε, // **πρῶτον** δὲ ἐπίτρεψόν μοι
v. 20b: καταφιλήσω τὸν πατέρα μου // καὶ [then JB/RSV]	ἀποτάξασθαι τοῖς εἰς τὸν οἶκόν μου.
(b) καὶ εἶπεν Ηλιου… v. 19: ἠροτρία, καὶ ἐπέρριψε τὴν μηλωτὴν αὐτοῦ ἐπ᾽ αὐτόν [v. 6: καὶ ἐπέβλεψεν] [Gen. 19.26: καὶ ἐπέβλεψεν εἰς τὰ ὀπίσω]	v. 62: εἶπεν δὲ ὁ Ἰησοῦς· οὐδεὶς ἐπιβαλὼν τὴν χεῖρα ἐπ᾽ ἄροτρον καὶ βλέπων εἰς τὰ **ὀπίσω** εὔθετός ἐστιν [New Testament: here; Lk. 14.35; Heb. 6.7 (cf. 6.1-8)] τῇ βασιλείᾳ τοῦ θεοῦ [intensifies v. 60].

Elijah's belated call (1 Kings 19, a variation on conventional prophetic calls)

Elijah flees death. [1]And Ahab told Jezabel his wife all that Elijah *had* done, and how he *had* skilled the prophets by the sword. [2] And Jezabel sent to Elijah, and said, If you are Elijah and I am Jezabel, may God do this to me, and more also, if I do not make your life like the life of one of them by this time tomorrow. [3] And Elijah feared, and rose, and departed for his life, and he came to Bersabee *to* the land of Judah, and he left his servant there.

1. The difficult/lonely journey in the wilderness (19.4-8)

Elijah is like his [dead] fathers; cannot stay lying down—food at head
[4] And he journeyed a day's road into the wilderness, and came and sat under a broom tree; and asked that his life die, and said, Let it be enough now. Pray take my life from me, Lord, for I am no better than my fathers. [5] And he lay down there under a plant and fell asleep.
And behold, someone touched him, and said to him, Arise and eat. [6] And Elijah looked, and, behold, at his head, a wheat cake and a jug of water, and he arose, and ate and drank, and he returned and lay down. [7] And the angel of the Lord returned a second *time*, and touched him, and said to him, Arise, and eat, for the road *is* far for you. [8] And he arose, and ate and drank, and journeyed in the strength of that food forty days and forty nights to Mount Horeb.

2. From preoccupation with death to anointing God's kings and proclaimer (19.9-18)

[9] And he entered there into a cave, and lodged there; and, behold, the word of the Lord *came* to him, and said,
>>> What **you here**, Elijah?
Death!   [10] And Elijah said, I am zealous, zealous for the Lord Almighty, for the children of Israel forsook
                you:
                they have destroyed your altars and killed your prophets by the sword; and I alone remain,
                and they seek my life to take it.
God!   [11] And he said, You shall go out to-morrow, and shall stand before the Lord on the mountain;
                behold, the Lord will pass by.
                And, behold, a great strong wind splitting the mountains, and crushing the rocks before the Lord;
                but the Lord *was* not in the wind;
                and after the wind an earthquake; *but* the Lord *was* not in the earthquake:
                [12] and after the earthquake a fire; *but* the Lord *was* not in the fire:
                and after the fire the voice of a gentle breeze, and the Lord *was* there.
[13] And it happened when Elijah heard, that he wrapped his face in his mantle, and went out and stood by the cave; and, behold, a voice *came* to him and said,
>>> What **you here**, Elijah?
Death!   [14] And Elijah said, I am zealous, zealous for the Lord Almighty, for the children of Israel forsook
                your covenant:
                they have destroyed your altars and killed your prophets by the sword; and I alone remain,
                and they seek my life to take it.
Mission: Go! [15] And the Lord said to him, Go, return on your road, and you shall come into the road way
                of the wilderness of Damascus, and you shall anoint Hazael to be king over Syria,
                [16] and Jehu the son of Namessi you shall anoint to be king over Israel,
                and Elisha son of Saphat from Abelmaoula you shall anoint to be prophet in place of you.
[17] And it shall be that the one that escapes from the sword of Hazael, Jehu shall put to death; and the one that escapes from the sword of Jehu, Elisha shall put to death. [18] And you shall leave remaining in Israel seven thousand men, all the knees that did had not bow a knee to Baal, and every mouth that did not worship him.

3. The plowman who first said goodbye, but did not look back (19.19-21)

>>> [19] And **he departed from there**, and he finds Elisha son of Saphat, and he was ploughing with oxen, twelve yoke before him and he with the twelve, and he came up**on** **on** him, and cast **on** his mantle **on** him. [20] And Elisha left the oxen, and ran after Elijah and said, I will kiss my father, and I will follow after you. And Elijah said, Return, for I have done for you. [21] And he returned from behind him, and took the yoke of oxen, and slaughtered and boiled them with the instruments of the oxen, and gave to the people and they ate, and he arose, and went after Elijah, and ministered to him.

Facing death, Jesus challenges disciples (Luke 9.57-62, a variation on prophetic calls)

1.The difficult/lonely journey evoking wild animals (9.57-58)

Mortal son of man, cannot lay down his head

[57] And as they journeyed on the road,
someone said to him,
I will follow you
wherever you go.

[58] And Jesus said to him,
Foxes…and birds…
the Son of Man [mortal] does not have
where to lay his head.

2. From preoccupation with dead father's burial to proclaiming God's kingdom (9.59-60)

[59] He said to another, [variation on 'someone', v. 57]
Follow me

But he said [Lord]
Permit me **first**
to **depart**
to bury my father.

[60] But he said to him, Leave
the dead to bury their dead.
>>> But **you, departing**,
proclaim the kingdom of God

3. First say goodbye? The plowman does not look back (9.61-62)

[61] Another said to him,
I will follow you, Lord
Permit me **first** (as in v. 59)
to say goodbye to those in my house

But Jesus said to him.
No one throwing **on** his hand **on** the plow
and looking back
is worthy (εὔθετός, in New Testament: here; Lk. 14.35; Heb. 6.7)
of the kingdom of God (as in v. 60)

Elijah's belated call (1 Kings 19, a variation on conventional prophetic calls)

Elijah flees death. καὶ ἀνήγγειλεν Αχααβ τῇ Ιεζαβελ γυναικὶ αὐτοῦ πάντα ἃ ἐποίησεν Ηλιου καὶ ὡς ἀπέκτεινεν τοὺς προφήτας ἐν ῥομφαίᾳ [2] καὶ ἀπέστειλεν Ιεζαβελ πρὸς Ηλιου καὶ εἶπεν εἰ σὺ εἶ Ηλιου καὶ ἐγὼ Ιεζαβελ τάδε ποιήσαι μοι ὁ θεὸς καὶ τάδε προσθείη ὅτι ταύτην τὴν ὥραν αὔριον θήσομαι τὴν ψυχήν σου καθὼς ψυχὴν ἑνὸς ἐξ αὐτῶν [3] καὶ ἐφοβήθη Ηλιου καὶ ἀνέστη καὶ <u>ἀπῆλθεν</u> κατὰ τὴν ψυχὴν ἑαυτοῦ καὶ ἔρχεται εἰς Βηρσαβεε τὴν Ιουδα καὶ ἀφῆκεν τὸ παιδάριον αὐτοῦ ἐκεῖ

1. The difficult/lonely journey in the wilderness (19.4-8)

Elijah is like his [dead] fathers; cannot stay lying down—food at head
[4] καὶ αὐτὸς ἐπορεύθη ἐν τῇ *ἐρήμῳ* ὁδὸν ἡμέρας
καὶ ἦλθεν καὶ ἐκάθισεν ὑπὸ ραθμ ἓν καὶ ᾐτήσατο τὴν ψυχὴν αὐτοῦ ἀποθανεῖν καὶ εἶπεν ἱκανούσθω νῦν λαβὲ δὴ τὴν ψυχήν μου ἀπ' ἐμοῦ κύριε ὅτι ~~οὐ κρείσσων ἐγώ εἰμι ὑπὲρ τοὺς πατέρας μου~~ [5] καὶ ἐκοιμήθη καὶ ὕπνωσεν ἐκεῖ ὑπὸ φυτόν καὶ ἰδού
τις ἥψατο αὐτοῦ καὶ εἶπεν αὐτῷ ἀνάστηθι καὶ φάγε [6] καὶ ἐπέβλεψεν Ηλιου καὶ ἰδοὺ πρὸς κεφαλῆς αὐτοῦ ἐγκρυφίας ὀλυρίτης καὶ καψάκης ὕδατος καὶ ἀνέστη καὶ ἔφαγεν καὶ ἔπιεν καὶ ἐπιστρέψας ἐκοιμήθη [7] καὶ ἐπέστρεψεν ὁ ἄγγελος κυρίου ἐκ δευτέρου καὶ ἥψατο αὐτοῦ καὶ εἶπεν αὐτῷ ἀνάστα φάγε ὅτι πολλὴ ἀπὸ σοῦ ἡ ὁδός [8] καὶ ἀνέστη καὶ ἔφαγεν καὶ ἔπιεν καὶ ἐπορεύθη ἐν τῇ ἰσχύι τῆς βρώσεως ἐκείνης τεσσαράκοντα ἡμέρας καὶ τεσσαράκοντα νύκτας ἕως ὄρους Χωρηβ

2. From preoccupation with death to anointing God's kings
and proclaimer (19.9-18)

[9] καὶ εἰσῆλθεν ἐκεῖ εἰς τὸ σπήλαιον καὶ κατέλυσεν ἐκεῖ καὶ ἰδοὺ ῥῆμα κυρίου πρὸς αὐτὸν καὶ εἶπεν
>>> <u>τί σὺ ἐνταῦθα</u> Ηλιου
Death! [10] καὶ εἶπεν Ηλιου ζηλῶν ἐζήλωκα τῷ κυρίῳ παντοκράτορι ὅτι ἐγκατέλιπόν σε οἱ υἱοὶ Ισραηλ τὰ θυσιαστήριά σου κατέσκαψαν καὶ τοὺς προφήτας σου ἀπέκτειναν ἐν ῥομφαίᾳ καὶ ὑπολέλειμμαι ἐγὼ μονώτατος καὶ ζητοῦσι τὴν ψυχήν μου λαβεῖν αὐτήν
God! [11] καὶ εἶπεν ἐξελεύσῃ αὔριον καὶ στήσῃ ἐνώπιον κυρίου ἐν τῷ ὄρει ἰδοὺ παρελεύσεται κύριος καὶ πνεῦμα μέγα κραταιὸν διαλῦον ὄρη καὶ συντρῖβον πέτρας ἐνώπιον κυρίου οὐκ ἐν τῷ πνεύματι κύριος καὶ μετὰ τὸ πνεῦμα συσσεισμός οὐκ ἐν τῷ συσσεισμῷ κύριος [12] καὶ μετὰ τὸν συσσεισμὸν πῦρ οὐκ ἐν τῷ πυρὶ κύριος καὶ μετὰ τὸ πῦρ φωνὴ αὔρας λεπτῆς κἀκεῖ κύριος
[13] καὶ ἐγένετο ὡς ἤκουσεν Ηλιου καὶ ἐπεκάλυψεν τὸ πρόσωπον αὐτοῦ ἐν τῇ μηλωτῇ ἑαυτοῦ καὶ ἐξῆλθεν καὶ ἔστη ὑπὸ τὸ σπήλαιον καὶ ἰδοὺ πρὸς αὐτὸν φωνὴ καὶ εἶπεν
>>> <u>τί σὺ ἐνταῦθα</u> Ηλιου
Death! [14] καὶ εἶπεν Ηλιου ζηλῶν ἐζήλωκα τῷ κυρίῳ παντοκράτορι ὅτι ἐγκατέλιπον τὴν διαθήκην σου οἱ υἱοὶ Ισραηλ τὰ θυσιαστήριά σου καθεῖλαν καὶ τοὺς προφήτας σου ἀπέκτειναν ἐν ῥομφαίᾳ καὶ ὑπολέλειμμαι ἐγὼ μονώτατος καὶ ζητοῦσι τὴν ψυχήν μου λαβεῖν αὐτήν
Mission: Go! [15] καὶ εἶπεν κύριος πρὸς αὐτόν πορεύου ἀνάστρεφε εἰς τὴν ὁδόν σου καὶ ἥξεις εἰς τὴν ὁδὸν ἐρήμου Δαμασκοῦ καὶ χρίσεις τὸν Αζαηλ εἰς <u>βασιλέα</u> τῆς Συρίας [16] καὶ τὸν Ιου υἱὸν Ναμεσσι χρίσεις εἰς <u>βασιλέα</u> ἐπὶ Ισραηλ καὶ τὸν Ελισαιε υἱὸν Σαφατ ἀπὸ Αβελμαουλα χρίσεις εἰς *προφήτην* ἀντὶ σοῦ [17] καὶ ἔσται τὸν σῳζόμενον ἐκ ῥομφαίας Αζαηλ θανατώσει Ιου καὶ τὸν σῳζόμενον ἐκ ῥομφαίας Ιου θανατώσει Ελισαιε [18] καὶ καταλείψεις ἐν Ισραηλ ἑπτὰ χιλιάδας ἀνδρῶν πάντα γόνατα ἃ οὐκ ὤκλασαν γόνυ τῷ Βααλ καὶ πᾶν στόμα ὃ οὐ προσεκύνησεν αὐτῷ

3. The plowman who first said goodbye, but did not look back (19.19-21)

>>> [19] καὶ <u>ἀπῆλθεν</u> <u>ἐκεῖθεν</u> καὶ εὑρίσκει τὸν Ελισαιε υἱὸν Σαφατ καὶ αὐτὸς <u>ἠροτρία</u> ἐν βουσίν δώδεκα ζεύγη βοῶν ἐνώπιον αὐτοῦ καὶ αὐτὸς ἐν τοῖς δώδεκα καὶ ἐπῆλθεν ἐπ' αὐτὸν καὶ ἐπέρριψε τὴν μηλωτὴν αὐτοῦ ἐπ' αὐτόν [20] καὶ κατέλιπεν Ελισαιε τὰς βόας καὶ κατέδραμεν ὀπίσω Ηλιου καὶ εἶπεν ~~καταφιλήσω τὸν πατέρα μου~~ καὶ **ἀκολουθήσω ὀπίσω σου** καὶ εἶπεν Ηλιου ἀνάστρεφε ὅτι πεποίηκά σοι [21] καὶ ἀνέστρεψεν ἐξόπισθεν αὐτοῦ καὶ ἔλαβεν τὰ ζεύγη τῶν βοῶν καὶ ἔθυσεν καὶ ἥψησεν αὐτὰ ἐν τοῖς σκεύεσι τῶν βοῶν καὶ ἔδωκεν τῷ λαῷ καὶ ἔφαγον καὶ ἀνέστη καὶ ἐπορεύθη ὀπίσω Ηλιου καὶ ἐλειτούργει αὐτῷ

Facing death, Jesus challenges disciples (Luke 9.57-62, a variation on prophetic calls)

1. The difficult/lonely journey evoking wild animals (9.57-58)

Mortal son of man, cannot lay down his head

Καὶ πορευομένων αὐτῶν ἐν τῇ ὁδῷ
εἶπέν **τις** πρὸς αὐτόν·
ἀκολουθήσω σοι ὅπου
ἐὰν ἀπέρχῃ. [Ruth 1.16]

[58] καὶ εἶπεν αὐτῷ ὁ Ἰησοῦς·
αἱ ἀλώπεκες φωλεοὺς ἔχουσιν καὶ τὰ πετεινὰ τοῦ οὐρανοῦ κατασκηνώσεις,
~~ὁ δὲ υἱὸς τοῦ ἀνθρώπου οὐκ ἔχει~~
ποῦ τὴν κεφαλὴν κλίνῃ.

2. From preoccupation with dead father's burial to proclaiming God's kingdom (9.59-60)

[59] Εἶπεν δὲ πρὸς **ἕτερον·**
ἀκολούθει μοι.

ὁ δὲ εἶπεν· (κύριε,)
~~ἐπίτρεψόν μοι~~ ἀπελθόντι
πρῶτον θάψαι τὸν πατέρα μου.

[60] εἶπεν δὲ αὐτῷ·
ἄφες τοὺς νεκροὺς θάψαι τοὺς ἑαυτῶν νεκρούς,
>>> σὺ δὲ ἀπελθὼν
διάγγελλε τὴν βασιλείαν τοῦ θεοῦ.

3. First say goodbye? The plowman does not look back (9.61-62)

[61] Εἶπεν δὲ καὶ **ἕτερος·**
ἀκολουθήσω σοι, κύριε·
~~πρῶτον δὲ ἐπίτρεψόν μοι~~
ἀποτάξασθαι τοῖς εἰς τὸν οἶκόν μου.

[62] εἶπεν δὲ [πρὸς αὐτὸν] ὁ Ἰησοῦς·
οὐδεὶς ἐπιβαλὼν τὴν χεῖρα ἐπ᾽ ἄροτρον
καὶ βλέπων εἰς τὰ ὀπίσω (Gen. 19.26)
εὔθετός ἐστιν τῇ βασιλείᾳ τοῦ θεοῦ.

Note: Some of Luke's words reflect his own distinctive vocabulary, e.g., διαγγέλλω ἐπιτρέπω ἀποτάσσωμαί ἐπιβαλὼν τὴν χεῖρά εὔθετός (Fleddermann 2005: 394, 396).

As already indicated, both main texts (1 Kgs 19; Lk. 9.57-62) consist essentially of three parts, and in giving a more detailed account of what Luke has done it is useful to follow the broad lines of the threefold division. The first part emphasizes the journey—that of Elijah into the wilderness to die, and that of Jesus towards Jerusalem.

1. *Restless: Cannot Just Lie Down (1 Kings 19.4-8; Luke 9.57-58)*
The accounts begin with Elijah's journey into the wilderness, and that of Jesus as he continues towards Jerusalem.

(a) On the road, Someone said...(Luke 9.57). The initial phrases have obvious similarities; the translation is literal:

1 Kgs 19.4	καὶ αὐτὸς ἐπορεύθη ἐν τῇ ἐρήμῳ ὁδὸν ἡμέρας.
Lk. 9.57	Καὶ πορευομένων αὐτῶν ἐν τῇ ὁδῷ.
1 Kgs 19.4	And he journeyed in the wilderness a day's road.
Lk. 9.57	And as they were journeying on the road

Luke's grammatical form (genitive absolute: 'as they were journeying') reflects his general style. The plural, 'as *they* were journeying' suits the context of having 'disciples' (9.54). Luke's abbreviation 'day's road' to 'road' retains and highlights a Lukan theme, the *hodos* (ὁδός), 'road/way'. Both journey-related phrases form beginnings. Elijah's attempt to just lie down and die is interrupted; and Jesus cannot just lie down. An unidentified τις, 'someone', speaks:

1 Kgs 19.5	τις ἥψατο αὐτοῦ καὶ εἶπεν αὐτῷ
Lk. 9.57	εἶπέν τις πρὸς αὐτόν
1 Kgs 19.5	Someone touched him and said to him.
Lk. 9.57	Someone said to him.

Again Luke abbreviates—both to suit his context and to construct the first of his seven miniscule introductory statements, all centred around εἶπέν, 'he said'. The words εἶπέν and τις are very common but the combination εἶπέν τις ('Someone said'), as a statement rather than a question, apparently occurs only three times in the Bible (Lk. 9.57; 11.1; Tit. 1.12) and the similar expression in the next verse of the Elijah account, τις...εἶπεν ('Someone... said'), also seems to be rare. The link between these phrases is supported by the addition of 'to him') (1 Kgs 19.5, αὐτῷ; Lk. 9.57, πρὸς αὐτόν).

In Luke, the unidentified '**someone**' says, 'I will follow you wherever you go', the first of Luke's three references to following—a reflection of Luke's expanding/dispersing of Elisha's statement, 'I will follow after you':

1 Kgs 19.20	ἀκολουθήσω ὀπίσω σου
Lk. 9.57	ἀκολουθήσω σοι ὅπου ἐὰν ἀπέρχῃ.
1 Kgs 19.20	I will follow after you
Lk. 9.57	I will follow you wherever you go

In this case, Luke not only disperses the crucial phrase about following; he also strengthens it, adding 'wherever you go', part of another famous statement of loyalty, that of Ruth to Naomi. Ruth (1.16) asked Naomi not to make her turn from going after her—'...from after you; for wherever you go...', ὄπισθέν σου ὅτι...ὅπου ἐὰν πορευθῇς. The detail of Luke's procedure becomes clearer when the texts are placed in sequence:

1 Kgs 19.20	ἀκολουθήσω **ὀπίσω σου**
Ruth 1.16	**ὄπισθέν σου** ὅτι...ὅπου ἐὰν πορευθῇς.
Lk. 9.57	ἀκολουθήσω σοι ὅπου ἐὰν ἀπέρχῃ.
1 Kgs 19.20	I will follow after you
Ruth 1.16	...from after you; for wherever you go...
Lk. 9.57	I will follow you wherever you go

Elisha's 'after you', ὀπίσω σου, is Luke's bridge to move to Ruth's 'from after you' (ὄπισθέν σου). And what he then takes up is the classic 'wherever you go', which he expresses not quite with 'where you go' (ὅπου ἐὰν πορευθῇς) but with 'wherever you go away/depart' (ὅπου ἐὰν ἀπέρχῃ). Both phrases are rare; apparently they occur nowhere else in the Bible, apart from the parallel in Mt. 8.19. Luke's preference at his point for 'depart/go away' (ἀπέρχομαι) seems to be a further element of the expansion/dispersal mentioned above—in this case his dispersal of the decisive 'went away/departed' (ἀπέρχομαι) that initiates Elijah's finding of Elisha (1 Kgs 19.19, 'and he went away from there and finds Elisha' (καὶ ἀπῆλθεν ἐκεῖθεν καὶ εὑρίσκει τὸν Ελισαιε). Reasons for adapting Ruth would be: the inherent affinity between the statements of Ruth and Elisha; the role of Ruth as model of a faithful Gentile; and the apparent role of the book of Ruth in inspiring the harvest imagery of the commissioning of the seventy.

(b) *Jesus replies: restless amid the wild (Luke 9.58)*. Jesus' reply to the would-be follower refers to animals—foxes and birds (ἀλώπεκες...καὶ τὰ πετεινὰ). The animals are associated with the wilderness ('like foxes in the wildernesses', ὡς ἀλώπεκες ἐν ταῖς ἐρήμοις, Ezek. 13.4), and birds were associated with the drought in the Elijah narrative (1 Kgs 17.4-6), so while Jesus may be journeying towards Jerusalem, his words evoke the sense of a walk like that of Elijah 'in the wilderness' (ἐν τῇ ἐρήμῳ, 1 Kgs 19.4). Three elements now occur in both texts in the same order:

Wilderness	Foxes
Elijah as mortal—[descended] from his [dead] fathers	Jesus as son of man
Cannot stay lying...And behold at his head	Cannot lay his head

When Elijah goes into the wilderness, he wants to die, seeing himself as no better than his (dead) fathers. The emphasis then is clearly on his mortality. Luke on the other hand speaks of Jesus as 'son of man/Son of Man'—fairly common in the LXX (about 100 times in eight books, mostly Ezekiel)—a phrase that as used in the New Testament is often taken as emphasizing humanity and mortality. Luke had last used this phrase, son of man, to refer to himself as 'eating and drinking' (Lk. 7.34). Now he uses it again apparently with essentially the same emphasis—as highlighting humanity, specifically mortality, on the road to fateful Jerusalem.

The references to 'my [mortal] fathers' (19.4) and 'Son of Man' (9.58) are followed immediately by references to lying down, but in both texts the lying down is not satisfactory: Elijah lies down literally but is told to arise and eat food, which is at his head; and the Son of Man, metaphorically, has nowhere to lay his head:

1 Kgs 19	v. 4: τοὺς πατέρας μου // v. 5: καὶ ἐκοιμήθη... v. 6: καὶ ἰδοὺ πρὸς κεφαλῆς αὐτου
Lk. 9.58	ὁ δὲ υἱὸς τοῦ ἀνθρώπου // οὐκ ἔχει ποῦ τὴν κεφαλὴν κλίνῃ...
1 Kgs 19	v. 4: my fathers // v. 5: and he lay down... v. 6: and behold at his head
Lk. 9.58	the son of (hu)man(ity) // does not have where to lay his head...

The words for 'lay down' are distinct. The verb in 1 Kgs 19.5, 6 (κοιμάω) is associated with falling asleep; and in Lk. 9.58 (κλίνω) with inclining or laying down. Here both these verbs are often translated as lay or lay down. Both texts tell of a person facing death, and both contain four elements: the basic idea of laying/lying down; desire to do so; not being able to rest in lying down; and mention of the head. The way in which Luke reshapes 'lying down' and 'head' is similar to the way in which he later reshapes the motif of the delay and the plough (1 Kgs 19.19-21; Lk. 9.61-62); in both cases there is a form, not so much of word-play—well known in biblical writing—as of image-play, the process sometimes associated with prophets.

The implication: while Luke's picture of Jesus as homeless builds on Jesus' rejection by the Samaritans, it also uses a series of elements from the Elijah account, and combines them into the single image of laying down one's head. But Luke maintains the sense of an unsatisfactory process: Elijah cannot just lie down; and the Son of Man cannot lay down his head. The essence of both texts is an evoking of the ambiguity of humans—bound to earth and mortal, but also having a further dimension that can wake them to something else and keep them restless until they engage the something else.

The reference to the birds is ambiguous. Unlike the foxes, who are clearly earthbound in their holes in the ground, the birds are described, unnecessarily, as birds 'of the sky/heaven', πετεινὰ τοῦ οὐρανοῦ. Like the references to the enigmatic 'someone' and to 'the messenger of the Lord' (1 Kgs 19.5, 7), it makes sense as a hint of relief from the homelessness, and, within Luke's surrounding text, forms part of a pattern linking 'heaven' to a wider world, ultimately to a divine dimension (Lk. 9.54, 58; 10.15, 18, 20). Unlike the dens of the foxes, the birds' nests, κατασκηνώσεις (twice in the New

Testament: here and Mt. 8.20) evoke places of deep rest, as indicated by the New Testament's four uses of the corresponding verb, κατασκηνόω (Mt. 13.32; Mk 4.32; Lk. 13.19; and esp. Acts 2.26). This ambiguity seems to correspond to something within Elijah. He is in the wilderness, and mortal; yet someone is calling him to something further.

What is essential is that, in the first exchange, every element of Luke's text, from the opening reference to journeying on the road to the final mention about laying down one's head, comes either from the scene of *Elijah's journey to Horeb* or from *elements associated with it* or from *Luke's own vocabulary*.

2. *From Preoccupation with Death/Burial to Proclaiming God (1 Kings 19.9-18; Luke 9.59-60)*

(a) *Preoccupation with death and burial (Luke 9.59)*. The second dialogue is unusual in having three parts, three 'he saids', rather then just two. Its initial 'Follow me', is a variation on 'I will follow (after) you' (1 Kgs 19.20). It is an imperative/command, the first in the triple challenge, and so clarifies the nature of the text as a call narrative (Fleddermann 2005: 393). The other dialogues have no imperative.

This second dialogue has two basic elements: preoccupation with burial; and a command to leave death/burial and proclaim God. Of these, one, the potential disciple's *request to first bury his father*, is modelled partly on Elisha's *request to first kiss his father goodbye* (1 Kgs 19.20, final scene); and the other element, the command to leave the dead and proclaim the kingdom of God, distils the large central drama of 1 Kings 19—an account of how, with intensifying imperatives, the awesome Lord moves Elijah from preoccupation with death to undertaking God's mission (19.9-18). In brief:

[1] *At Horeb: Focus moves from death to God.*	[2] Let me first bury my father.
[2] Elisha: I will (first) kiss my father.	[1] *Leave the dead; proclaim God.*

Details: As mentioned earlier, the opening reference to an indefinite 'other' ('He said to another', Εἶπεν δὲ πρὸς ἕτερον), is a variation on the initial indefinite 'someone' ('Someone said to him', εἶπέν τις πρὸς αὐτόν, Lk. 9.57; cf. τις...εἶπεν αὐτῷ, 1 Kgs 19.5).

The basic vocabulary of following, 'Follow me', ἀκολούθει μοι, relies largely on the earlier phrases—'I will follow after you', ἀκολουθήσω ὀπίσω σου / ἀκολουθήσω σοι (1 Kgs 19.20; Lk. 9.57), but its imperative tone, and the subsequent commands ('Leave the dead...; But you, going away, proclaim...') reflect the Lord's directive tone in the central scene at Horeb (1 Kgs 19.11, 15-18), especially 'Go; return...', πορεύου ἀνάστρεφε (19.15).

As already partly indicated, the potential disciple's request to be permitted to first go away and bury his father is a variation on Elisha's 'I will kiss my father and (then) follow after you:'

1 Kgs 19.20   καταφιλήσω τὸν πατέρα μου
Lk. 9.59   ...πρῶτον θάψαι τὸν πατέρα μου
1 Kgs 19.20   I will kiss my father
Lk. 9.59   ...first to bury my father

Luke's 'first', πρῶτον, makes explicit what the 1 Kgs 19.20 implied—that Elisha would *first* kiss his father. Some modern translations make a similar adaptation; they insert the word 'then' ('and *then* follow', RSV, JB) to indicate sequence/priority. 'Permit...', ἐπιτρέπω, is Lukan; it occurs only in Luke (Lk. 9.59, 61; Acts 21.39) apart from parallel Mt. 8.21, always as 'Permit me...', ἐπίτρεψόν μοι). Its courteous tone may reflect the tone of the exchange between Elijah and Elisha (19.20). The stark change in the reason for going back to one's father—not 'to kiss' but 'to bury'—is explained by the way death preoccupies Elijah (19.10, 14).

(b) *Jesus' reply: Leave death/burial and proclaim God (Luke 9.60)*. Luke distill Elijah's repetitive complaining by a sharp repetition involving just two short words, 'bury' and 'dead':

1 Kgs 19   ἀπέκτειναν...ἀπέκτειναν (19.10, 14), θανατώσει...θανατώσει... (19.17).
Lk. 9   θάψαι... θάψαι, τοὺς νεκρούς... τοὺς νεκρούς (9.59-60).
1 Kgs 19   killed...killed...(19.10, 14), put to death...put to death... (19.17).
Lk. 9   to bury...to bury...the dead...the dead (9.59-60).

The word 'put to death', θανατώσει, actually belongs not with Elijah's pre-occupation with death but with the Lord's response to it (19.17), yet it maintains some of Elijah's repetitiveness, and may have served Luke's overall emphasis on death and on seeing beyond death. The core of the entire Elijah chapter (1 Kgs 19) is the dynamic presence of the Lord, first the Lord's in-breaking on the mountain (19.11-12) and then the Lord's intensifying command to get moving: 'Go; return...and you will come...and you will anoint...and you will anoint...and you will anoint...' (19.15-18). The command to get moving is reflected in Jesus' dense command to leave the dead, and go:

1 Kgs 19   v. 15: πορεύου ἀνάστρεφε...καὶ ἥξεις... v. 19: καὶ ἀπῆλθεν...
Lk. 9.60   ἄφες...σὺ δὲ ἀπελθὼν
1 Kgs 19   v. 15: Go, return...and you will come... v. 19: and he departed
Lk. 9.60   Leave...but you, departing...

The 'leave', ἄφες, may involve some word-play with the LXX—a matter for another discussion. The emphatic 'But you, departing', σὺ δὲ ἀπελθὼν, telling the potential disciple to move elsewhere, brings together the repeated 'you', σὺ, in the pointed questions to Elijah about his location 'What you (σύ) here!?' (1 Kgs 19.9, 13), and combines them with Elijah's 'departing' in response to the Lord's command (19.19). The addition of δὲ, 'but', is Lukan. The anointing means turning the Lord's in-breaking into practical action—in this case by appointing two kings ('king...king'; βασιλέα...βασιλέα, 19.15-16) and, then climactically, 'you will anoint [Elisha] a prophet' (χρίσεις εἰς προφήτην), instead of Elijah himself. Such was the Lord's resounding commanded at Horeb, and Luke immediately tells of the clear command of Jesus: 'But you, departing, proclaim the kingdom of God':

1 Kgs 19.15-16	καὶ εἶπεν κύριος πρὸς αὐτόν πορεύου ἀνάστρεφε...καὶ ἥξεις καὶ χρίσεις εἰς βασιλέα...εἰς βασιλέα...καὶ...χρίσεις εἰς προφήτην ἀντὶ σου
Lk. 9.60	εἶπεν δὲ αὐτῷ...σὺ δὲ ἀπελθὼν διάγγελλε τὴν βασιλείαν τοῦ θεοῦ.
1 Kgs 19.15-16	And the Lord said to him, Go, return...and you will come and you will anoint as king...as king...and...and you will anoint as prophet in your place
Lk. 9.60	But he said to him... But you, departing, proclaim the kingdom of God.

The gap between the prophet (προφήτην) and proclaiming (διάγγελλε) is not great: 'Prophets are first and foremost proclaimers' (Sawyer 1993: 1). And while the Lord asks Elijah to anoint two kings (βασιλέα...βασιλέα, 19.15-16), Jesus commands the proclamation of 'the kingdom of God', τὴν βασιλείαν τοῦ θεοῦ (9.60). 'The verb [proclaim] διαγγέλλω is Lucan...[used] twice in Luke–Acts (Lk. 9.60; Acts 21.26)...and nowhere else in the gospels' (Fleddermann 2005: 394).

The phrase 'kingdom of God' is not in 1 Kings 19 but it was well-established as early as the Epistles (for instance, in 1 Cor. 4.20; 6.9, 10; 15.24, 50), and Luke had used it earlier (for instance, in 7.28 and 8.1) so it fits with his larger pattern of writing, particularly with his earlier reference to 'announcing the good news (εὐαγγελίζω) of the kingdom of God' (8.1). But as well as being in accord with Luke's own practice, the phrase 'proclaim the kingdom of God' also captures the heart of the drama at Horeb (1 Kgs 19), and it thereby captures something also from the background drama of Sinai (Exod. 19). Luke's distillation of Horeb—and ultimately of Sinai—forms a strong foundation for disciples, especially for the far-flung mission of the seventy.

In summarizing Luke's second exchange (Lk. 9.59-60) what is essential is that virtually every element in it is either a copy or variation of 1 Kings 19 or is a reflection of Luke's own distinct vocabulary.

3. *Turning Back from the Plough (1 Kings 19.19-21; Luke 9.61-62)*
(a) *Let me first say farewell (Luke 9.61)*. While the second dialogue focused on the kingdom of God, the third consolidates that focus by emphasizing perseverance—not looking back from the plough. The one who looks back is not worthy of the kingdom of God. In speaking again of the kingdom of God, this third dialogue goes over some of the same ground as the second. It begins again with a request from a potential follower to first take leave of his house, and, as in the case of the person who wanted first to bury his father, it too makes use of the account of Elisha first going to kiss his father goodbye.

The initial phrases ('Another said, I will follow you, Lord, but first permit me...', Εἶπεν δὲ καὶ ἕτερος· ἀκολουθήσω σοι, κύριε· πρῶτον δὲ ἐπίτρεψόν μοι...) all consist of repetitions or variations on the beginning of dialogue two (9.59).

The first distinctive phrase in this dialogue is the request 'to say farewell to those in my house', ἀποτάξασθαι τοῖς εἰς τὸν οἶκόν μου. While this repeats aspects of the earlier texts on parting from one's father, it also contains variations that reflect some of Luke's adaptations and distinctive vocabulary. The use of 'house' prepares for the fivefold reference to house (οἰκία, οἶκος) in the mission discourse (Lk. 10.5, 7). The rare word ἀποτάσσομαι, 'to say goodbye', is predominantly Lukan (only Lk. 9.61; 14.33; Acts 18.18, 21; Mk 6.46; and 2 Cor. 2.13). It is not clear whether Luke's use of ἀποτάσσομαι should be linked with its occurrence in 2 Cor 2.13.[6]

(b) *Jesus' reply: Ploughing...no turning back (Luke 9.62)*. As indicated, Jesus' response about perseverance/commitment, about not looking back from the plough, adapts the LXX picture of Elisha the ploughman turning from ploughing. Luke preserves the idea of a promising perseverance, but does so by reversing actions and image. Freedom to go back becomes an implicit warning about relinquishing the task; and the plough, instead of being burned, is kept in hand and before one's eyes.

Details: 'The use of οὐδεὶς ["no one"] with a participle and ἐπιβαλὼν τὴν χεῖρα / τάς χεῖράς ["throwing/putting one's hand(s)"] are both Lucan'

---

6.   Luke's use of ἀποτάξασθαι, 'say goodbye/take leave of', has affinity with 2 Cor. 2.12-13: both texts imply mission, travel, pressure, and sorting things out with people to whom one has ties (one's brother/'them'). Cf. 2 Cor. 2.12-13: 'When I came to Troas to preach the gospel of Christ, a door was opened for me in the Lord; but my mind could not rest because I did not find my brother Titus there. So I took leave of them and went on to Macedonia', Ἐλθὼν δὲ εἰς τὴν Τρῳάδα εἰς τὸ εὐαγγέλιον τοῦ Χριστοῦ καὶ θύρας μοι ἀνεῳγμένης ἐν κυρίῳ, οὐκ ἔσχηκα ἄνεσιν τῷ πνεύματί μου τῷ μὴ εὑρεῖν με Τίτον τὸν ἀδελφόν μου, ἀλλὰ **ἀποταξάμενος αὐτοῖς** ἐξῆλθον εἰς Μακεδονίαν. The identity of the αὐτοῖς, 'them', in ἀποταξάμενος αὐτοῖς, 'took leave of them', is obscure; cf. Lk. 9.61, **ἀποτάξασθαι τοῖς** εἰς τὸν οἶκόν μου, 'to take leave of those in my house'.

(Fleddermann 2005: 396 n. 27). But while thus maintaining aspects of his usual style, Luke also reflects details of specific aspects of 1 Kings 19, namely variations of 'on', ἐπ / ἐπ', in 1 Kgs 19.19. Very literally:

1 Kgs 19.19   καὶ αὐτὸς ἠροτρία...καὶ **ἐπῆλθεν ἐπ'** αὐτὸν καὶ **ἐπέρριψε** τὴν μηλωτὴν αὐτοῦ **ἐπ'** αὐτόν

Lk. 9.62   οὐδεὶς **ἐπιβαλὼν** τὴν χεῖρα **ἐπ'** ἄροτρον

1 Kgs 19.19   And he was ploughing...and he came-up**on on** him and he cast-**on** his mantle **on** him

Lk. 9.62   No one putting/throwing-**on** his hand **on** the plough

When Elijah first approached Elisha, he *threw* (ἐπιρρίπτώ) his prophetic mantle over/on him (ἐπέρριψε τὴν μηλωτὴν αὐτοῦ ἐπ' αὐτόν), and Luke refers to the potential followers as *throwing* (ἐπιβάλλώ, throw over) a hand *onto* the plough (ἐπιβαλὼν τὴν χεῖρα ἐπ' ἄροτρον). Thus Luke keeps the idea of throwing something over something else, but instead of ἐπιρρίπτώ he uses his generally preferred word, ἐπιβάλλώ. Luke also preserves the repeated use of on/over (ἐπ / ἐπ'). Luke is not just playing with linguistic trivia. He is keeping elements of the passing on of the mantle of prophecy. Elisha burned the plough to stay with the mantle, but in Luke's account of the call, the new mission still keeps the plough—as a metaphor, an indication of future fruitfulness and clear focus.

Luke's 'and looking back', καὶ βλέπων εἰς τὰ ὀπίσω, abbreviates the reference to Lot's wife looking back at the destruction of Sodom: 'and his wife looked back', καὶ ἐπέβλεψεν ἡ γυνὴ αὐτοῦ εἰς τὰ ὀπίσω (Gen. 19.26). Luke abbreviates to suit the context, uses the participle ('looking', βλέπων) as he did in the preceding phrase ('throwing', ἐπιβαλὼν), and provides an allusion to Sodom that prepares for the reference to Sodom in the commissioning (10.12).

Regarding 'is worthy of the kingdom of God', εὔθετός ἐστιν τῇ βασιλείᾳ τοῦ θεοῦ, in the New Testament the adjective εὔθετός, 'worthy', is Lukan insofar as Luke is the only evangelist to use it (twice: 9.62; 14.35). Otherwise, within the New Testament, it occurs only in Hebrews (6.8).[7]

Again, in the third exchange, virtually every element of Luke's text (9.61-62) is either a repetition/variation of 1 Kings 19 and related material or reflects Luke's own distinctive vocabulary.

---

7.   Heb. 6.1-8 talks of perseverance and has linguistic affinities with Lk. 9.60, 62; cf. Heb. 6.1-8, esp. 1-2: **ἀφέντες**... κατα**βαλλόμενοι**...**νεκρῶν**...**ἐπιθέσεώς**...**χειρῶν**... **νεκρῶν**... **εὔθετον**, 'leaving...throwing down...dead...laying on...hands...dead...worthy'. A colleague mentioned in conversation (Limerick, 7 July 2011) that in Papyrus 46 (c. 200 CE) Hebrews is placed after Romans.

Summary

The purpose of this chapter was to seek out if possible the literary back-ground or sources of Jesus' triple challenge to disciples (Lk. 9.57-62). The main results are as follows:

The context of the challenge—a journey with extraordinary features, including looming assumption, and the power to call down fire from heaven (Lk. 9.51-56)—immediately links the account of Jesus *in some way* with the Old Testament account that tells of Elijah as likewise able to call fire from heaven and as likewise setting out to be taken up (2 Kgs 1.1–2.2).

The essential Old Testament narrative concerning Elijah is scarcely eight chapters, so it does not take long to attempt an initial check as to whether Jesus' triple challenge owes anything to the rest of the Elijah narrative, and given that there is a frequently recognized link between Jesus' third challenge about not turning back from the plough (Lk. 9.61-62) and the third part of Elijah's crisis journey to Horeb, the part about calling the young ploughman, Elisha (1 Kgs 19.19-21), it makes sense of look more closely at the full account of Elijah's journey to Horeb (1 Kgs 19). The opening of Elijah's journey proper, the beginning of his journey in the wilderness (1 Kgs 19.4), provides immediate encouragement. Its eight opening words contain varia-tions on all six of the opening words of Luke about the journey of Jesus (Lk. 9.57).

Further investigation shows wide-ranging similarities and adaptations. The form used by Luke, that of three pithy repetitive exchanges, follows a form that he himself had used earlier in reporting John's replies to would-be doers (Lk. 3.10-14); and these exchanges also incorporate some of the repeti-tiveness of 1 Kings 19. Both 1 Kings 19 and Lk. 9.57-62 are essentially three-part, but in both cases the central part is more sharply challenging, and particularly in 1 Kings 19, more elaborate. The heart of both texts is a variation on the call of the Old Testament prophets. In addition, Luke turns elements of plot, actions described as really happening, into metaphors: not being allowed to stay lying because of food at one's head becomes not having a place to lay one's head; emphasis on the dead become partly a metaphor for the spiritually dead; God's appointing of kings becomes a basis for referring to the kingdom of God; and ploughing turns into the metaphor of the plough. In addition, Luke interweaves the use of 1 Kings 19 with the use of other texts, and he adapts the final shape of the text to his own context, both the immediate context of a journey to Jerusalem, the further missionary journey far beyond (Lk. 9.51–10.20), and the larger context of Luke's entire work.

Continued analysis shows similar procedures in the full detail of Luke's work. Even the repetitive use of indefinite pronouns to indicate Jesus' interlocutors, 'someone', 'another', 'another' (9.57, 59, 61), consists of repeating and varying the indefiniteness of the 'someone' who first speaks to Elijah in the wilderness (1 Kgs 19.5).

Likewise regarding the content *within* the framework. Essentially every word, every image of the entire text of the triple challenge is built either on the LXX (on 1 Kgs 19 plus associated references) or on Luke's distinctive vocabulary and purpose. Occasionally Luke's distinctive vocabulary has curious affinities with the Epistles, leading to the issue of Luke's relationship to these Epistles, but even without attempting to resolve that question, the essential fact remains: the combination of the LXX and Luke's literary capacity—his masterful skill as a Christian evangelist intent on communicating the message of Christ—explains the data within the text of the triple challenge.

At times Luke may seem to reflect material from another source, for instance in referring to the foxes and birds, but these animals fit perfectly with the image of the wilderness, and with other Septuagintal references to foxes and birds; and the description of the birds as birds 'of heaven' fits the birds into the context of repeated references to heaven in the surrounding text (Lk. 9.51–10.20). Even unusual words, such as 'permit', 'say goodbye/take leave of', and 'worthy' (ἐπιτρέπω, ἀποτάσσω/ομαι, εὔθετός) reflect Luke's distinctive vocabulary (Fleddermann 2005: 396).

Conclusion

The result of these procedures is that the sub-text, 1 Kings 19, is not just edited or redacted. It is transformed. Redaction is indeed present in the composition of the Gospels, and elsewhere in the scriptures, but, as the critique of John Van Seters (2006) has partly indicated, the role of redaction in the composing of the Bible has been exaggerated.

The role of redaction has been particularly exaggerated in discussions of Q. Since both Matthew and Luke used redaction in dealing with Mark there is often a presumption that they also used redaction in dealing with their other sources. As a working hypothesis such a presumption is reasonable, but it needs to allow for other methods of adaptation, including transformation.

There is no ready indication as to which texts are redacted and which are transformed. Each text has to be tested. In the case of Lk. 9.57-62, the transformation of the LXX—plus perhaps some indebtedness to the Epistles—is the simplest explanation of the data, and in scientific method the explanation that accounts for the data most simply is to be preferred. In this case, Q is unnecessary, and therefore unjustified.

Matthew's use of a similar shorter version of the challenge (Mt. 8.19-22) is relatively easy to explain: Matthew used this part of Luke's text but adapted and abbreviated it, as he frequently did with Mark's text. Of course this raises the question of Matthew's overall relationship to Luke, but that was already mentioned when outlining the sequence of the New Testament documents (Chapter 5), and has been discussed at length elsewhere— essentially to say that Matthew first used a brief Elijah-based version of Luke's work (a work containing Lk. 9.57-62), and that, as a later stage, canonical Luke–Acts used Matthew.[8] The credibility of the brief Elijah-based version of Luke—based on the whole Elijah–Elisha narrative—rests especially on the fact that, like Lk. 9.57-62, it is rooted solidly in an extant text, the LXX, and so, as the analysis in this chapter indicates, it is verifiable in a way that Q is not.

What is important is that, as Lk. 9.57-62 illustrates, the literary roots of the Gospel text can be traced, often in considerable detail. While it is useful and necessary to employ all the resources of historical investigation, of 'historical criticism', including archaeological excavation of sites, it is also necessary to try to trace the pen of the evangelist. Luke's reworking of 1 Kings 19 shows an extraordinary attention to the entirety of the older scriptures, everything from the scope and depth of their vision to the detail of their fabric. He distils the essence of 1 Kings 19, its increasingly sharp word to the dead heart, but he also harvests many of its actions as metaphors, and he gleans many details that preserve something of the texture of the old and that lend character to the new.

But the character of the new is another topic.

---

8. Brodie 2004: esp. xxvii-xxviii, 197-203, 260-67. Much further discussion is still necessary.

Part III

THE THIRD REVOLUTION:
LITERARY ART, INCLUDING FORM/GENRE

*Becoming aware how biblical writers redesigned
their materials into a new work of art*

Chapter 8

THE THIRD REVOLUTION:
ST LOUIS, 1984–1991

On my first morning in St Louis, in August 1984, as I looked out my sixth-storey window, I could see, on the western shore of the Mississippi, the soaring silver Arch that recalls the city's role as the Gateway for the opening up of a captivating frontier—the American West.

My own frontier, as I began teaching at Aquinas Institute on Lindell Boulevard, was miniscule by comparison, but for me was equally captivating. It was twofold: to clarify, in the classroom, the meaning and history of the Old Testament; and, through writing, to communicate the sources of the New.

However, I did not know what lay ahead.

The teaching of the Old Testament generally went well. The students were colourful and keen, and, compared to the New Testament scene, Old Testament studies seemed to have more ideas and movement. Much of this movement was coming from the first revolution—good old-fashioned historical criticism, including ongoing archaeology and a relentless search for the truth regarding the history of ancient Israel. Gone now was the possibility of maintaining what I had eventually taught in Trinidad in 1968, namely, that it seemed best to allow that some of the major figures of Genesis—Abraham, Isaac and Jacob—were significantly historical.

The unravelling of the historicity of Genesis took off in the 1970s. The works of Thomas Thompson (1974) and John Van Seters (1975) made it clear that, while Genesis is hugely instructive, its composition was late and it has little relationship to specific historical events. Thompson's presentation of his ground-breaking evidence did not immediately help his career. For a while he had to get work as a painter.

By 1986, when the down-to-earth John Hayes was still concentrating on ancient history rather than on his blessed cattle farm in Alabama, he co-operated with Max Miller in producing *A History of Ancient Israel and Judah* which reckoned that reliable history was lacking not only in Genesis, but in all six books from Genesis to Joshua's conquest, thus implying that the very nature or form of these books had to be rethought. Instead of being regarded as history, they should be classed as some form of instruction or prophetic teaching—an implication that corresponded significantly with the traditional Jewish view that the first five books were *torah*, 'instruction', and that Joshua belonged with the 'former prophets'.

Hayes and Miller had drawn the line at Judges. Here at last, in characters such as Deborah, Jephthah and Samson, they reckoned that the historian finds areas of solid ground. They relied on Judges because they saw its jumbled-looking sequence and style as reflecting oral tradition, and most scholars regarded oral tradition as somehow linked to past events.

In the classroom in St Louis, we too struggled with history, and then we moved on to the questions of theology—of ultimate meaning. Overall, progress was satisfactory.

* * *

However, back at my writing-desk, in trying to communicate the sources of the New Testament, my wheels were mired. The effort to get at John's sources, his raw materials, was proving inseparable from understanding John's ultimate meaning, from understanding the entire Gospel—both its content and form. To some degree, I was still focused on the healing of the man born blind (Jn 9), and on whether it had used the sight-related episodes at the centre of Mark (Mk 8.11–9.8), but more and more the meaning of John 9 was turning out to be inseparable from the meaning of much of the rest of John—the meaning, for instance, of depicting Jesus' ministry as spread over three years, rather than just one, as in the other Gospels. So, I began to look around to the larger narrative of John's Gospel. Then one day I woke up and realized I was being drawn into writing a commentary!

For days I walked the streets and parks of St Louis, often discussing it at length with a good friend, a Dominican sister. I frequently found commentaries difficult to read, especially when they were dominated by mountains of disconnected notes. Surely the world did not need another commentary on John. Besides, the thought of the work involved wearied me. Worst of all, I was being drawn away from identifying the use of extant sources—a key task that seemed largely neglected and to which I seemed called and suited. Cobbler, stick to your last!

On the other hand, I appeared to be hitting a seam of the Gospel that had not been worked before. Could I now walk away from it? My friend encouraged me to stay with it. What I was hitting, though I did not know it clearly, was an aspect of a third revolution—something that, to some extent, was already being developed in the work of others, for instance in Alan Culpepper's *Anatomy of the Fourth Gospel* (1983).

Anatomy! The body—the entire completed body, from brawn to brains and even to breathing, from toe nails to hair texture. I had spent over ten years engrossed with genealogy, with identifying the parentage of biblical books—their roots or sources. Parentage and anatomy are indeed linked. One generates the other. And a good family doctor will take account of both. But they are also very distinct. Just because you know the parents well does not mean that you know what the child will be like, what form of anatomy it will have. The famed exotic dancer, Isadora Duncan, once proposed to George Bernard Shaw that they have a child together.

'Think of it! With my body and your brains, what a wonder it would be.'

'Yes, but what if it has *my* body and *your* brains?'

A new anatomy was a new world. If I were to deal responsibly with John's Gospel, I would have to take account of both aspects—the sources that underlie it, insofar as they can be identified, and also the completed body, all the features of ancient rhetorical art, especially its basic *form* (is it a girl or a boy? is it history or story?).

The emphasis on *form* was not new. As we saw earlier, voices as diverse as Hermann Gunkel (1901, 1926, 1933) and a papal encyclical (*Divino Afflante Spiritu*, 1943) spoke of the need to identify ancient literary forms correctly, and so did 'form criticism' (*Form-geschichte*, 'the history of forms') with its special interest in trying to trace the identity and history of small episodes. Yet there was a huge gap between establishing a principle and applying it fully.

But now, in the 1970s and 1980s, the gap was being bridged. The emerging awareness brought attention to literary features further. As never before, literary criticism was seeking to identify not only the basic form (genre/nature) of a biblical writing but, again, all the specific features that held it together and shaped it. *Modern* literary criticism had arrived. Its efforts at taking off had moved almost imperceptibly from Leonardo da Vinci's flying machine to the Wright brothers. Biblical historians had found a rejuvenated ally.

Not everyone rushed to greet it. As things happened, especially in the 1980s, 'literary criticism' became associated in biblical studies with modern literary *theory*. This has its uses, but some of it was brittle, numbingly abstract and of doubtful relevance, and perhaps it was for this reason that Joseph Fitzmyer, one evening in July 1998, during a Colloquium panel session in Louvain (Leuven), declared boldly, even defiantly, that he did not engage in literary criticism.

But literary criticism at its best was here to stay—both a new way of searching for sources, and a new sense of how to look for a book's art (its identity/form/genre and also its specific features). In the final decades of the twentieth century these two kinds of literary criticism gained momentum in biblical studies, and certainly for me the recognition of their depth constituted revolutions.

With regard to appreciating the literary features of the finished text, especially the use of ancient art or rhetoric, the importance of using developed literary criticism appears at the very beginning of the Bible in the story of creation. As already seen, the existence of two accounts (Gen. 1.1–2.4a and 2.4b-24) can seem somewhat confused, the result of poor editing (or 'redaction'), and so it was that our medical man at the court of Louis XV, Jean Astruc, suggested that the variations between the two accounts represented the difference between two of Moses' sources. They did in fact reflect diverse ways of picturing creation, but when looked at more closely, when seen from another angle, they constitute an extraordinary unity; they complement one another deeply—like the two parts of the brain, or the two genders that constitute humanity. In other words, Genesis begins to emerge not as muddled, but as chiselled with supreme care. I will come back to Genesis later. What was instructive for someone like me who had swallowed the Astruc theory, was that at last, through literary criticism, through appreciation of literary art, the unity and purposefulness of Genesis became recognizable.

A similar process of recognition often comes easily when dealing with other works of art. It is taken for granted, for instance, that the strange spelling in James Joyce's *Ulysses* does not mean that there was a spelling disorder in Joyce himself or among the Jesuits at his Clongowes Wood high school, or among the people of Dublin. No, the strange spelling was done with purpose, especially to indicate sound. And it is taken for granted that Picasso's strange faces do not mean Picasso could not draw a face. But for several reasons, including at times a modern sense of superiority, the superb artistry of the ancient biblical writers had not been recognized. The ultimate value of the Bible had indeed often been invoked, including the role of God in inspiring it. But the role of the human authors, the detailed artistry with which they crafted texts and the way God was within that artistry, incarnated as it were, had been overlooked.

In studying John, it was impossible to avoid the issue of literary artistry. Was this text as jumbled as it looked, or was its curious shape—for instance, its gaps and contradictions—trying to say something?

The wake-up call to the full reality of what might be going on in John came to me not only through Culpepper's *Anatomy* but above all through Robert Alter's *The Art of Biblical Narrative* (1981). Alter was speaking of the way in which strange-looking Hebrew narrative, despite all its apparent oddities, including its repetitions, breaks and contradictions, was not at all lacking in unity, as was often assumed. Rather, 'the biblical writers…had certain notion of unity rather different from our own' (1981: 133)—a phrase that landed in my mind with clanging reverberations. Much research on John regarded John's oddities of style—his strange breaks or 'aporias'—as indications of disunity and as clues to the use of diverse sources, now lost, and much time was given to trying to reconstruct these lost sources, especially the hypothetical 'Signs Source'. But if Alter's reading of Hebrew narrative was a reliable clue, these breaks had almost nothing to do with the use of lost sources. Rather, like the seeming confusion of some writings and paintings—such as those of Joyce or Picasso—they were primarily expressions of art; they were trying to say something.

Alter not only startled me—he provoked a process of further reading: literary criticism, rhetorical criticism, authors such as Luis Alonso Schökel, Carol Newsom, Meir Sternberg, Jan Fokkelman, Phyllis Trible, Vernon Robbins, and Gail O'Day. Suddenly a mass of data in John, formerly assigned to a vague mixture of oral tradition, lost sources, and elusive stages of redaction, began to fall into place as the work of one accomplished writer. Strange syntax made more sense as artistry rather than as poor editing ('redaction'). C.K. Barrett's view of John as dialectical became clearer in light of Carol Newsom's work on the dialogical nature of biblical narrative. And the importance ancient writers attached to a work's beginning, middle and end helped explain many elements, including why at these three points Mark is most obviously related to the Elijah–Elisha narrative, and John in turn is most obviously related to Mark.

* * *

So, in the long term there was no way that I could give a full account of how John or any of the evangelists had used sources without asking what they were trying to produce—what form of writing and with what features. And so, eventually, reluctantly, I realized that writing a close commentary was an opportunity to engage the third revolution, and to make peace with it. Apart from issues concerning John's history and sources, I would try to be alert to the literary clues that might indicate how his work hung together, and what vision it was evoking. I wrote an introduction to the Gospel. But later I had to revise it. And eventually I rewrote the introduction five times. I had no illusions of having captured the whole Gospel fully, but at least each rewriting was much better than what had preceded.

I learned much about John 9. Here too was evidence of a single coherent author, a fully unified text, but with at least three levels: a biography-like account (*bios*) of Jesus; a reflection of the early church; and, surprisingly, an evoking of the stages of human living and believing. As in Shakespeare's seven ages, John goes from birth to (evoking) death, but while Shakespeare emphasizes *outer* detail, John had used a small selection of outer details to evoke stages that were largely *within*, particularly stages of believing.

Eventually, it began to become clear that, even if the Gospel used dozens of sources, every word from beginning to end had been chiselled by a single authoritative writer into its present shape, a shape with a specific artistic and theological purpose. The prologue's notorious variations of style, for instance, a spiralling change *from soaring poetry to mundane prose*, made complete sense in light of the prologue's central message—the change *from Word into flesh*. The distinctive portrayal of a three-year ministry likewise made sense, when analyzed closely, as a way of portraying major stages of a Spirit-led human life—a variation on the stages portrayed in John 9. And the problem of the 'double ending' (20.30-31; 21.24-25) fell into place as part of a choreographed three-part conclusion (19.35-37; 20.30-31; 21.24-25), for which Proto-Luke gives a partial precedent (Acts 1.1–15.35; cf. triple 'it seemed good', 15.22, 25, 28; note the references to writing; cf. Lk. 1.1-4).

Even the Gospel's startling conclusion, that *Jesus' words and deeds would not fit into the entire world* (21.25), fits perfectly as a well-crafted variation on the Gospel's opening, concerning *the Word who had made all things from the beginning* (1.1-3). The world-surpassing Word (1.1-3) has generated the equivalent of world-surpassing writings (21.25). Thus the final verse contains at least two literary features, balance (or inclusion) and hyperbole, but these features are not superficial decorations. They build towards one of the Gospel's primary aims—imparting a sense of wonder, a sense reflected in the final suggestion of being left guessing (*oimai*, 'I suppose/think').

So, for several years, including a number of secluded semesters in Germany—one in Tübingen where I attended Martin Hengel's seminar and received his support in joining the Society of New Testament Studies—I laid aside completely the question of John's sources, and concentrated on the methods of the third revolution, on developing awareness of how John's finished text, with all its gaps and tensions, forms a unified work of art. Not every detail was accounted for, but, overall, the evidence converged. From beginning to end the entirety of John's Gospel constitutes a literary unity that is tightly woven, and every sentence is shaped to contribute to that unity and to the Gospel's encompassing vision and meaning.

The emphasis on the story's meaning is so strong and coherent that the text requires no further explanation. In particular it does not require that the story be historical. In other words, explaining the data requires meaningful artistry, but it does not require history. What is not required by the data cannot be established. It may be conjectured, but it cannot be verified.

The result was that, having set out to trace John's reworking of extant sources—a method that already raised serious questions about the historicity of John's text—I had wandered into a quite different method which showed that history was not required. In the book that followed—*The Gospel according to John: A Literary and Theological Commentary* (Brodie 1993a)—I made no reference to the loss of a historical claim. That belonged to another place and time. Instead, I placed the emphasis where I believe it belongs—on John's positive message.

* * *

Eight years after my first New Haven attempts at resolving whether John 9 used Mark (Mk 8.11–9.8) I decided to give it another try. To ensure concentration I had arranged a semester in Walberberg, the Dominican house of studies outside Cologne, a quiet spot, near woods. I settled in quickly, just before Christmas, ready for another slow slog.

The slog never happened. Within a week or two the key pattern emerged almost effortlessly. Each text—Mark and John—may be said to consist essentially of six scenes or episodes, but John, instead of using each Markan episode to colour just one scene concerning the man born blind, had subdivided each Markan episode into three distinct aspects and had systematically *dispersed* these aspects among three scenes in John 9, somewhat like taking a red uniform and, instead of putting it on one policeman, distributing its three main parts—cap, jacket and trousers—among three policemen. The systematic dispersal explained the complexity of the data, and suddenly the essential pattern of the evidence became clear.

The basic idea—that John's Gospel dispersed the material in Mark—was not new. Almost thirty years earlier Raymond Brown had identified the essence of the phenomenon: 'Incidents that are Units in the Synoptic Gospels but Dispersed in St John' (1961). But, at a time when biblical scholars, especially Catholics, were still struggling to come to grips with historical criticism, Brown had not pursued its possible literary explanation. He had left it, as did others dealing with such data, to an undefined oral tradition.

Once the dependence of John 9 on Mk 8.11–9.8 had been secured as a test case it was possible to publish an outline of John's use of Mark, Matthew and Proto-Luke—*The Quest for the Origin of John's Gospel* (Brodie 1993b: 67-134). This book is not at all as detailed and articulate as I would have liked, but it is essentially true.

The outcome was anticlimactic. Scarcely any reviewer attempted to say whether the test case provided a valid argument. Apparently the material was too strange and time-consuming.

Part of the reason for the gap between me and reviewers became slightly clearer when, one day, along with many others at Aquinas Institute, I accepted an invitation to do the Myers Briggs psychological test, something completely new to me, and about which I felt dubious. The essence of the result for me was that among four key aspects of mind—Sense, Intuition, Thinking, Feeling—my level of Intuition was heavily disproportionate. For the first time, I began to understand why what seemed clear to me—for instance, in comparing texts—was not at all clear to those whose primary strength was in one of the other three qualities, especially in Sense, in other words, in gathering sense data such as measurable facts and details.

I was vaguely grateful for whatever intuition I might have, but was unsure how to assess it, and it was years later, in 2008, when Erin Brockovich visited Ireland, that I got some idea of how to regard it. Erin Brockovich was the whistleblower who recognized the havoc being wrought by a chemical company in California and whose role was played by Julia Roberts in the gripping film *Erin Brockovich*. Her interview with *The Irish Examiner* (19 September 2008: 9) showed that it was largely by intuition that she had known what was going on, but the proving of the facts had been painfully slow. 'I think intuition is a God-given gift', she said, 'it's just that we're taught not to use it. Or society tells us you can't rely on it.'

I do not mind that people will not rely on it. I did not live in Missouri, the 'Show Me' State, for seven years without developing a healthy need to see the colour of someone's evidence. The problem arises when people will not stop to look at the evidence, when they will not allow themselves to engage a world that seems strange or threatening, and will not take the time to be at home in that world.

Reviewers were not the only ones who needed more time. So did I, and it was not happening in St Louis. The Dominican community, centred on students, wanted me to be present at virtually all the community functions—including occasional evening meals that lasted hours, and occasional Saturday mornings spent on cleaning—functions meant to 'build community'. One of the senior men explained to me that the ethos of student communities had shifted in a few decades 'from the heroic model to the therapeutic model'—a phrase I had never heard before. Research and spending long hours in one's room did not always make sense to people. 'I want to know what is going in that room', one of the students said angrily at a community meeting.' I discussed it with the Prior and we agreed it would be better that I live in an apartment, which I did on West Pine Boulevard, for a year, travelling by bicycle, and learning to cook and to collect the bargain coupons at the nearby National food store—a slightly lonely year, but somehow very precious. I decided, for that year, to live without TV, and for the first time in my life, cultivated flowers. Then I rotated between living in a mostly student residence, De Matthias Hall, St Louis, and escaping for an occasional semester to Germany—generally to Walberberg, or to Biesfeld, outside Cologne, as a minimum-duties unpaid chaplain to the Dominican sisters.

Solitude in Germany provided time for research, but the Aquinas Institute needed someone who would be more available for regular teaching and some administration. The deepest problem was that even if all my time were free for research I would not be able to do what needed to be done. Historical criticism (the first revolution) would look after itself; but literary criticism, especially awareness of the vast phenomenon of rewriting (the second revolution), was desperately slow in catching on. In fact, some people seemed not to want to know about it. Fundamental tasks were lying untouched.

I was being driven came back to an idea that first occurred to me in Florida—the need for a research centre, where an entire team of people would work together on how the Bible, especially the New Testament, was composed. Florida seemed a good location, because specialized inter-seminary meetings were often held in Boynton Beach. Serious research might be challenging, but in winter the sun would be attractive.

During a visit to Ireland, the Irish Dominican Provincial, Tom Jordan, asked me if I would consider returning to Ireland. I said I had an inescapable commitment to research, but if Ireland allowed the research to continue, then it would be possible to come back. To initiate the process, we agreed that I would come to Ireland in September 1991 for a sabbatical year in my former place of studies, in Tallaght, Dublin.

Ireland? Would returning really be a good idea? To cope with the coming adjustment I spent a week at Eckhart House, Dublin, a form of retreat house run by my old friend Miceál O'Regan, and during that time we regularly sat in silent meditation, trying as far as possible to empty our minds completely—no easy task. During one of these sessions, when my mind had in fact reached an unusual stillness and emptiness, something came to me strong and clear: 'Ireland is young. Ireland is a young country.' I realized then that, without being aware of it, I had been thinking of Ireland as old, tired, weighed down by centuries of oppression and hardship, but in fact, at that moment, I also realized that, at a level I could not articulate, Ireland is just beginning.

Soon afterwards, in September 1991, I was back in Tallaght and began a careful academic presentation on the dependence of part of Matthew on part of Deuteronomy—work I had first attempted in 1973 in Jerusalem, and, as already mentioned, eventually, almost twenty years after I had tried to formulate it, it was published in the *Revue Biblique* (Brodie 1992a).

Chapter 9

THE THIRD REVOLUTION DEEPENS:
AFRICAN GENESIS 1992–1995

If you were writing a narrative about Jesus, why model it on the two-part story of Elijah and Elisha? Why not choose one of the older biblical narratives—that of Abraham, for instance, or of Jacob, Joseph or Moses? Or of David—since Jesus was said to be his son? Or of the major prophets—Isaiah, Jeremiah or Ezekiel?

The question had hit me in 1972/3, in the earliest stages of linking the two testaments, but ten years later, even after completing a dissertation on Luke's use of the Elijah–Elisha text, I was no wiser, and, as the years went on, I could see no prospect of the matter ever becoming clearer. I was perplexed too by the overlap between the two, between Elijah and Elisha. Why two, and why so much overlap? Explanations had been hopelessly vague.

Meanwhile, there was another question that went back long before 1972—some kind of a call to Africa. As a teenager I had applied to the Kiltegan-based mission to Africa, because, if I had to be a priest—if there was a genuine vocation as we generally understood it—Africa seemed to be the place that most needed anything I had to offer. Besides, I had been invited to go there by some Dominicans from South Africa, and by the end of July 1992 I had landed at the airport of the busiest port in Africa, Durban, and there was met by a Dominican colleague I had known for years—Paul O'Leary from Cork. 'You begin teaching the day after tomorrow', he said as we drove inland for over an hour to the multi-faceted theology school at Cedara, near Pietermaritzburg, state capital of Natal, now Kwa-Zulu Natal, 'John's Gospel'.

South Africa had eleven languages, and some of the students were from other countries, including Mozambique, where the second language was not English but Portuguese, yet across the diversity of languages, tribes and countries, John's Gospel spoke to all. The Gospel's dramas clarified the situations of their own lives, and they used John's six stages of the man born blind as one way of measuring their own maturity, including their relationship to parents, to authorities, and to a down-to-earth God.

A year later, when I met a classroom of high-school girls in Zimbabwe—at the Dominican school in 4th St, Harare—they too enjoyed the man's drama, but they also wanted to compare it to Shakespeare's seven ages. Harare had its own stages. One of the Dominican sisters led me through its worst slum, where everybody seemed to know her, but which even then, in 1993, was explosive.

Back in Natal, in Cedara, the Dominican house was conducive to work—set in open country, ten minutes' walk by dirt road from the seminary, with a view for miles, often including the Drakensburg Mountains away in the distance, sometimes snow-capped. The Dominican community consisted of students, administrators, teachers, and Jackie—a black Labrador. I had never in my life had a dog, and Jackie belonged to the community, not to me. But Jackie and I used to go walking nearly every day after lunch, and often we ended up tracking springboks—gazelles. Jackie was impatient with tracking; he wanted to chase the springboks. So did I of course, but I knew that by running we would probably lose them.

From time to time Paul and I would buy pasta and a bottle of local wine, and around 8 pm, when Paul had cooked the pasta, we would go to my room and have a feast. During this feast the conversation could be about anything, and it could also refer without inhibition to any aspect of Ireland and of the Irish Dominicans.

Most of the writing work consisted of developing and refining what had already been outlined in earlier years, particularly of clarifying further details in Luke's use of the Elijah–Elisha narrative. As for the question of *why* Luke chose the Elijah–Elisha narrative as a model, I had almost ceased asking. Just get the details, I told myself, never mind the why.

* * *

However, somewhat as had happened in St Louis with the commentary on John, I was being drawn off course by the idea of a further commentary—on Genesis. When giving occasional talks, it seemed increasingly appropriate to use Genesis. Various groups, especially the Portobello Dominican sisters, nearly all Zulu, seemed at home in it. And so the commentary called. But unlike the anguish around the John commentary, this time I went willingly.

I love Genesis—despite its limitations. I love its sense of the depth and wildness of things, its mixture of rawness, subtlety and evocative power, and also its capacity to hold opposites together. It gives an ideal of monogamous marriage—it begins with Adam and Eve, and ends with Joseph and Asenath—but, without ever abandoning the ideal, it also makes room for the complexities and confusions that overtake people's lives. Having taught Genesis over and over since 1968, I had come to hope that, if I ever had a long healthy retirement, I would write a commentary on it. Now, suddenly, I had time.

Part of my interest in Genesis was in its kinship with the prophets, especially with Isaiah, Jeremiah and Ezekiel. My first direct contact with Brevard Childs of Yale was built on his willingness to assess an article I had drafted regarding similarities between Genesis' account of the return of Jacob from his long sojourn abroad (Gen. 31–33) and Jeremiah's prophetic account of the return of the exiles (Jer. 30–31). As far as I could see, Genesis depended on Jeremiah. Childs appreciated the similarities, but then he asked, 'How do you know the dependence is not in the other direction?' The question had pushed me to closer scrutiny of the relationship of Genesis to the prophets, but my suspicions had increased.

However, my main interest in Genesis was not in its sources but in its meaning, the meaning of the finished text. Of course I still had to pay some attention to possible sources—not extant texts, such as the book of Jeremiah—but sources or documents that have been lost and that, if they had been used as some researchers suggested, would have undermined the possibility that Genesis is a coherent book.

As we saw earlier, the idea of older lost documents had begun to become popular since 1753 when Astruc interpreted the perplexing variations in Genesis as reflecting diversity of sources. Like a hardworking detective, he observed, for instance, that the two creation accounts (Gen. 1–2) use diverse names for God, 'God' in the first account, and 'Lord God' (or 'Yahweh God') in the second. And then he drew his conclusion: Genesis must be a combination of diverse documents, documents now lost, and despite Astruc's emphasis on being conjectural, the idea of lost documents caught on, and it opened the way to various forms of documentary hypotheses.

There were two main problems with these hypotheses. First, they did not work; in fact, they led to endless confusion about lost documents and traditions, and sometimes generated proposals that were incoherent. Second, they distracted attention from the one thing that was certain—the present form of the book of Genesis, essentially the only Genesis document that has ever been verified.

Astruc had made a real contribution in noting variations, as did others after him, but was it possible that, like a detective who gathers data, but then misreads it—or like a doctor misreading symptoms—he had drawn the wrong conclusion? Since around 1970 a handful of researchers who were experienced in literary appreciation had been taking a second look at the data, at the curious mixture of variations, and were proposing a whole new kind of explanation. The variations seemed to correspond to the kinds of variations found in writing that, far from being confused, were highly organized and sophisticated, writing that was artistic.

This made sense to me, especially as I had seen how the apparent instances of confusion in John's Gospel—features such as the variations in style within the Prologue (Jn 1.1-18)—had turned out to be the result not of confusion or lost sources, but of literary artistry with a meaning.

In inquiring about the unity and artistry of Genesis I particularly wondered whether, as modern researchers had sometimes implied, the book was carefully organized into a series of paired texts—beginning most obviously with a pair of creation stories (Gen. 1–2), a pair of sin stories (Adam and Eve; Cain and Abel), and two complementary genealogies (4.17-26; and ch. 5). And I had often been struck, sometimes with promptings from other researchers, by further apparent pairings of texts throughout the book. But there had never been enough time to check whether these pairings were real.

Now, inch by inch, I worked my way through Genesis, combining close attention to the details of making a literal translation with standing back and trying to catch the larger story. All seemed to be going well—everything organized in pairs—until I got to Genesis 11, the story of Babel. Babel was unique in the Bible, the one and only tower reaching for the sky. There seemed to be nothing paired with it, in fact nothing in the nearby text that was remotely like it. Babel stood out in the imagination like the ultimate unforgettable skyscraper, but the second part of Genesis 11 was just a boring genealogy.

Boring?

Yes.

Well, maybe not completely.

Oddly, the ending after the genealogy—the end of Genesis 11—had some of the same phrasing as the beginning of the Babel story. And the numbers in the genealogy were curious: overall they kept getting smaller. In fact, looking at it more closely, it was clear that while the genealogy had started as some-thing very imposing, it ended as a fragile family going nowhere. And so the balance between the two parts of Genesis 11 eventually emerged: there were two collapses, one of the great city of Babel, the other of the imposing family; one of the outside world; the other closer to home.

The effect of the two evocations of collapse was to heighten the sense of the fragility of life, to show human striving as ending in a place that is desperately bleak. Life is going nowhere. The scene is empty, obscure, almost numb. But the deadly pairing has a purpose. It is the background for the story of the faith of Abraham.

Eventually it became clear that the pairing of texts filled all of Genesis, one of several patterns that, despite great diversity, formed the book into a profound unity. I still do not fully understand the reasons for organizing a book into paired texts, but such pairing helps to keep the mind open to the complexity of reality, to the existence of another way of viewing things.

In the two creation stories, for instance, humans are shown first as like God, then as made of clay; first as ruling the earth, then as serving it; first as marrying to have children, then as marrying for companionship. These two creation stories may have had complex roots in older writings, especially in those of Mesopotamia, but as they now stand on the page—the only place they have ever been seen—they are, as we said, as closely united as the two sides of the brain. Even the opening phrases match one another:

> In the beginning God created heaven and earth. (Gen. 1.1)

> In the day Yahweh God made earth and heaven. (Gen. 2.4b)

Each component of the second line is a down-to-earth complement of its counterpart in the first. The mysterious time-reference 'In the beginning' is matched by a time-reference that is colloquial, 'In the day'. 'God' is matched by 'Yahweh God'—a name associated with God's down-to-earth compassion (Exod. 3.15). 'Created' gives way to the ordinary word 'made'. And 'heaven and earth' is reversed so that priority goes to earth. All the pieces fitted. And essentially the same was true for Genesis as a whole. Though the book had often been dismembered into disjointed bits and pieces, it emerged as a finely wrought unity, its diverse parts as integrated as the parts of the human body.

The struggle to connect the diverse parts of Genesis was taking place amid the much more dramatic struggle to connect the diverse parts and peoples of South Africa, and at times the political struggle took priority, especially in the tension preceding and surrounding the 1994 election that ended apartheid—I was given the job of chauffeuring a pro-Mandela Zulu woman who was responsible for moving around to check the progress of voting in several polling stations situated in territory that was largely pro-Buthelezi and that sought to break away from South Africa—but eventually it was possible to return to the unity of Genesis, and not just the unity of Genesis within itself, but the unity of Genesis with the subsequent epic that runs all the way from Genesis and Exodus to the fall of Jerusalem (2 Kgs 25). In one sense the outcome of the inquiry was almost predictable. It was obvious that, despite its diversity, the whole corpus of nine books (Genesis–Kings) has some kind of unity.

What surprised me was the degree of that unity. By taking a number of soundings, it began to become clear, as others had suggested, that Genesis was tied soul and sinew to the entire epic, right down to the fall of Jerusalem.

It was also tied to the Elijah–Elisha narrative.

The pace of the investigation changed. I had often heard that Elijah was a new Moses, but I had never connected Elijah to Genesis. Yet the evidence began to emerge. The great opening drama in the Elijah story—*how God punished the earth with drought*—involved a distilling of Genesis, especially of the account of *how God punished the earth with a deluge*. Deluge and drought, two faces of the same coin. And Elijah's next episode, crossing the desert to meet God at Horeb, distilled the account of Moses and Moses' long journey to Sinai—otherwise known as Horeb. And so on: section after section of the Elijah–Elisha narrative systematically distilled almost the entire epic of Genesis–Kings.

Eventually the Elijah–Elisha narrative emerged as a distinct text which belongs to the Genesis–Kings epic but which, like a church steeple, stands somewhat apart and reflects the larger building. The evidence pointed clearly to a deliberate and precise process of composition. The author of the Elijah–Elisha narrative (whether or not identical with the author of other parts of Genesis–Kings) had generally:

- taken one key episode from the various books or blocks of Genesis–Kings—episodes such as the deluge from Genesis, or Sinai from Exodus—
- adapted that episode in some bold way, and then
- expanded the adapted episode by adding other features of the book or block in question.

The result: the Elijah–Elisha narrative is a ready-made synthesis of the Old Testament's foundational epic (Genesis–Kings), of its narrative and theology. If you were writing a narrative about Jesus, and wanted to ground that narrative in the older scriptures, you could scarcely find a more suitable foundation than the ready-made synthesis, the Elijah–Elisha narrative.

Choosing the Elijah–Elisha narrative as foundation had strong implications. It showed Jesus not just as an individual belonging to one generation, but as containing in himself the stories of all humans, right back to the beginning, and even as containing or evoking the Genesis story of creation.

I contacted Mark Twomey of Liturgical Press, Collegeville, Minnesota, and asked him what was the smallest size book the press would publish. He said sixty-four pages, but when I submitted the equivalent of sixty-four pages, the Press judged it unsuitable. Luckily, one of the editors, Linda Moloney, advised me to rewrite it, and some years later it became a small book: *The Crucial Bridge: The Elijah–Elisha Narrative as an Interpretive Synthesis of Genesis–Kings and a Literary Model for the Gospels* (Brodie 2000).

It was difficult to leave Africa, but I had to do it if I was to refine and communicate all I had been working on. Africa and its people get into your bones. You become part of its tribe, so I knew leaving would be difficult. But I did not know how difficult it would be to say goodbye to Jackie.

Chapter 10

FROM HOMER TO 4Q525:
TALLAGHT, BOSTON 1995–2000

Back in Ireland, early in September 1995, I was seriously distracted by a hurling match and my mother's brief hospitalization, but eventually I regained focus on the research, glad of the promise given in 1990 that I would be allowed to concentrate on it. Much as I appreciated the Dominican Order, I had a far clearer sense of an inescapable draw towards biblical research. I simply could not walk away from it.

My plans were reasonably clear. First I would seek to complete the two tasks that had emerged in Africa—unravelling Genesis and clarifying the nature of the Elijah–Elisha narrative—and for this it seemed best to do further work in Tallaght, and then, for the later stages of writing, to take up a research fellowship at Weston School of Theology, in Cambridge, Massachusetts, near the many schools in the Boston area. The second plan was to return as soon as possible to communicating what I believed about the origin of the New Testament.

So, once more to Genesis. I was not discussing its sources, just its present shape and meaning. It often looks jagged, but inch by inch that jagged shape had begun to make more sense, and there was always something new to discover in it. I had often read and studied the story of Abraham, yet it came as a surprise to realize clearly that the first two crises of his life revolved largely around two of the most combustible elements in human life—beauty and wealth (Gen. 12–13). Sarah was too beautiful for her own good—or Abraham's good. And Abraham and Lot had too much property to live together in peace.

At some stage that year I broke free of my usual schedule late one lovely morning. At the last minute, I joined a group that was leaving to climb the mountains above Glendalough, in County Wicklow. In my eagerness to see space and breathe it, I climbed ahead of the others. At the top was solitude. Lakes, mountains, distant sky, another world, another time, another space.

'Elijah vertical, Elisha horizontal. That's why two. One heaven, the other earth.'

I was talking to myself. Without the faintest awareness of recalling the problem, it was suddenly clear why the number of prophets in the Elijah–Elisha narrative is two. Like the two creation stories, one emphasizes closeness to God, the other closeness to earth. Later, I verified the details, but I was aware that I could have spent decades in libraries and never have connected the two with the simple variation between heaven and earth.

Meanwhile, writing on Genesis was going fairly well until I tried to find a single word that would summarize Jacob. His story is so complex, and his character so many-sided, that, despite the danger of over-simplifying, it seemed that it would be useful to identify a central characteristic. I was stumped because in searching for a suitable word I kept coming back to 'wily'.

Wily was off limits. It was already patented by Homer as the number one word to describe Odysseus. There was no way I could use it of Jacob. Surely amid the richness of the English language there must be another word to capture the essence of Jacob. Yet I could not get wily out of my head. Later, in a footnote to *Genesis as Dialogue* (2001b: 452), I recounted what happened:

> While searching for a single adjective to describe Jacob (February 2, 1996), the word that came was 'wily', but this seemed unusable because the same word is often applied to Odysseus, and to use it of Jacob would be confusing and misleading. Still, the coincidence was perplexing, and I mentioned it soon afterward to a Dominican colleague, Philip McShane. He immediately referred to the Jewish philosopher, Emmanuel Levinas, whom he had known while studying in Fribourg, Switzerland. Levinas had explicitly contrasted Jacob and Odysseus. A search through several of Levinas's works yielded nothing except an obscure Abraham-related reference to an unavailable work in Dutch (de Broux, 1972). McShane said that perhaps the contrast had been made in conversation. Emmanuel Levinas had died on December 25, 1995.
>
> Resuming the study of Jacob, the account of moving the great stone (Gen 29:1-10) recalled the Odyssey's story of the Cyclops moving a massive stone (Od. 9:24). On checking the Homeric passage, other connections began to emerge.
>
> The connection with the massive stone would not have been made perhaps but for Oona Ajzenstat of Ontario. In conversation, and in a paper to the SBL (Philadelphia, November 18, 1995) she had emphasized the influence of the story of the Cyclops.

The idea that Genesis was in some way connected to Homer was intriguing, but I did not want to know about it. Homer was another world, and trying to incorporate him into a commentary on Genesis could engulf the whole project. Besides, I simply did not have the time. Genesis was supposed to have been reserved for my seventies if they ever happened, when I would already have communicated the essence of my New Testament research.

While I was glad to work on Genesis, and was grateful that that work had helped to clarify the origin and role of the Elijah–Elisha narrative, researching connections with Homer could take the rest of my life. And even if I was able to work out the relationship with Homer—it was possible that even after prolonged work I would in fact find nothing significant—the highlighting of Homer could kill the commentary in the eyes of many potential readers. Was it not enough to say that Genesis used the prophets without adding that it also used a rollicking story-teller from another world? Forget him.

I checked where Homer stood in the eyes of Old Testament research. I looked up one of the flagships of biblical studies, the six-volume *Anchor Bible Dictionary* published a few years earlier, a work I treasured. The entry on Homer stood out:

> **HOMER** [Heb *hōmer*]. See WEIGHTS AND MEASURES.

This seemed to confirm that I should indeed forget Homer. Besides, as I say, I did not have the time. Yet to just forget him, to neglect completely a possible lead, seemed wrong. I discussed it with a friend and decided to give it three weeks.

At the end of the three weeks, the evidence was already strong. So I added further time, and eventually it was possible to trace the main lines of dependence. Yet there was no practical possibility of developing the investigation fully. I summarized my findings in about fifty pages and placed them in what seemed an inoffensive position—in an Appendix. The basic conclusion:

> The investigation of Genesis' relationship to the Odyssey will require years of research—detailed analysis and thorough application of the criteria for [judging literary] dependence—and until such research is developed it is difficult to draw definitive conclusions. But, as with the case of Genesis and the prophets, there is already sufficient evidence to propose that Genesis' use of Homer is a reasonable working hypothesis.[1]

As far as I know no reviewer has attempted to judge whether in fact the working hypothesis is reasonable. But, independently, awareness of Homer is entering biblical studies through researchers such as Dennis R. McDonald.

The writing of the appendix on Genesis' use of the Odyssey dragged on for months. It was slowing work on the Genesis commentary, and ultimately delaying getting back to the New Testament, yet it also seemed that in the long term it might somehow contribute to understanding how the New Testament was composed.

Cambridge, MA (from early September 1996) presented many opportunities, including the meetings of the Boston Theological Institute where it was possible to test the thesis that Genesis is structured into paired texts or

---

1. Brodie 2001b: 492. See Burkert 1992.

diptychs, and to clarify the idea that one structure does not exclude others. Michael Barré suggested that, like the ancient god Janus, the second creation account (Gen. 2.4b-24) is two-faced: it looks back to the first creation account, so that the two accounts form a pair, a diptych; but it also includes features that look forward to the account of the fall (Gen. 3).

With encouragement from Helmut Koester and François Bovon, I was invited to the Wednesday afternoon doctoral seminars at Harvard Divinity School. And I was glad to present the seminar with the case for Proto-Luke. But I did it badly. I did not have enough time and was insufficiently prepared. I had forgotten how strange it can seem at first.

By the Summer of 1997 I had essentially finished the manuscript on Genesis, *Genesis as Dialogue*, and was able to focus more fully on the Elijah–Elisha narrative—on its origin, shape and meaning, and on its role as a model for later writers, especially Luke and Mark. Things were going well, and I was set to stay on in Cambridge for a second year.

Soon afterwards I received a letter from the Dominican Provincial in Dublin saying that the Regent of Studies, Paul O'Leary, needed me to come back to teach a course in the new year in Tallaght. The prospect of returning to Tallaght concentrated my mind concerning the future, and it was about this time, probably in October 1997—when most of the basic work on Genesis and the Elijah–Elisha narrative had been done—that I stayed up late one night on the ground floor in Kirkland St going through the files of my computer and printed out all the diverse material, published and unpublished, that would go into my basic book on the composition of the New Testament. Apart from the gentle chugging of the printer all was quiet in the house as the material emerged slowly and began to pile up. By around 3.00 am I had about 1400 pages—material to form the book that hopefully would substitute partly for the unpublished manuscript of 1975.

Having returned to Tallaght to teach in 1998, the issue arose about what to make of my proposed 1973 version of Matthew's *Logia*, 'Sayings'—the short arrangement of Beatitudes, Antitheses, and a Hymn, the arrangement with its own distinct dependence on Deuteronomy, and to some degree, Sirach. These Matthean sayings (from Mt. 5 and 11) were as follows:

The Logia/*Sayings in English (based on the* Logoi/*Deuteronomy)*

Beatitudes

5.5	Blessed are the gentle,	for they shall inherit the land.
5.6	Blessed are those who hunger and thirst for rightness,	for they shall be satisfied.
5.7	Blessed are the merciful,	for they shall receive mercy.
5.8	Blessed are the clean of heart,	for they shall see God.
5.9	Blessed are the peacemakers,	for they shall be called children of God.

Law

Law: Prelude

5.17   Do not think that I came to undo the law or the prophets;
                    I came not to undo but to fulfil.

5.18   For amen I say to you;
                    until heaven and earth pass,
                    not one iota or dot will pass from the law
                    until all is accomplished.

Law: Antitheses

5.21   You have heard that it was said of old, 'You shall not kill, and
         whoever does kill
                    shall be liable to judgment'
5.22a   But I say to you that all who are angry with their brother
                    shall be liable to judgment.
5.27   You have heard that it was said, 'You shall not commit adultery'.
                    But I say to you that whoever looks at a woman with desire
                            has already committed adultery with her in his heart.
5.33   Again you have heard that it was said of old, 'You shall not break your oath
                            but shall carry out your oaths to the Lord'.
5.34   But I say to you, do not swear at all
                            neither by heaven   for it is God's throne
5.35a   nor by earth   for that is his footstool.
5.38   You have heard that it was said, 'An eye for an eye and a tooth for a tooth'.
5.39a   But I say to you, do not set yourself against (the) evil (one).
5.43   You have heard that it was said, 'You shall love your neighbour and hate
         your enemy'.
5.44a   But I say to you, love your enemies.

Law: Sequel

5.45   So you may become children of your father in heaven,
                            for he raises his sun on the evil and the good
                            and it rains on the just and the unjust.
5.48   You shall therefore be complete
                            as your heavenly father is complete.

Call/Cry of Revelation/Wisdom

11.25b   I thank you, father, Lord of heaven and earth
                            for hiding these things from the wise and understanding
                            and revealing them to infants.
11.26   Yes, father, for such was your gracious will.

11.27   All has been handed over to me by my father,
                            and no one knows the son except the father,
                            just as no one knows the father except the son
                    and anyone to whom the son chooses to reveal him.

11.28   Come to me all you who labour and are burdened
                            and I will give you rest;

11.29   take my yoke upon you and learn from me
                 for I am gentle and humble of heart
11.30   and you will find rest for your souls;
                 for my yoke is easy
                 and my burden is light.

At some stage during or after the discussion of these verses, someone—
either me or one of the students—became aware of the existence of a Qumran
document that had been discovered in 1952, partly published in 1988, and
more fully published in 1991. In translation:[2]

Beatitudes   [Blessed is the one who speaks truth] with a pure heart
               and does not slander with his tongue.
               Blessed are those who cling to her statutes
                       and do not cling to paths of iniquity.
               Blessed are those who rejoice in her
                       and do not babble about paths of iniquity.
               Blessed are those who search for her with clean hands
                       and do not seek after her with a deceitful heart.
               Blessed is the man who has attained wisdom

Law   and walks by the law (*torah*) of the Most High
                       and fixes his heart on her ways,

               gives heed to her admonishments
                       delights al[way]s in her chastisements,
               and does not forsake her in the stress of [his] trou[bles];
                       (who) in time of distress does not abandon her
               and does not forget her [in days of] fear,
                       and in the affliction of his soul does not reject [her].
               For on her he meditates,
                       and in his anguish he ponders [on the law];
               and in all his existence [he considers] her
                       and [puts her before] his eyes

                       so as not to walk in the paths of [   ]
                       [   ] his [   ] together,
                       and he perfects his heart for her [   ]
                       [and she will put a crown upon] his [hea]d
                       and make him sit with kings
                       [   ] he will *pr*[ ] brothers [   ]
                       [   ]   [   ]

Wisdom's Call   [And now, children, listen to me, and] turn [n]ot away from…

2.   The translation is from Fitzmyer 1992b: 512-13; see also Puech 1988a: esp. 66,
and, again, Puech 1991.

This Qumran document had been designated 4Q525 (4Q indicates its place of origin, Qumran's fourth cave; 525 identifies it among the cave's many other documents). It was often called the Beatitudes document, but did not consist of Beatitudes alone. Its second section on the Law, emphasized a form of antithesis—antithesis between following and not following the Law. And its third section apparently consisted of the beginning of a climactic Call, like Wisdom's Call to listen and not turn away. This Qumran document was obviously shorter than Matthew's *Logia*, but this was partly because most of its final Call section was broken off.

Whereas I am certain the Elijah–Elisha narrative provided a model for Luke, I am not equally sure that the Qumran 'Beatitudes' document provided a *specific* model for Matthew's logia. The physical distance between the author of the Sayings/Logia (Matthew?) and a copy of 4Q525 seems likely to have been greater than that between Luke and the Septuagint, and there is not as much material to work with, so it seems better to leave a final judgment to others. But 4Q525 does provide an example of a form of writing that could have provided a *general* model for Sayings. The students in Tallaght enjoyed the discussion and we let the matter rest.

Two days before I was due to leave for the SBL conference in Boston (mid-November 1999), the Provincial, Larry Collins, called me to his office and said Paul O'Leary was unwell and would have to be relieved of the responsibilities of being Regent of Studies. Would I take the job? It was my nightmare scenario, a time-consuming administrative job—responsibility for studies at a time when faculty were insufficient and when studies as a whole needed reorganizing in the run-up to a major meeting, a Provincial Chapter, due in June 2000. At an earlier stage the Provincial had asked me lightly if I would like to be house bursar in Tallaght, and in that case it was easy to decline. This was different. He would give me time to consider. However, I just nodded dumbly and said OK, I would do it—until June, when Paul's four-year term was due to finish, and when the Chapter was due to make a fresh decision about the situation.

In the following months, while preoccupied with administration, my research work on the composition of the New Testament came to a halt—a sobering situation that finally gave me the impetus to do something that otherwise might not have happened for a long time. I wrote to David Noel Freedman, one of the most well known figures of twentieth-century biblical research, and asked if he would look at an extensive manuscript. He agreed, and when he had received it, he sent a critique, and a general comment: 'It is original, but not off the wall'. He also began to investigate how it might be edited and published.

During discussions about the future of the Tallaght house of studies (*Studium Generale*) I was invited to Limerick to discuss cooperation with Mary Immaculate College, a century-old College that worked in association with the brash new University of Limerick. It was soon clear however, that the proposal was not workable. Later, we sauntered back for a cup of coffee with the College President at 3.30 before I would take the train back to Dublin. Over the coffee I again explained that unfortunately Tallaght could not help. They agreed that it was better to accept the reality of the situation, and they assured me not to worry in the slightest. I was relieved.

Then I heard myself saying, 'How about a biblical research centre?'

Chapter 11

LIMERICK:
THE DOMINICAN BIBLICAL INSTITUTE

The Irish Dominican Chapter of 2000 surprised itself. Given the jubilee year, it seemed appropriate to look afresh at things, but it was also a further year in the deepening crisis of the Irish Church, deeper some say than has been experienced for centuries—a withering storm of modernity, money and numbing scandal—and the chapter made considerable changes, including the setting up of two centres of study which later became known as the Priory Institute in Tallaght, Dublin, and the Dominican Biblical Institute (DBI), Limerick. The working of the DBI was greatly helped by the purpose-built facility that opened in 2006 with a library that, within its means, covers all methods of biblical study.

The Limerick project eventually proved complex, and for about three years I awoke most mornings around 5 am in a cold sweat. Limerick sought to have the biblical centre for a region that could offer opportunities but lacked biblical resources. Scarce funds come largely from the Irish Dominican Province and partly from a few precious private donations. The DBI for its part tries to reduce expenses. As circumstances allow, the DBI seeks collaboration with other institutions, especially the Priory Institute, Mary Immaculate College/University of Limerick, Glenstal Abbey, and St Patrick's College, Maynooth.

This short account of the DBI will give, first, an overview of some plans and activities; and, second, brief reports on a conference and on research.

Overview of Some Plans and Activities

The biblical centre in Limerick was founded primarily on a sense of being led rather than on a prior plan, but, once the idea was approved, it was appropriate to plan, and to do so in a way that took account of the crisis in parts of Christianity and the Church.

The centre's vision has three aims, three levels or phases that may overlap: (1) short-term, to provide immediate service; (2) medium/long-term, to provide research that clarifies the roots of Catholic/Christian faith; (3) long-term, to help integrate Christianity with other truths.

Short-term: Supplying Immediate Programmes
Among DBI programmes and activities that seek to make an immediate contribution, three are especially noteworthy:[1]

(1) *Diploma in Biblical and Theological Studies.* The main programme offered by the DBI has been the three-year part-time Pastoral Scripture Programme begun in 2008, and accredited in 2011 by St Patrick's College, Maynooth, as a Diploma in Biblical and Theological Studies. Each year since it began, the programme has taken in over twenty new students, generally people who are mature and self-motivated. They come especially from the dioceses of Limerick and Killaloe, but also from Kerry, Cork-and-Ross, and Cloyne. Those who completed the programme in 2011 seemed to benefit deeply from the course. Most of them were sponsored by their parishes, and have committed themselves to work for their parish communities.

(2) *Lectio divina.* Like the stream which Ezekiel saw flowing from under the Temple and growing into a great life-giving river, so *lectio divina* (literally, divine/spiritual reading) has spread through the Church since the Second Vatican Council. The DBI has made it an integral part of its ministry from the beginning. In the early years, courses in *lectio* were offered at the DBI; in more recent years we have gone to groups in the parishes, particularly in Advent and Lent. The twenty-five students in the pastoral scripture course who graduated in 2011 are equipped to bring *lectio divina* back to their parishes; a number of the seventy plus who are in the three-year course at present are already leading *lectio* groups. Brendan Clifford has worked for a number of years with a group in Moyross, a group in the city, and with a group in the Methodist/Presbyterian Church.

(3) *Public talks.* Talks at the DBI have become a regular part of the Church's life in Limerick, particularly in Advent and Lent. We have tried to attract a general audience but we depend a lot on regular church-goers; religious sisters also give us good support.

We marked the Year of St Paul with lectures by Jerome Murphy O'Connor, Morna Hooker of Cambridge University, Ciaran O'Mahony O.S.A., and Thomas Brodie.

---

1. This account of DBI activities was supplied by Brendan Clifford.

Speakers on the crisis facing the Church included Bishop Willie Walsh, Mary T. Malone, Ethna Regan, Bishop Kieran O'Reilly, Michael Campbell-Johnston, John Waters, Joe Kavanagh and Donagh O'Shea.

Speakers on the economic crisis and social issues included Peter McVerry, Maureen O'Sullivan T.D., John Lonergan and John O'Shea.

Medium/Long-term: Researching the Roots
The purpose of biblical research at the DBI has been to help clarify the roots beneath Christianity, especially its biblical roots. One way of doing this is by tracing how the *texts* were formed, something that gives clues to how the *Church* was formed, which in turn provides background that makes it easier to renew the church—to address the problems from those roots rather than from some superficial level.

The two levels of engaging scripture, the intellectual quest to identify roots through research, and the spiritual quest to generate fresh life through exercises such as *lectio*, complement each other. At times the mind/intellect leads, gathering and processing new knowledge. In other ways, the spirit can lead the way, and, where necessary and possible, the inquiring intellect—the search for understanding—can catch up later.

Long-term: Integration of Christianity with other Truths
The clarifying of Christian origins and Christian faith will make it easier to integrate the truth of faith appropriately with the truth that is in culture, art (including literature), world religions, and science. Such integration—the formation of a modern *summa* of basic understanding—may seem an unreachable goal, but some element of it is already indispensable. Things have fallen apart. Many people are walking around carrying within themselves an indigestible mixture of culture, world religion, science and Christianity or at least the bones of Christianity, and something cries out, not for uniformity—'*vive la différence*' at several levels—but for a reasonable amount of integration, harmony, and meaning.

In forming an integration, two aspects of the challenge seem to stand out: first, how to achieve some such integration in theory, on paper as it were; second, how to communicate it. One possible way of making it available to a large audience would be through an exhibit (not funded by Dominicans) that uses the best of modern communication technology—early Christians made much use of the latest means of communication, the codex—and so the Dominican Biblical Institute has made some attempts to promote the idea of some such exhibit in or near Limerick. And the idea may be of use to some other city. There are dozens of ways to foul up both the theory and the communication, but the mission is not impossible.

Brief Reports on a Conference and on Research

Lectio divina *conference*

The challenge of bringing the Bible directly into people's lives was entrusted primarily to Brendan Clifford, a gifted communicator who combined insight and generosity, and who had spent decades reviving and developing *lectio divina*. Part of Brendan's inspiration around *lectio divina* had come from years of work in Trinidad with Michel de Verteuil. Further inspiration came from the down-to-earth work of Carlo Martini, former Rector of the Pontifical Biblical Institute, Rome, later Cardinal Archbishop of Milan, and apparently an unwilling candidate for Pope in the conclave of April 2005. And yet more inspiration came from Pope Benedict XVI, who in September 2005 declared concerning *lectio divina*: 'If effectively promoted, it will bring to the Church—I am convinced of it—a new spiritual springtime'.

In discussing *lectio divina*, we wrestled with the obscurity of its Latin name. But we could not resolve it. We could not find a concise English formula that expressed *lectio divina*'s dynamism, its spirit-to-life drama, and the way it can take words that lie lifeless on an ancient page and bring them alive in the soul and sinew of daily experience.

What we *were* able to do, in November 2006, was summon help. We convened a conference to discuss *lectio divina*, particularly its relationship to the historical-critical method, and we sought a wide range of speakers. Despite disparaging comments from those around her, our secretary, Peig McGrath, stayed working the phone until she located Cardinal Martini in Jerusalem, and spoke to him directly.

No, he was unwell—he had Parkinson's disease—and he could not come. But could he recommend someone?

He took his time, and then he did.

In the event the main speakers at the conference were as follows, in order of appearance:

Carlos Mesters, mostly Brazil

Frances Young, University of Birmingham

Martin Drennan, Bishop of Galway, formerly St Patrick's College, Maynooth

Pat Elie, Trinidad, co-worker of Michel de Verteuil

Seamus O'Connell, Maynooth

Chris Hayden, formerly St John's Seminary, Wexford

Ludger Feldkamper, Rome/Philippines

Luciano Monari, Bishop of Piacenza-Bobbio, recommended by Cardinal Martini

and Cecil McCullough, Queen's University, Belfast.

The title for the conference papers emphasized life—*Reading Scripture for Living the Christian Life* (Treacy 2009)—and certainly the conference itself was lively. The place was packed and animated, and many said they found it inspiring. Cecil McCullough, a Northern Protestant, brought encouragement by indicating some of the similarity between the ways in which Catholics and Protestants struggle with the Bible in real-life situations. However, the conference also highlighted a tough question: what is the relationship between prayerful application and solid history? Can one rely on Scripture without having verified its historicity?

At one point the focus turned anxiously to the wedding feast of Cana.

'Did it really happen?'

The question fell to Father Ludger Feldkamper, S.V.D., long-serving secretary of the vast Catholic Biblical Federation.

'What a European question! In Asia they would ask "What does it mean?"'

The reply was calm, assured, but there was no shortage of discussion.

Research

During the process of research in Limerick, the historical existence of Jesus was not discussed; it was taken for granted, and left undisturbed—probably the only practical way to proceed initially. As I see it, proposing Jesus did not exist historically is like a heart transplant; you either do it fully or not at all. Instead the research had other features and dealt with other topics. In summary:

(1) *Priority for literary issues, especially sources.* As already said, modern biblical research has many aspects of investigation, many 'criticisms', and while building on historical criticism, the Limerick centre has gone on to highlight two main branches of literary criticism—the quest for the text's sources, and the quest for its art. This does not mean that literary criticism is more important than other methods, but simply that, in the order in which things need to be done, it has a certain priority. And since the quest for the text's sources is particularly in need of development, it has received special attention.[2]

---

2. The methods that the DBI follows and develops have been discussed and generally promoted by official church documents, especially the three main documents since 1893:

1893: Emphasized use of the critical *historical* method—Pope Leo XIII, *Providentissimus Deus*.

1943: Emphasized need to identify *literary* form/nature—Pope Pius XII, *Divino Afflante Spiritu*.

The process of research started in a disused disco hall, moved after five years to the new purpose-built building, and quickly developed its library from two books to over ten thousand, with more than a hundred journals. The wide-ranging choice of journals, commentaries and monograph series ensured that the small group of researchers could stay aware of virtually any aspect of biblical studies. Limerick's special interest in literary criticism, particularly the quest for extant literary sources, extends also to the Hebrew Scriptures/Old Testament, but in practice progress on the Old Testament has been slow at the DBI. A post-doctoral researcher did preliminary work on Genesis' reshaping of the book of Jeremiah in the Jacob story, but efforts to find a suitable candidate to examine the reworking of Homer's *Odyssey* in Genesis 11–50 have so far failed. Still, Old Testament studies being done elsewhere remain encouraging.[3]

1993: Identified *five main kinds of methods, especially historical and literary*—Pope John Paul II/Pontifical Biblical Commission, *The Interpretation of the Bible in the Church.*

A commentary on this text has been produced by Joseph A. Fitzmyer: *The Biblical Commission's Document 'The Interpretation of the Bible in the Church': Text and Commentary.* Despite some limitations (insufficient awareness of rewriting and of Gunkel's limitations), this book is extremely useful.

3.   When the prospects for the idea of rewriting seemed bleak in the late 1970s, I had drawn inspiration from Calum Carmichael, beginning with his pioneering study of how Deuteronomy's laws reshaped women-related episodes in Genesis (Carmichael 1979). Since then many others have done pioneering work on the inner rewriting of the Hebrew Scriptures and Septuagint. Thirty years after I first encountered Carmichael, when I paused one night before I fell asleep to glance at a newly arrived book by a certain David P. Wright, further inspiration appeared. Wright's book concerned an apparent link between the Covenant Code (much of Exod. 20–23) and the Laws of Hammurabi, king of ancient Babylon (c. 1750 BCE), and, as I opened it casually, I suspected that the link would turn into something vague and long-distance. But the link was immediate and what turned out to be long was the night. Wright (2009: 3-4) was proposing, persuasively, 'a profoundly new understanding of the composition and nature of the Covenant Code... This law collection, the pinnacle of the revelation at Mount Sinai...is directly, primarily, and throughout dependent upon the Laws of Hammurabi. The biblical text imitated the *structure* of this Akkadian text and drew upon its *content* to create...casuistic...as well as apodictic law... This primary use of the Laws of Hammurabi was supplemented with the occasional use of material from other cuneiform law collections and from native Israelite-Judean sources and traditions... Moreover, because the Covenant Code is largely a creative rewriting of Mesopotamian sources, it is to be viewed as an academic abstraction rather than a digest of laws practiced by Israelites and Judeans over centuries'. In a variation on Carmichael—and since 1979, Carmichael has published other like works—Wright was setting forth solid evidence for a new model of how the biblical text was composed. Later Wright emailed me: 'If you like the notion of "rewriting" the Bible, see...Jeffrey Stackert, *Rewriting the Torah*, 2007. Also influential in my approach is Bernard

The Gospels and Acts

In practice most of the research done at the Limerick centre has been in New Testament, and as one of our starting points we often used my own *Birthing of the New Testament. The Intertextual Development of the New Testament Writings* (2004). The title could have been clearer, and the conclusion (Chapter 26) certainly holds back. I made the mistake too of including some examples that were weak (for instance, Chapter 52, on Judg. 21 and the Last Supper). I believe such examples are true, but they are indeed weak, and insistence on what is weak, whether by someone presenting the argument or someone opposing it, confuses the discussion. As in a courtroom, the issue is not whether some evidence is weak, but whether there is enough evidence that is strong. *The Birthing of the New Testament* is also incomplete, but that was inevitable. It will be decades before anyone can give a reasonably full account of how the New Testament books used the Old Testament and non-biblical writings and one another. Besides, to save space I reduced discussion of the epistles. Yet, in many ways, at least as far as I can see, *The Birthing of the New Testament* goes further than any other existing work in providing a skeleton outline of how the New Testament documents were composed. But the skeleton needs to be further tested and elaborated, and much of the work at the Limerick centre, while undertaken with an independent spirit, contributed to such testing or elaboration:

(1) *John Shelton and the centurion's servant.* An example of the need for testing and elaboration emerged in examining Luke's account of healing the centurion's servant (Lk. 7.1-10). I had indicated that Luke's text depends on the older account of Elijah saving the widow's children (1 Kgs 17.1-16).[4] However, when John Shelton of Oklahoma was working on his dissertation in Limerick—dissertations at the DBI were approved through Mary Immaculate College, Limerick, and the University of Limerick—he provided powerful evidence that while Luke's text had indeed used the episode from the Elijah narrative, he had made even greater use of the account of the healing of Namaan the Syrian commander (2 Kgs 5.1-19).[5] Even Jesus' climactic pronouncement about the centurion's faith (Lk. 7.9) is modelled closely on Naaman's faith-filled climactic pronouncement about God (2 Kgs 5.15), but the relationship between the two pronouncements is one not of verbatim

Levinson's *Deuteronomy and the Hermeneutics of Legal Innovation*, 1977. One can put the three studies together to establish a chain of legal revision/creative rewriting: Hammurabi to the Covenant Code (Wright), the Covenant Code to Deuteronomy (Levinson), and the Covenant Code and Deuteronomy together to the Holiness Legislation (Stackert).'

    4.   Brodie 2004: 294-301.

    5.   Shelton 2012.

similarity but of intricate complementarity. Shelton's work indicates that Luke's use of the Elijah–Elisha narrative is more complex than I had realized. At the same time, it confirms the evidence that Luke's account of the healing of the centurion's servant comes not from the hypothetical source Q but—like Jesus' triple challenge or call to disciples (Lk. 9.57-62)—primarily from Luke's own intricate transformation of the Septuagint, especially the Septuagint as filtered through the Elijah–Elisha narrative.[6]

The clarifying of the opening episode of Luke 7 (the centurion's servant) serves in turn to bolster the already existing evidence that all three other episodes of Luke 7—the raising of the widow's son (7.11-17), the vindication of John the Baptist (7.18-35), and the woman's anointing of Jesus' feet (7.36-50)—likewise originated largely through Luke's literary transformation of accounts from the Elijah–Elisha narrative.[7] Of these three, the one concerning John the Baptist is again an account that is usually attributed to the hypothetical Q.

One of the results, then, of Shelton's work is to solidify the dependence of an entire chapter of Luke (Lk. 7) on the evangelist's transformation of the Elijah–Elisha narrative, and, when taken with the case of Jesus' triple call (9.57-62), to indicate that in at least three cases, texts often attributed to Q can be accounted for far more verifiably through the Elijah–Elisha narrative. Thus the evidence increases that there is indeed a Q, a *Quelle* or source, but it is not lost; to a significant degree it is the Septuagint. This does not immediately solve the puzzle of the relationship between Luke and Matthew, but it indicates a line of inquiry that is more verifiable than invoking an unseen source that does not have so solid a literary foundation. Once Luke has been clarified through this more verifiable process, the way is open for a well-grounded discussion of Luke's relationship to Matthew.

(2) *John's transformation of the Synoptics: Anne O'Leary and Martin Heffernan.* While the theory of Q has dominated much of the discussion of sources regarding the Synoptic Gospels, John's sources have often seemed equally elusive—a hypothetical Signs Source, a hypothetical source of Revelation Discourses, or else independent tradition. But the doctoral theses of two students, Anne O'Leary and Martin Heffernan, indicated what many had long suspected or maintained: John's main sources were much closer to home—the Synoptic writers. O'Leary showed in detail that Matthew's reworking of Mark was done in accordance with the literary practices of antiquity, and, with a passion born from her previous studies in Maynooth

---

6. See Brodie 2000.

7. On Lk. 7.11-17, see Brodie 1986b; on Lk. 7.18-35, Brodie 1994; and on Lk. 7.36-50, Brodie 1983b. Or, on all of Lk. 7.11-50, see Brodie 2004: 302-38.

and Manila, O'Leary also showed that John in turn had adapted sections of Matthew.[8]

Heffernan's work on John 1–4 opens the way to showing that the journey most repeatedly emphasized in John, Jesus' journey from Jerusalem and Judea to Samaria and Galilee (Jn 2.23–4.54)—which does not remotely correspond to the journey most repeatedly emphasized in Matthew, Mark and Luke (the journey *to* Jerusalem)—corresponds in basic outline to the progression most emphasized in Acts, namely, from Jerusalem and Judea to Samaria and beyond (Acts 1–8, esp. 1.8, and 8.1). The similarity of the central geographic pattern is not only strong; it is unique. John's account of Jesus' journey is inextricably linked with Acts 1–8. The adaptation is surprising, but it makes sense. The narrative of Acts 1–8 is filled with 'this Word of God... this Word concerning Jesus' (Haenchen 1971: 98), and so it is appropriate that the journey of the Word in Acts be adapted to portray the journey of the Word made flesh. Heffernan's dissertation does not discuss the journeys directly, but it provides dozens of corroborating details.[9]

(3) *Slowly clarifying some of Mark's sources: Adam Winn and Thomas Nelligan.* For many decades of the twentieth century Mark was regarded as unliterary or clumsy, and his sources as hopelessly uncertain. But Mark's literary character has slowly been appreciated—in 1991, for instance, it was described as interwoven tapestry (Dewey 1991)—and some of his sources have begun to emerge in the work of Adam Winn and Thomas Nelligan. Winn's post-doctoral work has gone far in spelling out the detail of a long-standing view that Mark is modelled on the Elijah–Elisha narrative, and Nelligan's dissertation has taken an idea that has been recurring for 150 years, namely, that Mark's work reflects that of Paul, and has begun to unearth evidence that, at least in the case of part of 1 Corinthians, Mark's

---

8.   O'Leary 2004: 513 + eight appendices. The first half of this dissertation was published as O'Leary 2006.

9.   Heffernan 2009. Heffernan divides Acts 1–8 and Jn 1–4 under eight headings: Prologues, John and Ascent/Descent (Acts 1.1-11; Jn 1.1-34); Formation of Disciples (Acts 1.12-26; Jn 1.35-51); Outpouring of the Spirit/Wine (Acts 2; Jn 2.1-11); Temple Clash (Acts 3.1–4.22; Jn 2.12-22); Gamaliel/Nicodemus (Acts 4.23–5.42; Jn 2.23–3.21); the Characters of Stephen and John (Acts 6.1–8.1a; Jn 3.22-36); the Mission to Samaria (Acts 8.1b-25; Jn 4.1-42); the Royal Officials (Acts 8.26-40; Jn 4.43-54). John's distillation of Acts 1–8 has some similarities to the distillation of 1 Kgs 19 in Lk. 9.57-62 but, along with Acts 1–8, it involves the transforming and interweaving of at least one other major source. The cleansing of the temple in Jn 2.12-22, for instance, involves a blending and transforming of the Mark/Matthew account with a distillation of the temple clash in Acts 3.1–4.22, plus an adaptation of all the source materials to John's own narrative and theological purposes.

link with Paul is not just theological; it is precise and literary.[10] The works of Winn and Nelligan, when combined, give new meaning to Dewey's picture of Mark as interwoven tapestry.

The works of these researchers—Shelton, O'Leary, Heffernan, Winn, and Nelligan—touch all four Gospels and Acts, and when taken together they help to confirm the evidence that many of the evangelists' sources are extant and that the literary dependence is traceable.

(4) *The question of Luke's first Elijah-related version*. So far no doctoral or post-doctoral student at Limerick has tried to assess directly the merits of the proposal that Luke–Acts first existed in a brief Septuagint-based version (Proto-Luke, or whatever we call it). Hesitation is understandable. It means invoking an unseen document, and in that sense it is like Q. Q can seem like its enemy, because it seeks to replace Q. But Q is also its friend, because Q is a reminder that in tracing the relationship between the Gospels, some literary source is missing. The case for an early version of Luke–Acts is more complex than that for Q, but it has at least two key advantages: it is more solidly grounded, especially because of the verifiability of its relationship to the Elijah–Elisha narrative; and it works better, it explains far more about Gospel relationships, even if again the explanation is complex. It not only clarifies the perplexing issue of the relationship between Matthew and Luke; it also provides a precedent for Mark, Matthew and John. And it clarifies the reality behind Raymond Brown's view (1971) that the Elijah–Elisha account is the best literary model for all four Gospels.

Though Brown saw the essential continuity, he worked in a context where literary questions often seemed secondary, and where it was not clear that the Elijah–Elisha narrative had synthesized much of Genesis–Kings, so he did not pursue his insight in a literary way, in dialogue with literary studies and ancient practices of literary transformation. Such dialogue is needed, and in particular dialogue among Gospel researchers between those who propose Q and those who see a role for a brief early version of Luke–Acts based on the Elijah–Elisha narrative.

It was partly to promote such dialogue that, in 2008, on the margins of a high-powered Oxford Conference on the Synoptic Problem, Limerick organized a week-end seminar on The Composing of the Gospels (4–6 April 2008), with nine visitors from Canada, USA, UK and Belgium. The papers from that seminar, edited by John Kloppenborg and assigned the provisional title *The Elijah–Elisha Narrative in Luke: Proceedings of the Limerick Conference*, are devoted primarily to the role of the Elijah–Elisha narrative, but they reflect something of the creative tension with Q.

---

10. Winn 2010; Nelligan 2012.

The Pauline Epistles

Great as is the importance of the Gospels and Acts, it is widely agreed that, as they were being composed, many or most of the Epistles bearing Paul's name already existed, and therefore any attempt to account for what the New Testament says about Christ must give a key role to the Epistles. So the first conference in Limerick, in May 2005, tried to get a general sense of the Epistles' origin and nature. This conference—twenty-five scholars from nine countries in a rented room of a Georgian house—explored the epistles' triple intertextuality, meaning how the epistles:

- used older writings, particularly biblical texts
- used one another
- were in turn used by the evangelists

The contributions were published in *The Intertextuality of the Epistles*,[11] and were reviewed in the *Catholic Biblical Quarterly* (Crawford 2009: 221) as containing 'essays [that] herald a promising new approach'.

But when I tried, both during the 2005 conference and afterwards, to organize a really good conference on the composition of 1 Corinthians, on its sources and on its final purposeful shape, I was not able to do so. So it seemed best to let the matter sit. However, since 2010 seminars within the Society of Biblical Literature and the Society of New Testament Studies have provided fresh impetus, and 1 Corinthians has now become the DBI's main research focus.

---

11.   Brodie, MacDonald and Porter 2006.

Part IV

THE FUNERAL

Becoming aware of the need
to lay some theories to rest

Chapter 12

THE FUNERAL:
'ORAL TRADITION' AND ITS WORLD

Twentieth-century biblical studies were probably at their slackest in discussing oral tradition. When I was growing up I was taught that the Gospels were the product of four great writers, divinely inspired, their splendour symbolized by visionary animals, including the soaring eagle for John. However, in the 1960s I learned of processes of composition where the central energy underlying the Gospels came from oral tradition. The idea seemed plausible, and even when it was becoming clear that the New Testament drew much of its material from written sources, from reflective literary adaptation of the Old Testament, the idea of oral tradition lingered on.

Robert Alter (1981: 50) woke me up when he described reading Robert Culley's presentation of the patterns of oral transmission in Genesis:

> As I stared at Culley's schematic tables, it gradually dawned on me that he had made a discovery without realizing it. For what his tables of parallels and variations actually reveal are the lineaments of a purposefully deployed literary convention. The variations in the parallel episodes are not at all at *random*, as a scrambling of oral transmission would imply.

Alter's analysis demonstrated that Culley had misread a literary phenomenon as oral, but it did not explain why Culley, along with other biblical scholars, first came to the idea that biblical narrative depends on oral tradition. Why impose an oral model on a literary phenomenon? And if oral tradition was questionable in the older scriptures, then even more so in the New Testament, where the time span between events and writing was generally less than a lifetime.

The answer seemed elusive. Speech is so basic to humans—obviously far more than writing—that the idea of oral communication has an immediate plausibility. This is doubly so regarding the ancient world where few people could read and the culture was radically oral. And when I looked into the matter—I ended up reading Walter Ong and once travelled from Florida to St Louis just to talk to him—I found that even writing, for most of its history, resonated with orality. All ancient writing, until the eighteenth century, reflected orality or oral rhythms; it was aural, geared to the ear, to being heard—unlike modern writing, geared primarily to the eye. Virgil's epic was highly crafted writing and a distillation of earlier literature, but it was saturated with orality; it was geared to oral communication, to being heard, and in fact was being read aloud in Augustus's imperial court even before it was complete. But such orality was still not oral tradition, not oral *transmission*, it was simply a quality of ancient writing.

Studying non-literate tribes did not help. For them oral transmission was largely the only option, and their ability to remember masses of very old material did not solve the essential problem: How do you deduce from a piece of writing that it is based on oral transmission? If the variations in the tribes' accounts corresponded broadly to the variations between the Gospels, then oral transmission could account for Gospel relationships. But tribal variations did not correspond to Gospel variations. And neither did the variations within rabbinical methods of memorization. Joseph Fitzmyer, for instance, praised Birger Gerhardsson's investigation of rabbinic methods, but noted that it did not account for much of the Gospel data.

Searching further I found a claim to oral tradition at the heart of Judaism. The Pharisees had justified their practices by appealing to an oral tradition. The claim was an accepted Pharisaic convention, and, if Paul is seen as a former Pharisee (Phil. 3.5), 1 Corinthians could be regarded as following the Pharisee convention. This Jewish claim would have provided context for analogous Christian claims, particularly the claim that there was a tradition underlying the teaching concerning the Eucharist and Christ's death and resurrection (1 Cor. 11.23-27; 15.1-8). Taken in isolation, the role of this convention in Paul is difficult to assess, and we will need to come back to it.

Eventually something obvious began to come into focus—the influence of form-history ('form criticism'). Form critics, especially Gunkel and Bultmann, made a major contribution in recognizing diverse literary forms in the Bible, but their presuppositions about the development of history and peoples led them to interpret those forms as tied to local communities and, above all, as oral, not literary. One of the clearest clues to the logic occurs in the Introduction to Gunkel's seminal commentary on Genesis. As I noted earlier, when first talking about the historical method (Chapter 1), Gunkel located the biblical people among the *uncultivierten Völker*, 'uncultured peoples',[1] and because such people were uncultivated, undeveloped, incapable of composing complex works of art, the method of communication was oral; and therefore their writings resulted from oral tradition. The point bears repeating because Gunkel's influence has been massive.

The idea of oral tradition spread not only to students of Genesis such as Robert Culley, but also to New Testament scholars, especially Schmidt, Dibelius and Bultmann. The idea then passed to Gardner-Smith (1938) who

1. Gunkel 1901: i; Eng. trans., 1997: vii.

used it to explain the similarities and differences between John and the Synoptics. The result is well known: John became cut off from the Synoptics, isolated; and his mantle of oral tradition endowed him with the potential for carrying an independent historical tradition.

To this day few researchers attempt to spell out the logic underlying the claim to oral tradition. With admirable honesty James Dunn states that oral tradition is a presumption, and he justifies that presumption by saying it is inescapable (2007: 157). With due respect, it is not. The core presumption is that Jesus Christ was a specific historical person, and within that theory, something is needed to bridge the gap between the death of Jesus (generally placed around 30 CE) and the composition of the Gospels (generally placed around 70–100).

Even if the theory were true, the gap could be filled by saying that the evangelists were either present at the events or spoke directly to people who had been. I know, for instance, the precise wording of how the 1922 assassination of Michael Collins, Chairman of Ireland's Provisional Government, was announced in one rural household. My mother was an eight-year-old child when her father came up from the village one morning and said to his wife, 'Michael Collins went over the bridge last night'. The meaning was obscured, but something about the moment and the phrase was unforgettable. And my father told me calmly and clearly what it was like as a teenager selling horses to men from the British Army who attended the fair at the Cross of Spancil Hill during World War 1, how the army men were so keen that, in the pre-dawn darkness, they would judge the horses by the light of a match. Because he was there, I now know, almost a hundred years later, both the mood and the detail of the scene. And I likewise know, because my grandmother told me, that when Charles Stewart Parnell, the controverted Protestant leader of the Irish Parliamentary Party at Westminster, died prematurely in 1891, people in the Irish countryside cried, at least in County Clare. She was there and she saw them. It is possible to bridge a gap of almost a century, or even more than a century, without relying on an ill-defined and unpredictable process of oral tradition, and it would make elementary sense, if the evangelists wanted to bridge a gap of several decades, that they would speak directly to those who had been present.

Sometimes of course it is easy or convenient to invoke oral tradition. Certainly, it is incomparably easier to call on irretrievable oral tradition than to try to follow the retrievable but complex processes of literary transformation and genius. And when an undefined oral tradition is combined with an undefined link to the Synoptics, then all bases seem to be covered. But the result is a world of vagueness where, despite fine erudition, logic is lost. The problem with the role given to oral tradition in twentieth-century discussion of the Gospels is not just that it did not account for the data, but that its fog of confusion absorbed energy and blocked progress on central issues.

* * *

Two essential phenomena remain. The variations among the Gospels, including John, fit well among the variations of ancient literary rewriting, but they
do not fit well among the variations of oral transmission. And the Gospels'
orality, strong though it is, fits well not into oral tradition but into the orality
of all ancient *writing*.

The way back from invoking oral tradition will not be easy. I remember
listening to Louis Martyn, speaking to the SBL in Anaheim, California,
probably in 1989. He described the notion of the Johannine community,
including his own version of it, as a genie which, when released, had gone
out of control and was proving very difficult to bring back. The same is true
of oral tradition. Once the genie was released it took on a life of its own.
Three generations have become so accustomed to the idea that a radical
review seems unthinkable.

Martyn was right, but as well as speaking of a genie, we should mention
scientific theories. As Thomas Kuhn (1996) has shown, such theories tend
to drag on for a long time. It is always tempting to try another expedition to
Mount Ararat. But eventually, such theories can allow something else to
emerge. For centuries, physics was haunted by the theory of an all-pervasive
substance called ether—light-bearing ether ('luminiferous ether') as distinguished from medical ether—which was believed in the nineteenth century,
for instance, to act as a medium for transmitting electromagnetic waves such
as light and X-rays. Slowly, however, as researchers began to understand the
nature of light and the structure of matter, it became clear that ether was not
needed to explain the data, and gradually the theory of ether has been laid to
rest.

The tenacity of Gunkel's mixture of insight and misreading is seen in *The
Interpretation of the Bible in the Church*, published in 1993 by the Pontifical
Biblical Commission. The document surveys and assesses diverse methods of
biblical interpretation, and as mentioned earlier, the document is very useful,
particularly as published along with Joseph Fitzmyer's commentary and
bibliographical notes, but it effectively endorses Gunkel and does not distinguish between the value of recognizing forms and the confusion of asso-
ciating these forms with undefined oral tradition and with an oversimplified
model of how the Pentateuch and Gospels developed.[2]

---

2. Fitzmyer 1995: 34-36. The document discusses narrative art but not its full dimensions and implications (1995: 50-59). It notes (p. 29) that 'literary criticism came for a
long time to be identified with the attempt to distinguish in texts different sources'.
It also discusses ways in which biblical books 'reinterpreted' or 'reread' earlier texts
(pp. 68-78, 134-39) but not the ancient practice of systematic rewriting and the present
possibility of tracking literary dependence on extant sources.

Oral tradition is like a theory of ether that has clouded form-history ('form criticism') and created a vast vague world, often of simple isolated people or communities telling developing stories, a theory that by its very vagueness is evocative and engaging. It is time that this theory be laid to rest, time to free the study of forms from unnecessary complications and to bring it to a new level of maturity. We need a gentle funeral.

Chapter 13

THE QUEST FOR HISTORY: RULE ONE

On leaving the foggy swamp created by the theory of oral tradition I came again to the search for well-grounded history, and was brought back to the person who, amid hundreds of ancient rules, asked Jesus, 'Which is the greatest commandment?' And so amid the complexity of searching for history, I wondered if there was a Rule One.

At the SBL meeting in San Diego in 2007, Richard Bauckham, who was then at St Andrews, Scotland, reminded his huge audience that he was unusually well qualified in history. It seemed then that Rule One was: 'Attend to History'. At one level this made sense. The search for history— 'historical method'—is invaluable. History is like an extension of life, and in the quest for understanding, knowledge of the past is generally useful and often indispensable. To avoid historical criticism is to deny evidence of reality. History is particularly important to Christianity, because Christianity at its best has a keen awareness of the presence of God in the world and in people's day-to-day historical lives.

For our much-loved Brevard Childs, in New Haven, Rule One was not history, not something in the Bible's background, but in effect theology, meaning. Childs had been through the prolonged discussions of historical background, and came to believe it was necessary to move on to something clearer and more solidly founded. So instead of the elusiveness of the Bible's historical background, he maintained there was more clarity and authority in the Bible itself—the finished text that the early believers had chosen as an appropriate guide or rule (*canōn*). So Rule One was to ask the meaning of the finished ('canonical') text.

I highlight Bauckham and Childs because I have a special regard for them and they have taught me much. At different times in my life they appeared like lighthouses in the darkness, and I read them with relief and gratitude. Childs gave me constant encouragement, and it was from Bauckham I received encouragement for maintaining that early Christians were in communication with one another.

Yet something was missing. I remember one day in class, as Childs was holding forth with strength and depth, he noticed how the text seemed to be structured or organized in a very specific way, and wondered if the structure was significant—in effect wondered if a purely literary feature, neither history or theology, made any real difference. He paused, and then, almost verbatim:

'We have no evidence that these things were important.'

The moment passed, and we returned to theology.

Ultimately Bauckham and Childs are right. Mastery of history is a central asset, and, in the long term, the theology of the entire Bible—its overall meaning—is of supreme value.

And yet, and yet, and yet. Being first in importance does not necessarily mean being first in the order of investigation. The first thing to be sorted out about a document is not its history or theology—not the truth of background events or its ultimate meaning—but simply its basic nature. For instance, before discussing a will—its possible many references to past events, and its provisions for distributing a legacy—the first thing to be established is whether it is genuine, whether it is a real will.

Some years ago, when setting the scene for examining Genesis, I tried to summarize the problem:

> The text, the finished writing, is the number one artifact, and no amount of historical background or theological acumen can substitute for taking that artifact seriously. Before asking 'What was the historical background?' one must first ask 'Historical background of what?' To do otherwise is like trying to figure out 'who done it' without knowing what was done...
>
> As an artifact, an object, Genesis is literary, at least in the basic sense that it consists of writing—words and sentences on pages of some kind. And the first step in taking it seriously is to be sensitive to writing—to the full text and to the procedures normally involved in writing, in other words, to literary procedures. The literary aspect has 'operational priority' (Robert Polzin, *Literary Study*, 1980, 5-7, esp. 6). [Or as David Gunn said: 'Write the history of the literature, and then the [wider] history...can be written'—meaning 'the history of "Israel" or "ancient Israelite religion" or Old Testament theology' (Gunn 2001: 182)]. Literary procedures are like the foundations of a house: on their own they are unimpressive and almost useless, but to build without them is to invite disaster.

Coming back, for instance, to the Jericho wall that 'fell flat' (Josh. 6.20), the evidence from archaeology is now sometimes disputed (Joines and Mitchell 2003: 888), but it still seems the Jericho site contains no remains from the centuries when the conquest is said to have happened. However, without ever lifting a spade, the literary aspect provides a further clue. The drama surrounding Jericho—success at Jericho and failure at Ai (Josh. 5.13–8.29)—is part of a larger pattern of texts concerning success-and-failure, texts that ultimately reflect the Bible's foundational drama of success-and-failure, namely, the creation-and-fall (Gen. 1.1–4.16). The details deserve a special study, but the operating principle behind the construction of the narrative is clear: the dynamics at work in creation and the fall are still at work in history.[1] The total compliance of the wall in falling is a variation on the process of command-and-compliance that began when 'God said "Let there be light", and there was light'.

What is essential is that literary context gives decisive clues on how to understand a text. If a newspaper announces cheap flights to Mars, it is important to note whether the advertisement occurs in the Travel Section or in the Cartoons-and-Jokes Page. Clarity on the literary factor is Rule One.

Richard Bauckham has made a major contribution to biblical studies by helping to show that oral tradition does not work in explaining the development of the Gospels, and he has gone on to replace oral tradition by invoking formal transmission and eyewitnesses. This makes immediate sense, because the proposed time-lag between Jesus' ministry and the composition of the Gospels could be bridged by long-lived eye-witnesses or by people who knew eyewitnesses well, and because the New Testament contains references to processes of transmission and witness (e.g. 1 Cor. 11.23; 15.1-8; Lk. 1.1-4; Jn 21.24-25; cf. 19.35-37; 20.30-31). Bauckham uses the New Testament references to transmission and witness as a starting point for building an elaborate history—a reconstruction of the identity of the eyewitnesses and of the processes of transmission.[2]

However, there are problems with Bauckham's proposal. John N. Collins of Australia maintains that Bauckham misreads Luke's prologue (Lk. 1.1-4); Luke is referring back not to eyewitnesses but to a process that is literary.

> Bauckham's…picture…of 'some process of teaching and learning'…within the Gentile churches contributes to his construction of 'eyewitness testimony'. However, it takes little more than a glance at the preface of Luke to realize that Luke's focus is [not on 'some process of teaching and learning' but] upon a literary tradition.[3]

The idea of *literary* tradition is not new,[4] and Collins touches a key feature of Bauckham's work: it shows historical erudition but without the necessary preliminary literary homework. Bauckham reads the New Testament data on

---

1. Note reflection of creation in Exodus's plagues (a variation of God's power over creation); in Num. 1–2 (a two-fold census); and in Deut. 1 (Deut. 1.1-18, creation/compliance; Deut. 1.19-46, failure/fall).

2. Bauckham 2006 and 2007.

3. Collins 2010: 451.

4. See Svebakken 2010: 94-95: 'While…interpreters naturally disagreed with the work of their predecessors on certain points, they tended not to reject it openly, because they considered themselves heir to a venerable tradition. They struck a delicate balance between continuity and change, honouring traditional interpretations by reusing them in whole or in part but often reworking them to suit their own interests.' See also Tobin 1983.

transmission and witness as historical,[5] without asking sufficiently whether it is actually historical or whether it is simply written to look *like* history.

John has ample reason to make his account look like history. He is writing in the tradition of Hebrew narrative, which, even when it is not history, is significantly history-like (Alter 1981: 23-46), and besides John is telling of the Word made flesh. God's Word is not distant; it is in life, and life is inextricably historical. Flesh means history in all its detail. It is appropriate to John's theological vision of the Word made flesh that his presentation of the Word be in the shape of history. But whether it is actually historical must be decided on grounds other than its appearance.

The beginning of John's Gospel (Jn 1–4), for instance, with its account of Jesus' journey from Jerusalem and Judea to Samaria and Galilee, may look historical because, among other things, it shows precise knowledge of places, and 'a good historian was expected to have a thorough knowledge of the places where the events of his history took place' (Bauckham 2007: 95).

But knowledge of places is not history. Virgil, for instance, in describing the incident of the wooden horse at Troy, describes the island of Tenedos where the Greek ships hid: *Est in conspectu Tenedos...insula...*, 'Within sight [of Troy] is the island of Tenedos...' (*Aeneid* 2.21-22). And elsewhere too he shows precise knowledge of places (e.g. *Aeneid* 3.506; 5.124). But that does not turn Virgils's account of Aeneas's semi-mythical life into history. And in St Louis I lived for years beside the building used by film-makers to show Superman taking flight, and I could give much precise knowledge of the location—on Lindell Boulevard, near the junction with Grand Avenue, close to Aquinas Institute, to the Fox theatre, and to Wendy's restaurant—'Quality Fast Food Made the Way You Want'. But that too does not make Superman historical. And likewise, John's precision in mentioning places may give a close imitation of the style of historians, but again that alone does not make history. Style is not substance. What Bauckham has clarified is not that John is a historian but that he has imitated the conventions of historians. He has made his work history-like. This is an important contribution to clarifying John's literary form, but the issue of history must be decided on other factors.[6]

---

5. Bauckham 2006: esp. 114-54, 264-89.

6. Bauckham 2007: 95-100. John's *concluding* imitation of the conventions of historians, his claim to eyewitness testimony, is a variation on Luke's *opening* imitation of the convention of the historical prologue (Lk. 1.1-4). And Mark also may be called a form of history, 'an eschatological historical monograph' (Yarbro Collins 2007: 42-44). The practice of making texts look like history is compounded by the ancient practice of making texts sound old, archaism; former writers were as focused in invoking what is old, on an appearance of age, as present-day people are on what is new (see, for instance, Craig 1927; Callebat 1964).

Other factors include especially the identifying of John's sources and how he uses them. As mentioned earlier, the journey most emphasized in John, Jesus' journey from Jerusalem and Judea to Samaria and Galilee (Jn 2.23–4.54) is unlike any journey in the Synoptics but corresponds in outline to the journey of the Word of God in Acts 1–8 (cf. esp. Acts 1.8, and 8.1, 40), and there are many details to corroborate John's literary dependence on Acts 1–8 (Heffernan 2009). Such adaptations, such creative rewritings, were not unusual. They were central to ancient literary composition. So it is impossible to make a historical claim about John 1–4 without first examining its dependence on Acts 1–8.

But some who claim to find history in John do not examine such literary links. In September 2007, I contacted Richard Bauckham to ask if, in examining the perplexing relationship between John and the other evangelists, he had ever set the problem in the context of the literary relationships of the ancient world, Greco-Roman and Jewish. A few days later, on 26 September, he replied and said quite simply 'No'.

I had to admire his promptness and honesty. But it reminded me of London's Metropolitan Police when they were first offered fingerprinting. The Metropolitan Police were no slouch outfit. Based in Scotland Yard, they had a proud professional tradition. It was they who maintained order in the capital city at the heart of the largest empire the world has ever seen. They did not need these flimsy-looking spider-lines.

Tracking creative rewriting is like looking for fingerprinting. In comparing texts it often shows similarities that may appear as virtually invisible as fingerprints. But the phenomenon of creative rewriting is not going away. It is like a technology that is improving steadily. Virtually every year now brings some new discovery of how it contributed to the making of a biblical or biblical-related text, and with each discovery comes an increased opportunity to learn how rewriting can work. New Scotland Yard and London's Metropolitan Police have long since become leaders in solving difficult cases. Solving what exactly John did will take time. Even the use of Acts 1–8 in John 1–4 needs much further work. But the clock will not be turned back. Fingerprints will always be useful in detective work. And the fingerprints left by the use of Acts 1–8 on John 1–4 will always be pivotal clues to John's use of diverse sources and to the nature of his final work.

Failure to connect John with Acts is part of a larger neglect around literary matters—whether about sufficiently recognizing literary art, including literary form, or the strange ancient method of creatively adapting sources. This neglect violates Rule One of historical research.[7]

---

7. Similar problems occur in reconstructions such as those of James Dunn. For instance, while granting that the speeches in Acts owe their presentation to Luke, Dunn claims that their distinctive material 'points to the conclusion that Luke has been able to

The irony of Bauckham's historical hypothesis is that, having helped to lay one ghost, that of oral tradition, he has released another. The theory of eyewitness testimony forms such an imposing construction, it has such a mixture of initial plausibility, erudition and complexity, that it is easy to be drawn into it and to forget that it lacks the indispensable foundation that comes from an understanding of literature. One forgets there is a chasm beneath the impressive edifice.

The chasm is so deep that, like the theory of oral tradition, it threatens to devour decades of research energy, until, someday, some future Bauckham will arise and say 'That dog don't hunt! It does not deal with the data—with the text and its links to other texts.'

The problem is not solved by moving from one imaginary foundation to another—from eyes to memory, in other words from eyewitness testimony to social memory.[8] There is indeed such a thing as social memory—the way societies remember events and people—but social memory does not necessarily prove the historical existence of the individual remembered. There is a social memory of Superman, though generally without details of the location of the building from which he flew. The discussion of the social memory of Jesus rests on the presupposition of Jesus' historicity—a presupposition that is particularly clear in Robert McIver's opening sentence: 'Jesus was crucified within a few years of 31 C.E....' (McIver 2011: 1). Historical existence provides a foundation for social memory; but social memory does not provide a reliable foundation for historical existence.

And so, later still, in the long lingering silence that follows the funeral's oration, a yet younger Bauckham will cry out 'What is Rule One?'

---

draw on and incorporate tradition...so it would be unwise to conclude that the speeches simply reflect Luke's own interests or that he imposes his own perspective entirely on the material' (Dunn 2009: 89). Dunn has detected that Luke is using something distinctive, but rather than check distinctive verifiable literary possibilities, particularly whether Luke is using the epistles and translating them into new form, Dunn invokes undefined tradition, thus embarking on a trail that is vague and out of scholarly control.

8. For introductory discussion and references, see, for instance, Le Donne 2009: 41-64; McIver 2011: esp. 81-121. See also Holmberg 2004; Byrskog 2004; Dunn 2004.

Chapter 14

THE SHIPPING FORECAST:
DEEPS BELOW AND A STORM AHEAD

> Once the narrative genie has been let out of the bottle, not least in a world with
> its eyes newly opened by contemporary literary study, you can't get it back in;
> and now all kinds of aspects of Paul are being tested for implicit and explicit
> storylines.
>
> —N.T. Wright, *Paul* (2005: 7).

> The [writer] need not cite [the] source-text [but...] can treat it in a limitless
> variety of perspectives... It is up to us to recognize and reconstruct the parti-
> cular force of relation.
>
> —George Steiner, *After Babel* (1975: 424-25).

One of the people I met in New Haven in the early 1980s was the newly
arrived young professor of New Testament at Yale Divinity School—the tall,
calm Richard B. Hays. Our interests overlapped. Hays's recently finished
doctorate, at Emory University, Atlanta, had discussed how part of the
Epistle to the Galatians evoked a much larger narrative about Jesus and some
of the Old Testament (Hays 1983), and one day he invited me to make a
presentation to his New Haven class regarding the use of Old Testament
narrative in the Gospels, especially in Luke.

Since then Richard Hays has become a pioneer in narrative theology—in
showing how New Testament narrative often builds a story or narrative that
is grounded on that of the Old Testament, and his work is now complemented
by that of many others, for instance, N.T. Wright of Durham, Francis Watson
of Aberdeen, and in another way by Carol Stockhausen of Marquette University, Milwaukee. Such writers often say the New Testament contains
'echoes' (Hays's word) of the Old Testament, or has 'allusions' to it. Their
work is a real advance for New Testament research.[1]

---

1. In 2006, when David Horrell of Exeter revised his valuable *Introduction to ... Paul*,
the main change was an expanded section (pp. 58-60) concerning Paul's reliance on a
storyline and the storyline's link with the Old Testament.

Yet there is a problem. Terms such as 'echo' and 'allusion' do not do justice to the complexity of how the New Testament uses the Old Testament.[2] 'Echo' is appropriate insofar as it pictures the transfer of sound or words from one place to another. But in an echo, the energy for the transfer comes from the source, whereas, in the various forms of rewriting, the energy that forms the echo comes especially from the destination, from the writer who takes the older text and gives it a new existence and often a new shape. So 'echo' tends to underplay the active role of the later writer. And sometimes the situation is not helped by using the word 'intertextuality'.[3] This lack of clarity needs attention.

2.   The advance in narrative theology has been won at a price. Hays's vision is primarily about theology. But what Richard Sarason once said of history, is true also of theology: the historical (or theological) question is posed prematurely (1981: 61). Hays speaks of 'discerning literary, thematic and theological linkages within the biblical canon', and he explicitly omits questions of history, *including further literary issues*—issues about 'sources' and 'processes of transmission' (Hays 2009b: xiii). It is true, in the context of historical criticism, that the examination of 'sources' and 'processes of transmission' often seems unfruitful. But within literary criticism at its best and its broadest, these factors have another meaning—processes of transmission become processes of literary adaptation—and ultimately they contribute to theology.

For instance, the continuity between Luke's narrative (Luke–Acts) and the narrative of the Old Testament gives a theological result: it shows the reader the continuity and reliability of God's plan, and thus gives the reader 'assurance' (Lk. 1.4); in other words, the assurance and reliability is a statement about theology, about the reliability of God's plan (Hays 2009a: 103, 116).

But one of the most basic factors in God's plan was the composing of scripture. If attention to the process of composition, including the ways in which sources were used, can clarify how God's plan was implemented, how the scriptures were actually composed, that needs to be taken into account. It does not seem to make sense to theologize about God's plan without making a reasonable effort to find out how God's actually worked.

3.   See Brodie 2004: 74. The recently formed term 'intertextuality' is primarily anthropological; it refers to interaction *between whole cultures* (Roudiez 1980: 15). However, partly because of research on intertextuality in the broad anthropological sense, literary scholars have become more attuned to the influence of one particular written text on another, and so the term 'intertextuality' is now frequently used precisely to refer to the relationship *between written texts*. (On Julia Kristeva, originator of the term 'intertextuality', see Roudiez 1980: 1-20; Lechte 1994: 141-44.)

Insofar as the emphasis on 'intertextuality' heightens awareness of literary connections, the term is welcome. But insofar as the term obscures ancient terms and phenomena, it is to be treated with caution. Dale C. Allison's *The Intertextual Jesus: Scripture in Q* (2000), takes 'intertextual' in a broad sense as referring to allusions, and on that basis Allison produces a valuable map of the way the Q material alludes to other texts.

However, the kernel of ancient writing was not in allusions; it was in taking hold of entire books and transforming them systematically. Virgil did not just *allude* to Homer; he swallowed him whole. And there are comparable systematic transformations within the Bible. Allusions and quotations were often little more than decorations and embellishments.

A Key Practice:
Transforming Texts beyond Immediate Recognition

A striking episode in Luke's Gospel tells of the centurion whose servant is sick (Lk. 7.1-10) and, across the years, many writers and speakers have discussed both the episode itself and related episodes in Matthew (8.5-13) and John (4.43-54). A significant percentage of those who discussed Luke's account were aware of the Old Testament episode concerning Naaman, the Syrian commander (2 Kgs 5.1-19), but almost no one noticed—certainly I didn't—that, to a decisive degree, the centurion consists largely of a transformation of Naaman. The differences between the texts are great, and it needs careful examination to see the central continuity between them, yet, as mentioned earlier, John Shelton, building on brief comments by a few earlier scholars, has put Luke's systematic dependence on the Naaman account beyond reasonable doubt.[4] The Naaman text has been transformed beyond immediate recognition.

The background to such transforming of texts is complex, but one significant part of it is connected to the ancient preoccupation with preservation. Generally speaking, human attitudes to preservation vary radically. What one individual keeps, another discards. Preservation orders are often contentious. One generation distrusts the past, another treasures it. And while such variations may be striking, they are miniscule compared to the radical difference between the way literary texts are composed in modern times and the way in which they were composed by ancient writers.

At the heart of the composition of ancient texts, including biblical texts, lay a visceral instinct for literary preservation.[5] The reason for this deep-seated custom of preservation and re-use seems to lie, in part at least, in a feeling that existing knowledge, stored largely in precious handwritten texts, was not to be taken for granted but was to be thoroughly understood, imitated (*imitatio*; Greek, *mimēsis*), emulated (*aemulatio*; Greek, *zélos*), rewritten (in diverse forms, Near Eastern and Mediterranean)—and thereby preserved. This feeling lasted until about 1800, that is, until the continued use of the printing press, especially as manifested in the French *Encyclopédie* (1751–1772), finally led to a situation in which ancient knowledge was taken for granted. The purpose, then, was both to preserve what existed, and simultaneously to ensure that it was available in fresh form for a further generation. The essential was preservation, not recognition.[6]

---

4. Shelton 2011.
5. For some details and references, see Brodie 2004: 3.
6. The situation is somewhat like food aid for the hungry. It is sometimes appropriate that those receiving the food recognize where the food comes from. Such recognition

So when texts are used, some are indeed recognizable, *but many others are not*. They are hidden, and unless the researcher is alert to the diverse ways in which they may be disguised, they remain hidden—thus concealing much of the heart of the matter.

The problem can scarcely be overstated. The process of tracing literary links or establishing literary dependence is often very difficult. The project needs fresh energy. To begin, it would be good if the entrance to every biblical department in the world could be knocked down and rebuilt to become an arch of black marble, and, on the black marble, George Steiner's words from *After Babel* (1975: 424), engraved in gold:

> The [writer] need not cite [the] source-text
> [but...] can treat it in a limitless variety of perspectives...
> from interlinear translation...
> to the faintest most arcane of allusions
> It is up to us to recognize and reconstruct
> the particular force of relation.

So, black and gold. Or whatever you are having yourself—whatever helps beginners to avoid having their imaginations imperceptibly so programmed that they stay within a very limited number of literary relationships, the relationships reflected, for instance, in Aland's (useful) *Synopsis*, in discussions about Q, and even in discussions of narrative theology, so programmed that, as the years go on, they will never envisage the full range of possibilities. They will never recognize...

Among the 'limitless variety of perspectives', narrative theology has an honoured place, but it is best set in the context of three uses that are particularly pertinent in biblical studies.

Quotation
The precise definition of a quotation is disputed, but generally the presence of the older text is clear, and the purpose of quoting is to give authority (see esp. Stanley 2004: esp. 36, 173, 182-83). Quotation requires recognition; if hearers or readers do not recognize the source, the authority and effectiveness of the quote is largely lost.

means that, apart from being nourished, they have a reassuring sense of connection to a larger reliable world. But not every can of beans has to be stamped with 'FROM THE PEOPLE OF...' What counts most is that the food itself not be wasted—in that sense it is preserved—and that those who need it receive it. At times, of course, investigators need to know the origin of certain food. In that case, the matter can generally be resolved, even if it means prolonged inquiry and slow work in a laboratory. However, generally, the essential need is for preservation and delivery, not for recognition.

Narrative Allusion/Echoes/Reception
In this case the presence of the older text is generally less clear, less direct, but it can evoke a whole narrative and theology. The exact meaning of terms such as 'allusion' and 'echo' is debated, but workable summaries are available.[7] Somewhat like quotation, so also allusion and echo generally require recognition; if hearers or readers do not catch the sound of the older text, do not recognize the source, the effectiveness is largely lost.

Transformation
In this case the older text is so thoroughly reworked that at first sight it is not recognizable. The purpose of this transformation was not to hit people with a clear authoritative quotation (à la Chris Stanley), or subtly to evoke a theological narrative within some hearers (à la Richard Hays), but to respect and preserve the text in adapted form so that it fulfils some other function.

The variations between these three models (quotation, allusion, and transformation) are like the variations, when moving house, between (1) keeping the old name plate or name; (2) keeping some key furnishings and some photos of the old house; and (3) taking the old house itself, and using its materials as one component, major or minor, to help build the new, even if the stones in the old sandstone walls are reduced to gravel for the driveway so that, at first sight at least, they are unrecognizable.

The issue is pivotal. Many biblical researchers tend to reject literary dependence if the dependence is not easily recognizable, if the hearers would not detect it. However, what counts for the investigator is not easy recognition, but whether, with due inquiry and patient work in the laboratory of literary comparison, in other words, in meticulous application of appropriate criteria, the hidden connection can be established. And the hidden connections are vast—far, far greater in number and volume than connections that are easily recognizable. Recognizable connections are like the few fish that occasionally break above the surface of the ocean. The overwhelming majority of the fish are out of sight, in the depths. The time has come for biblical research to move out into the deep.

The deep in this case involves degrees of transformation that may seem alien, transformations in which texts are given a thoroughly new appearance. Obviously, as a general principle, some kinds of transformation are familiar and welcome—the Spring sun that transforms the frozen earth, the organ transplant that effectively creates a new body, and the transformation of inert food and drink into energy and vitality.

However, not all things seem open to transformation. Manhattan is built on granite, and its foundations are unlikely to be transformed, at least for

---

7. See, for instance, Porter 2006: 107-109.

now. And in a world where 'the facts is the facts', and where, for a long time, science meant certainty, many people have a sense of solid certitudes, including solid gold. And diamonds are forever.

But in asking about the widespread acceptance of the idea of transformation we are looking at the ancient world, and 'the past is a foreign country: they do things differently there' (L.P. Hartley, *The Go-Between*, 1953, opening line). Heraclitus compressed his philosophy into just two words: *panta rei*, 'everything flows', meaning that everything is constantly changing. Alchemy was concerned not only with changing one metal into another. It constituted an entire philosophy—ancient, widespread. And when Ovid was synthesizing ancient mythology into an epic, he filtered its many narratives through the prism of transformation, and entitled his work *Metamorphoseon*, a Latinized form of Greek—in English, *Metamorphoses*. His book was near completion in 7 CE, just before Emperor Augustus exiled him from the comfort of Rome to end his days forlorn on the shores of the Black Sea, at age sixty-one. Despite the exile, his friends in Rome rescued his work, thus preserving a writing of singular influence and, as its beginning indicates, vast scope:[8]

> My mind is bent, to tell of bodies changed (*mutates*) into new forms (*formas*).
> Ye gods, for you yourselves have wrought the changes (*mutastis*),
> breathe on these my undertakings
> and bring down my song in unbroken strains
> from the world's very beginning (*ab origine mundi*)
> even unto the present time (*ad mea tempora*).

The concept of transformation is not alien to the New Testament. It occurs at a key point in Mark's Gospel, at the literary centre, in the account of the Transfiguration, where it says that Jesus *meta-morphōthē*, literally 'was transformed' (Mk 9.2; cf. Mt. 17.2).

What is important is that within the ancient world the general concept of transformation was familiar, so it is relatively easy to understand why processes of transformation were so acceptable within literary composition. Instances occur across virtually the entire range of ancient literature, non-biblical and biblical, Old Testament and New, and the evidence of processes of transformation is increasing rapidly.[9]

So, to summarize. Three of the main methods of using existing texts are: quotation, allusion and transformation. Among these three, biblical research

---

8. Loeb translation, line arrangement added.
9. See, for instance, Brodie 1978; Fishbane 1985: esp. 383-91, 500-505; Harrington and Horgan 1986: 239-47; Fischel 1975; D.P. Wright 2009. Note the idea of writing as weaving: Scheid and Svenbro 1996. For an example of what a detailed analysis might look like, see esp. Steiner 1975: 296-470.

has gone far in articulating one and two—quotation, and (narrative) allusion. The third method, insofar as it involves major transformation, is still largely unexplored.

Narrative theology is like Columbus. It has accomplished a pioneering voyage. But now, like Columbus, it needs to stand back and take a fresh look at the continent on which it has landed. The way ahead is not into semi-familiar India. It is moving into a whole new world, and the sense of accomplishment gives way to that of an infant who looks out at the world in wide-eyed wonder. The infant image is not new. 'Literary analysis of the Bible…is only in its infancy', said Robert Alter (1981: 12). And likewise Luke Johnson (1998: 10): 'Literary analysis of the New Testament writings as literary compositions is still in its infancy'. The sign that now stands before these newly awoken wide-eyed explorers is not 'Here be Dragons', but 'Here be Transformed Texts—More Transformed than is Dreamt of in Your Philosophy, or Theology'.

* * *

Dealing with a Strange World:
Criteria for Recognizing the Presence of Transformed Texts

Recognizing the presence of an underlying transformed source can be like recognizing a transformed human being. When Odysseus finally arrived home to Ithaca, it seemed at first that no one could possibly know him. Ten years of a foreign war had taken their toll, as had ten years more of wandering. Besides, he was thoroughly disguised as an old beggar, and no human could see through his dirty clothes. He needed, in his first approach to the house, to avoid recognition.

However, as a young man, before he left Ithaca, he had hunted with a dog. And while it was true, as he now entered, that people paid him little heed, the dog was still present. However, the dog was now desperately old, just lying there:

> But 'the dog that lay there
> Lifted up his muzzle, pricked his ears'.[10]

He had sensed a presence he once knew. For a moment it looked at if Odysseus would be recognized. But the weight of age and the excitement were too much for the faithful animal and, before he had a chance to reveal the identity of his master, he suddenly died (*Odyssey* 3.317-60).

---

10. *The Odyssey* 3.317-18 (trans. Fagels).

All was going well for Odysseus until, as a gesture of welcome, it was decided to wash his feet, and the washing fell to the nurse who had cared for him as a youth. As she washed, she saw a scar, and she knew there was only one such scar—the result of a youth's encounter with a wild animal more than twenty years previously. She said nothing, but he knew she had recognized him, and as inconspicuously as possible he threatened her fiercely not to say who was present.

The initial process of recognizing the presence of an underlying literary source—recognizing for instance that within Genesis lies a transformation of Homer's *Odyssey*; or that within Matthew lies a transformation of Romans—can sometimes resemble what happened within the dog and the nurse. Some kind of scent. Or a telltale detail. And suddenly you know. Or at least you have a strong suspicion. But no matter how strong the suspicion, no matter how accurate the nose, the claim that one document used another needs to be backed by systematic investigation. A strong suspicion is useless in court. You need evidence—plus clarity.

One of the features of recent biblical studies is that several researchers, including those concentrating on the presence of allusion/echo, have begun to spell out the criteria for claiming that one document depends on another. In my own case it took me several years to go from strong suspicion and scattered evidence to being able to lay out the evidence in a reasonably orderly way. In brief, the criteria of dependence fall into three categories:[11]

Initial plausibility, including accessibility. For instance: Was the document—for example, the *Odyssey*—already in existence when Genesis was being fashioned? Would it have been reachable? Is it likely that the composer of Genesis would consult such a document, or would ever make systematic use of such a document? Even after seeing the document, is it likely that the composer would transform it? And never quote even one full line of it? This first criterion proves nothing. It simply asks if the case seems worth pursuing, and its result may in fact be a clear 'No'.

---

11.   The clarifying of criteria for detecting literary dependence is generally a fairly recent development. See Hassan 1977; Koch 1986: 11-24; Hays 1989: 29-32; Van Ruiten 1992; Porter 1997; Allison 2000: 9-13; MacDonald 2000: 8-9; Brodie 2001b: 421-32; Kowalski 2004: 52-65; Brodie 2004: 43-49.

The formulation of criteria shows considerable divergences. For instance, in detecting allusions, Allison (2000: 10-13) uses: the history of interpretation; some shared elements (words; word order; imagery; structure; circumstances), especially if the shared elements are unusual; the prominence of the subtext in the tradition and interest of the later writer. However, Van Ruiten and Kowalski rely considerably on more quantifiable criteria: a quotation is indicated by five words in the same order as the Old Testament; and an allusion by two substantial words. In practice, Van Ruiten and Kowalski are attentive to other factors, so the divergence from Allison is not as great as it may seem.

Significant similarities between the two documents, beyond the range of coincidence. This is the crucial category of evidence. Similarities can include genre, theme, plot/action, pivotal clues, order/sequence, completeness, telltale details, including details of wording. Like a fingerprint, a detail can be very significant. The issue here is not whether some of the evidence is weak, but whether there is enough evidence that is strong. As already mentioned, insistence on what is weak, whether by the one presenting the evidence, or by someone questioning it, obscures the key issue: Is some of the evidence strong—beyond the normal range of coincidence? The debate at times is like that of a courtroom.

Interpretability—or the intelligibility of the differences. Sometimes the differences between the two documents are massive—like the difference between a supermodel in New York and her aged father, a farmer in a small French village, married to a woman from Cameroon. Despite all the differences, the New York supermodel contains the French farmer within herself, but transformed and interwoven with other factors. The issue, then, is not whether there are differences, but whether the differences are intelligible.

The meticulous application of these criteria sometimes leads to the realization that even in the case of texts that are very different, one may be deeply dependent on the other. One contains a transformation of the other, so that the emergence of that transformation, that dependence, brings a sharp surprise. And the gradual emergence of the full extent of these processes of transformation, right across the whole New Testament, begins to open a new world.

This new world is not a passive place. The New Testament authors did not just lie back and, in a process of hearing or re-reading, simply let the Old Testament flow over them. Far more than readers, they are writers, holding sensitive instruments in their hands. They bring to the older text the full apparatus of their sophisticated wide-awake craft, and they generally bring that craft not to isolated quotes but to the texts in their entirety. They are proactive. Some texts they swallow whole, almost; others they distil; or reverse; or adapt in ways that are strange—so that the old cloth become a new thread. And having thus produced something new—the new thread—the active writer does not cease. In a highly complex process, the thread is interwoven with other threads to produce a new text, literally a new *textus*, 'woven' (Latin *texere*, 'to weave'), and the pattern of the weaving can open up a new country. So when the twenty-seven countries are placed together—the twenty-seven books of the New Testament—a whole new continent lies open. The image of a new continent—new at least to me—had already hit me in 1980 when Joseph Fitzmyer's challenging question had driven me into finding for myself what many others already knew—the multiple forms of literary imitation and rewriting. And the image may be adapted. By following the process of New Testament weaving we both see a continent coming into being, and also see it as it emerges into its final shape.

The moment is pivotal. New continents affect people in diverse ways. For some the reshaping of an old text may seem boring. But not to John Keats when he saw what Chapman's translation had done to Homer:

> Then felt I like some watcher of the skies
> When a new planet swims into his ken;
> Or like stout Cortez, when with eagle eyes
> He star'd at the Pacific—and all his men
> Look'd at each other with a wild surmise—
> Silent, upon a peak in Darien.

Not all are so wide-eyed. Some of those with Columbus wanted to go back. And many of those with Alexander the Great, coming to India from the other side, did not want to know anything more. They just wanted to see home again. New continents are unsettling. Just when research into New Testament use of the Old Testament is poised to open its eyes to the vastness and richness of what lies before it, it seems that it is meeting problems. In 2008, while trying to do justice to the Year of Paul, and particularly to some talks I was due to give, I was struggling once more with Paul's use of extended narratives such as those of Abraham and the Exodus, and also with 'the new perspective'—E.P. Sanders's proposal that first-century Judaism was much more positive than the epistles imply[12]—when I came across a passage from N.T. Wright in which he referred to some scholar's 'determination not to see'. Wright is no flyweight. And he measures his words. Besides, it is unusual, in biblical scholarship nowadays, to speak plainly about a negative attitude in another scholar. But there is was: 'It is hard to argue against such determination not to see what is in fact there in the text'.[13]

Part of me understands failure to see. I have done so countless times. But Wright was not talking simply about not seeing. He was talking about determination, about an unwillingness to see that the Pauline writings are engaging large narratives from the Old Testament. Slim chance here of a 'conversion of the imagination'—to adapt Richard Hays's phrase (2005: esp. 10). Then, on the next page, reflecting on what is going on, Wright spoke of an 'unearthing' process that leads to revolution and resistance:

> Paying attention to the underlying narrative structure of Paul's thought, then, is not simply a matter of recognizing the implicit narratives in Paul and drawing out their implication for detailed exegesis. Something much deeper, more revolutionary, is going on when we start to unearth these implicit stories,

---

12. Sanders 1977. For brief discussion, see Horrell 2006: 92-95.
13. N.T. Wright 2005: 10.

and I suspect it is resistance to this element that is currently driving both the resistance to recognizing narratives at all and, more particularly, the increasingly forceful resistance to the 'new perspective'.

Much of my own initial work in unearthing underlying sources had been done by a form of inarticulate instinct, and I have learned slowly that inarticulate instinct does not suffice in communicating how the New Testament was composed. The relationship between texts needs to be spelled out clearly. But Wright's words were a sobering indication that clarity alone would not guarantee smooth sailing. The shipping forecast seems to include storms.

Chapter 15

PAUL'S BIOGRAPHY—INCREASINGLY DIFFICULT:
FORDHAM, THE BRONX, 2008

I had never wanted to write about Paul. Though I had treasured aspects of
the Epistles—passages we memorized as teenagers, inspiring pictures of
wisdom and generosity, the experience of teaching Romans in Trinidad—my
primary interest from the beginning, and especially after linking Matthew
with Deuteronomy in September 1972, was in the Gospels, not the Epistles.
In Trinidad, when I had first begun to write for the public—short columns in
newspapers—and when I wondered if I should ever consider writing something longer, it seemed it would be good to write one book about the basic
meaning of one of the Gospels. Get the essence, and let it connect with life.
Afterwards, as I came to love Genesis more and more, first in Trinidad and
later in the US, I hoped, given time and health, that I would write a commentary on Genesis. But Paul! Too complex to write about. No, leave Paul in
peace, and myself too.

However, as I already recounted, eventually I had no choice. I had to
accept that without the Epistles it was impossible to understand the origin of
the Gospels, and so through a massive shift of interest and energy, I began to
engage the Epistles seriously in the early 1970s. Then I was dragged in
deeper, first into the way the Epistles had used one another, and later into the
way they had used older writings, especially the Greek Old Testament, the
Septuagint. I ended up in a Pauline ocean. The ocean was wonderful, and it
provided further insight into the vast depths underneath the Gospels.

In trying to get a sense of the dynamic among the epistles, it seemed as if
it would be helpful to identify which was written first, and which came
next—like sorting out relationships within a clan or large family. Eventually,
in April–July 1974, the evidence highlighted 1 Corinthians, an epistle that
showed radical dependence on older scriptures, especially Numbers and
Deuteronomy, and that, if not first among the epistles, certainly had a key
role in how other epistles developed. So eventually a line of development
emerged: from 1 Corinthians into a succession of epistles and finally into the
Gospels. The order of succession—the sequence—needed further work, yet it
looked like a reasonable working hypothesis.

But the Pauline ocean also posed a dilemma. If I tried to include a detailed account of the epistles in my presentation of the origin of the New Testament, in the volume I had begun assembling in the late 1990s, I wondered would it be unwieldy.

So when the volume was finally published in 2004—*The Birthing of the New Testament*—the account of the epistles was severely curtailed; it was often relegated to appendices or simply omitted. Paul was again on the sideline.

Effectively it was put on hold for another time. Some day it would surely be possible, first to provide a much more thorough analysis of the sources of 1 Corinthians, and then to give a fuller account of the development of the other epistles. However, as John Lennon said, 'Life is what happens while you are making other plans'. It was difficult amid so many other things to once again summon a primal passion for Paul. A few years went by.

Then in 2005, as already recounted, when we held a conference on the epistles in Limerick, we hoped a later conference would focus on 1 Corinthians, but it was not possible to organize the kind of conference that the problems in 1 Corinthians seemed to need.

However, something else did emerge. While working with Mary T. Brien on the presence of dialectic or dialogue in Romans, I chanced once again to be reading Robert Alter's *Art of Biblical Narrative* and noticed, almost as never before, his chapter on the role of dialogue in Hebrew narrative. Could the central role of dialogue in the Bible's foundational narrative have something to do with the dialogical nature of Romans?

The two seemed planets apart—jagged Hebrew narrative and a magisterial letter to the Romans. One was ancient and distant, a world evoking dusty deserts, the other seemed much closer, and it was regal Mediterranean Rome. But if you laid aside the two elaborate stage settings that clutter our imaginations, and concentrated instead on the texts, it seemed that there was indeed some basic continuity between the two. Something of the very fabric of Hebrew narrative was in the Pauline epistle, something of the actual way of constructing the text.

It eventually became clear that dialogical thinking is not just an occasional feature of Romans. It is a key to its structure. Romans not only has two introductions (1.1-7 and 1.8-15) and two conclusions (15.14-33 and 16.1-27), features already often recognized. The entire body of the Epistle was composed of diptychs or dyads, ten of them, all in two-parts—except for number seven (chs. 9–11) which, with climactic grandeur, consisted of three parts. This diptych (or triptych) structure is not a matter of trivial curiosity. It sets Romans more firmly within the larger biblical tradition, and it provides a clue to its meaning and to emphasis.

8 CE and All That: Research Report at Fordham

By 2008 something else had happened. Some bright spark had calculated that 2008 was the 2000th anniversary of the birth of Paul, and would it not be a great idea to mark the occasion in a really special way? So the Pope had declared the Year of Paul—a twelvemonth period following June 2008—a time in which all those interested in Paul were particularly encouraged to hear and study the epistles.

The year helped to give me fresh energy. I felt a kind of broad support somewhere out there. So I started reading afresh and undertook a number of assignments on Paul: a research report at the meeting of the Catholic Biblical Association of America (CBA) in Fordham; a public lecture here in Limerick, one of a series we organized on Paul; and a two-day series of talks at the Irish College in Rome. And since the designation of the Year of Paul was under way and as it implied a specific date for the beginning of his life, I was drawn back not just to the epistles but to the life behind the epistles, Paul's biography—in effect the quest for the historical Paul.

At first the task may seem easy. We have two main sources: Luke's vivid account of Paul in the Acts of the Apostles (Acts 7.58–8.1, plus most of Acts 9–28); and the collection of thirteen letters or epistles, all bearing Paul's name, and often giving rich detail about him.

Yet the challenge is extremely difficult: first, because the two sets of sources—Acts and the epistles—are often at odds with one another;[1] second, because each source has its own problems. Many researchers see evidence that Luke's account in Acts is historically unreliable. And as for the thirteen epistles, they are so divergent from one another in content and style that the vast majority of investigators cannot accept that they were all written by one person. Among the thirteen, most scholars reckon that Paul probably wrote seven (the first four in the New Testament collection: Romans, 1 and 2 Corinthians, and Galatians; plus three others: 1 Thessalonians, Philippians and Philemon). As for the remaining six (2 Thessalonians, Colossians, Ephesians, and the three to Timothy and Titus), they are ascribed to various elusive authors. So, in this view, seven are from Paul and six are from other writers.

Yet a problem remains. The criteria for distinguishing the seven are unreliable. Some of the seven are as different from one another as the seven are from the six (Horrell 2006: 129). For instance, 'the stylistic difference between 1 Corinthians and 2 Corinthians is far greater than that between, say, Romans and Ephesians, but nobody supposes for that reason that one of them is not by Paul' (N.T. Wright 2005: 19). This is true even of Ferdinand

---

1.   For the differences between the two sets of sources, see Fitzmyer's outline (1990: 79:4-13, esp. p. 1331).

Christian Baur of Tübingen, whose key work appeared in 1845. Though he limited Paul's authorship to just four epistles, those four still included both Corinthian epistles.[2] So who really follows these criteria that in principle nearly everybody accepts? And if scholars are not following these criteria, then what are they following? How much did Paul write? We have the thirteen epistles, an invaluable collection, but how many writers were involved? How much do we know about Paul's life?

For over two centuries researchers have tried to reconstruct Paul's life and work. But the project has not succeeded. In 1996, for instance, Jerome Murphy-O'Connor of the *Ecole Biblique* made a remarkable attempt at reconstructing Paul's life (*Paul: A Critical Life*). Murphy-O'Connor set Paul's birth not at 8 CE, but about 6 BCE.

However, within ten years of Murphy-O'Connor's work, Gregory Tatum, who also now works at the *Ecole Biblique*, could begin his study of Paul with a simple declaration: 'The jigsaw puzzle of Paul's life and thought lies in disarray... Older syntheses of Pauline biography and theology have been demolished by successful critiques' (2006: 1, 3).

So, long before I went to Fordham to give the research report, the building of Paul's biography was already in serious trouble, and the quest for the historical Paul was in danger of obscuring the significance of the body of writings that bear his name.

The words Tatum applied to Paul's biography, 'disarray' and 'demolished', may once have been used of the Bronx also, but not today, and certainly not the green spaces of Fordham, nor the adjacent zoo, one of the world's finest. The place was inviting. On a couple of occasions, over the years, I have pre-pared conference presentations to which nobody came, but for the research report at Fordham, on 3 August 2008, the room was crowded. The procla-mation of the Year of Paul had strengthened interest in the great figure, and people were also drawn by the title, 'The New Testament Use of the Septuagint and the Increasing Difficulty of Writing a Life of Paul'. They already knew that the basic task of writing a life of Paul was in trouble, and they also knew that the picture of Paul was being changed by increasing awareness both of its diverse backgrounds, Jewish and Greek, including its indebtedness to the great narratives and theology of the Greek Old Testament.

However, my focus was not on great narratives, not on theological themes. It was on the way that down-to-earth details concerning Paul are composed on the basis of specific Old Testament texts—details of plot and scene and emotion. The handout that day was extensive—twenty pages, two of them in Greek, with links highlighted in red and blue (red for correspondence of wording, blue for correspondence of content).

---

2.   Cf. Kümmel 1972: 135.

The main links between the texts centred on three moments of Paul's life and work—moments concerning anger, order and travelling as a captive.

Paul's Anger

Colin Powell, former US Secretary of State, once said he liked to rattle people's cages, because seeing someone rattled helps you meet the real person. So when Paul suddenly becomes angry in Galatians and calls the people stupid (literally, 'mind-less', without nous, *a-noetos*, Gal. 3.1) you feel this is the real thing. And when he repeats it a little later the effect is even stronger: 'Are you *so* stupid? (Gal. 3.3). OK, so that's the kind Paul was.

But, as indicated earlier, when you look closely at the text as a unit (Gal. 3.1-3) and, when you reconnoitre in the Old Testament, especially in the Greek version, you find a similar text in Jeremiah, where the great prophet effectively calls the people mindless, and then repeats it with intensified effect (Jer. 5.21, 23). Of course there are huge differences between the texts. In the Old Testament the mindlessness is a failure to respond to nature—first to the sea, and then to the rain (Jer. 5.22, 24). In Galatians the mindlessness concerns a failure to respond to the new message—first to Jesus Christ crucified, and then to the one who gives the Spirit (Gal. 3.1, 4). And so on: the elements of the older text are reflected in the new, but in forms that are variously distilled, updated, and adjusted to the context of the later writing. The overall relationship between the full texts (Jer. 5.21-25; Gal. 3.1-5) is complex and precise.[3] Galatians is not raw emotion. It contains a rehearsed literary adaptation of ancient Jeremiah.

Order: A Crisis Scene in Corinth and the Need for Wise Judges (1 Corinthians 6.1-11)

One of the crises addressed by Paul concerns the lack of justice and *wise judges* within the Corinthian community, and the consequent danger of *losing inheritance* (of not inheriting God's kingdom). The scene looks very real and Paul sounds quite spontaneous. He is using his experience to respond to the Corinthian situation.

However, an examination of the Septuagint reveals a close relationship between the Corinthian scene and the opening scene in Deuteronomy (Deut. 1)—a chapter that begins happily by speaking of the need to choose *wise judges* within the desert community (Deut. 1.9-18) and concludes with failure and *loss of inheritance* (not inheriting God's land; Deut. 1.19-39). The emphasis on inheriting, which frames most of Deuteronomy 1, frames the later part of the Corinthian scene (1 Cor. 6.9-10). And the account of *daring and defeat*, which occurs at the sad conclusion of Deuteronomy 1 (1.40-46),

---

3. I had given some details of the correspondence in *Birthing of the New Testament* (2004) and I used a copy of the relevant page (p. 591) when speaking at Fordham.

finds an equivalent in the frame around the beginning of the Corinthian scene, when Paul refers to *daring and defeat* (1 Cor. 6.1, 7).

There are a whole series of precise links between the texts, and the plot thickens when it emerges that the beginning of Deuteronomy (Deut. 1) is not about something trivial, some bizarre change of fortune which went from goodness to losing the land. It is itself a distillation of the narrative at the beginning of Genesis, when humanity went from goodness to losing its original place with God (Gen. 1.1–4.16). Paul's scene at Corinth emerges as a distillation and adaptation of the dramas surrounding the emergence of God's people, the emergence even of humanity.

The comparison of the texts (Deut. 1 and 1 Cor. 6.1-11) needs about thirty pages, not just these few words. In Fordham we examined both texts in Greek and, at a sharp pace, we made some progress.

The Climactic Journey of the Captive Prisoner: Paul Comes to Rome
The final great drama in Luke–Acts tells in vivid detail of the epoch-making journey whereby prisoner Paul was brought from Caesarea to Rome (Acts 27–28). Adding to the sense of drama is the presence of a first-hand narrator ('We...'). And the worn pages of my beloved *Jerusalem Bible* add a note: 'The precision of the narrative suggests a carefully kept diary'.

The narrative is indeed precise, but the precision does not necessarily come from a diary. It has now been established that the account of the first great adventure of the voyage—the storm and shipwreck (Acts 27.9-41)—is modelled on well-known literary accounts of storms (Robbins 2010).

The focus at Fordham was on the rest of the account—coming ashore in Malta and then going on to Rome—and the brief discussion, again with the Greek in front of us, focused on one fact, namely, the striking similarities between Luke's *finale about the journey that brought Paul to land and on to captivity in Rome* (Acts 27.41–28.31) and the extraordinary Old Testament *finale about how the people were deported from their land and brought to captivity in Babylon* (2 Kgs 25). The sequences of events match one another, except that the episode of the commander with the power of life and death is brought forward in Acts (2 Kgs 25.18-21; Acts 27.42-44), and to significant degree, the events are reversed: what is brutal in the journey to Babylon is matched by kindness on the way to Rome: the commander who kills the prisoners in 2 Kings 25 is matched in Acts by the commander who saves them. And after an account of the Judeans' internal drama (2 Kgs 25.22-26; Acts 28.17-28), both conclude by telling of a prisoner who in fact is free, the king in Babylon, and Paul in Rome (2 Kgs 25.27-30; Acts 28.30-31). Again the texts need prolonged analysis, especially because the account of being brought to Babylon provides just one component of the account of being brought to Rome.

I concluded the talk by looking again both at the three texts (from Gal. 3; 1 Cor. 6; Lk. 27–28) and their unacknowledged indebtedness, and by asking whether they could be used reliably for reconstructing Paul's life.

The questions afterwards included one from Terry Keegan of Providence College concerning the role of coincidence and unconscious recollection, the way in which, for instance, Ronald Reagan, while speaking spontaneously and concentrating on some question he was asked, would give an answer that contained one or more allusions to films.

I did not answer the question well. I was not clear about the key issues of complexity and precision. The relationship between the previously mentioned New Testament texts and the Old Testament is incomparably more complex and precise than the relationship between President Reagan's answers and the films to which he alluded. Highly precise literary complexity is not achieved without careful crafting. Recalling books or films spontaneously does not give the same precision as writing. 'Reading maketh a full man…and writing an exact man', as Francis Bacon once said. The parts of a Mercedes may perhaps be adjusted and shaped to form a particular model of Toyota, but it does not happen simply by juggling the pieces spontaneously, no matter how skilled the juggler. Detailed conscious work is needed. The way the Old Testament is used in Galatians 3, in 1 Corinthians 6, and in Acts 27–28 is incomparably more precise and complex than the way Ronald Reagan used film narrative.

There was an idea too that I had begun to formulate to myself before the talk but had not included clearly in the handout. In the detail of the epistles, adaptation is so pervasive, intricate, and coherent that authorship seems inextricable from the person holding the pen—often not Paul. In 1 Corinthians, for instance, there is an indication that the letter as whole is not actually penned by Paul; he just adds a greeting and his name near the end (1 Cor 16.21). If Paul is not the person holding the pen, then he is not the author.

The situation in crafting an epistle like 1 Corinthians is not like chess, where someone on the sideline can dictate the moves and so effectively play the game from a distance. Rather, it involves a degree of complexity and precision, a degree of inner coordination in the person holding the pen, that, like holding a golf club (or bat/hurley/tennis racquet), the decisive movement of playing must come from within the player, and no mentor can be said to be the main player.[4]

---

4. A similar idea on the inseparability of a specific book's substance from its authorship occurs in K.J. Van Hoozer's analysis of the Fourth Gospel: 'It is difficult to see how the substance of the witness could be preserved if the beloved Disciple were not also responsible for its…finely tuned…form' (2002: 262).

Overall the talk made a reasonable case that increased awareness of the role of the Septuagint adds a new level of difficulty to the task of writing a life of Paul. While much work remains to be done on the epistles' use of the Septuagint, it is clear that the three passages mentioned above from the epistles and Luke cannot be taken at face value in writing a life of Paul. And these three are not an isolated phenomenon. Recent years have seen a steady advance in awareness of the use of the Septuagint in the composing of the New Testament. Overall, this increasing awareness of the use of the Septuagint makes writing a life of Paul extraordinarily difficult.

It was only when I got back to Limerick and started doing further work in preparation for the talks at the Irish College that something much clearer dawned on me. Luke's account of the conversion of Paul (Acts 9.1-30)— which I had previously linked to Damascus-related events in the Elijah–Elisha narrative (2004: 421-35)—seems also to be based strongly on one of the most seminal of all Old Testament texts—the call of Moses (Exod. 2–4). The emergence of the role of Moses strengthened the evidence for what I had presented at Fordham.

Meantime, however, between submitting the title of the Fordham talk in February 2008 and delivering it in August of that year, something further had happened.

Chapter 16

PAUL: THE PENNY FINALLY DROPS

One day in 2008, one beautiful morning in May, as I was walking across the library floor, I was struck out of the blue by the depth of the similarities between the Pauline Epistles and Hebrew narrative. For over twenty-five years I had periodically reread or perused Alter's *Art of Biblical Narrative*, all the time trying to get a better sense of what kind of writing we are dealing with in the Old Testament, and it was with Alter's analysis in mind that I had first wondered if one feature of Old Testament narrative, the role of dialogue, had contributed to what Mary T. Brien had said about Romans' use of dialogue, about dialogical structures and thinking. And the answer seemed to be 'Yes': on the question of dialogue, Romans is somewhat similar to Old Testament narrative. The dialogue in Romans is adapted—it is updated to be more like a philosophical dialogue—yet it is dialogue nonetheless.

But that May morning brought something else. The repeated perusals of my well-marked copy of Alter meant that I knew his chapter headings and some key sentences almost by heart. As I left my office I was not thinking just of dialogue. In fact, I was not thinking of Alter at all. However, as I walked between the rows of books, near where *The Art of Biblical Narrative* was lodged, suddenly almost every chapter of Alter's book connected with the epistles. I turned back, found the book on the shelf, and started checking the table of contents. Yes, yes, yes. Like Hebrew narrative, the epistles are reticent. And composite. And repetitive. And, standing out from the list: like Hebrew narrative, the epistles are historicized fiction.

Historicized fiction.

A mass of data had suddenly fallen into place.

What hit me was that the entire narrative regarding Paul, everything the thirteen epistles say about him or imply—about his life, his work and travels, his character, his sending and receiving of letters, his readers and his relationship to them—all of that was historicized fiction. It was fiction, meaning that the figure of Paul was a work of imagination, but this figure had been historicized—presented in a way that made it look like history, history-like, 'fiction made to resemble the uncertainties of life in history' (Alter 1981: 27).

The idea of composing letters and attributing them to someone else, real or fictitious, is not unique. Examples vary from the fictitious correspondence between Paul and Seneca—a series of letters that were not composed until around 300 CE[1]—to modern letters that are lighter in tone, such as C.S. Lewis's *The Screwtape Letters* (1942), or humorous, such as John B. Keane's *Letters of a Love-hungry Farmer* (1974). The picture of John B. Keane's farmer may be fictitious and humorous, but he is not vague. The love-hungry John Bosco McLane is fully historicized, complete with life-like details. The letters bearing Paul's name are in a different league, but some of the same principles apply. For the sake of communicating a message, it is possible to compose letters that evoke a vibrant character and an epoch-making vision.

So—and this reality took time to sink in—the figure of Paul joined the ranks of so many other figures from the older part of the Bible, figures who, despite the historical details surrounding them, were literary, figures of the imagination.

This did not make these figures without value, any more than the figure of the Good Samaritan on his way from Jerusalem to Jericho is without value. The Good Samaritan represents radical truth concerning a central issue of human existence—how to treat others, especially those who are different. The figure of Paul does likewise, but covers a vast range of issues, virtually encyclopaedic—God, creation, people, relationships, community order, diversity of roles, love, past, future, and death. Many of these subjects are difficult, but the drama surrounding the figure of Paul helps to hold them together and to present them in a way that is unforgettable. The story of Paul, as told in the epistles, encapsulates the essence of Christianity and of human existence. As portrayed *within scripture*, in the epistles—and Acts—the account of his life is inspired and inspiring; 'Paul is a representative figure for all of Christianity' (Martini 2008: 15).

The scriptural account of Paul's life, with its details, from womb to old age, links him both to God and to human existence. Under Jesus, he is presented as someone to be imitated, a central model. 'Everything was given to him [Paul] so that he could be for all peoples a *sign* of the merciful God' (Martini 2008: 24). The scriptural figure of Paul, then, is a permanent treasure, and still not fully fathomed. Alain Badiou, Chair of Philosophy at the *Ecole Normale Supérieur* in Paris, described Paul as a revolutionary thinker whose invention of Christianity weaves diversity of truths together in a way that is still relevant (Badiou 2003).

The idea that that Paul was a literary figure did not remove the possibility that behind the epistles lay one outstanding historical figure who was central

---

1. Cf. Sevenster 1961.

to the inspiring of the epistles, but that is not the figure whom the epistles portray. Under that person's inspiration—or the inspiration of that person plus co-workers—the epistles portray a single individual, Paul, who incorporates in himself and in his teaching a distillation of the age-long drama of God's work on earth.

On that May morning in 2008 in the library the idea that the figure of Paul is literary rather than historical hit me with a shock. It also hit me quite simply as the truth. Yet just then I did not have time to look at the idea closely, to test it more critically, nor would I have the time to incorporate it into the talks I was due to give in the following months. I would have to go ahead with those talks without mentioning it. I felt that to dish it up half baked would be disastrous, but I also knew that, whether I liked it or not, it would impinge on my presentations. When in Rome, for instance, what was I going to say during the ceremony at the traditional site of Paul's martyrdom at Tre Fontane?

Eventually, over a year later, on Saturday, 11 July 2009, I began to check to see if the idea of Paul as a non-historical figure was new, and had to go no further than an article in the *Jerome Biblical Commentary* (1968: 41:7)—a John Kselman article I had read decades ago—to find that 'B[runo] Bauer (1809–1882) removed what historical foundation [D.] Strauss had allowed and left only myth, concluding that Jesus and Paul were non-historical literary fictions'.

Searching further I found that Bauer's stance was largely followed by 'Dutch, German, French and Anglo-Saxon scholars at the end of the nineteenth and the beginning of the twentieth century' (Kümmel 1972: 447), but the methods used by these scholars were very undeveloped and their proposals faded. When Bauer reached his conclusion he had nowhere to go; he

> eventually abandoned academic life to become a farmer (in German, a *Bauer!*); he died a confirmed skeptic, in the words of Albert Schweitzer, 'a pure, modest, and lofty character' (Baird 1992: 278).

More than a century later, at the beginning of 2008, the thesis that Paul was a literary figure was not even an idea, at least for me. Despite Bauer, it had never crossed my mind as a genuine possibility. In fact, the celebration of the Year of Paul made the Apostle more vivid and historical than ever. Yet by 2008 the situation had changed since the days of Bauer. The methods of research had greatly improved, and evidence had been gathering slowly that the epistles are not what they had seemed to be.

* * *

The evidence concerning the epistles and the figure of Paul as literary may be called both direct and circumstantial. Direct evidence comes from the epistles themselves; circumstantial from biblical studies as a whole. All I give here is a minimal outline.

* * *

Paul as a Literary Figure: Direct Evidence—from the Epistles Themselves
(1) *Authorship.* The idea that Paul is not the author of several of the epistles is no longer a minority opinion; it is now widely accepted among scholars. Once the principle is established that Paul's name, plus details about his life, do not necessarily establish the history of Paul, then the road is open for further questions about Paul's history. The situation becomes even more unstable when the criteria (such as content and style) for establishing Pauline authorship are not reliable. And while N.T. Wright (2005: 19) could take is as certain that no one questioned Paul's authorship of 1 or 2 Corinthians, close analysis of the discussion of the need for wise judges (1 Cor. 6.1-11) indicated strongly that in fact Paul was not the actual author of 1 Corinthians. As already mentioned in the previous chapter, the composition of 1 Corinthians is so complex and precise that—like the person holding the golf club—authorship must be granted to the person holding the pen. Adding a signature, as Paul is said to do (1 Cor. 16.21) could not constitute authorship. The picture of adding a signature was another piece of narrative fiction, one that fitted well with the larger fiction of Paul's own life and also with the contemporary convention whereby secretaries often penned epistles that others signed. In other words, the reference to a secretary would seem to be a fiction that brings the epistle into line with the contemporary practice of sometimes using secretaries. And once Paul's authorship of 1 Corinthians goes, Paul's authorship of all the epistles becomes open to question.

(2) *Genre/form/kind/nature.* Identifying the genre or form of a writing is pivotal—what kind of document it is, what is its nature, whether novel, economic report, science fiction, biography—but the process of identifying the genre or nature of the epistles has not been easy; it is a work in progress. For a while in the early twentieth century the documents with Paul's name were being classed with very simple writings, with plain letters. These thirteen documents are indeed dressed broadly in the mantle of ancient letters, like spontaneous letters to specific individuals.

But that mantle of spontaneous simplicity seems interwoven with other features. Under closer scrutiny the documents have emerged as more sophisticated. For instance, in varying ways they use careful rhetoric. Furthermore, the very size of the epistles makes them stand out, and asks if they contain more than normal epistles. On average they are over ten times longer than papyrus letters, and more than two to eight times longer than the sophisti-cated epistles of Seneca and Cicero.[2] They are in a league of their own. If the epistles are in a league of their own, what makes them different? Does some line separate them clearly from the others?

In general it is not easy to draw clear lines between ancient letters. The most basic distinction frequently used is between spontaneous 'letters', which are generally brief, and carefully composed 'epistles', which are like essays. Scholars have also used the term 'letter-essay' or, switching the emphasis to the letter aspect, 'essay-letter' (*Lehrbrief*, 'didactic letter') (Fitzmyer 1992b: 68-69). The Pauline documents are frequently described as 'letters', since they do indeed look spontaneous, but a small minority of scholars hold to 'epistle' because beneath that spontaneous appearance lies something like a meticulously shaped essay, better classified as an epistle. So the Pauline writings have a double identity, and 'epistle' seems the better term because it captures the essence; but 'letter' is important as reflecting the deep connection between the studied epistle and daily spontaneous life, the fierce historicity of now. The Pauline documents have further deep-seated identities insofar as they encapsulate many older forms of writing, and it seems to be this commitment to reinterpreting ancient traditions for a new time that tends to make them stand out.

The basic idea of diverse identities is not new. A single human being can be a combination of several diverse races. And a single writing can be a synthesis of diverse forms or genres of writing. Years ago I visited David Damrosch, when he was working on his doctorate, and one of the things I had learned from him was that Genesis is a synthesis of genres—several forms of writing all blended together. Seneca's letters too involve blending; they are 'essays in disguise'.[3] Likewise the Pauline epistles, but more so. They look like letters, but they are essays in disguise, they are multi-faceted epistles.

(3) *Autobiographical passages.* The epistles' autobiographical passages appear quite spontaneous and realistic, perfect material for a historian. How-ever, comparison with other ancient authors shows that Pauline autobiogra-phy is part of a larger literary practice and that the epistles deliberately use material that appears autobiographical for pedagogical purposes. George Lyons concludes (1985: 171, 224-26):

> Various strands of evidence come together to support the conclusion that Paul presents his 'autobiography' as a paradigm of the gospel of Christian freedom...

2. Average number of words in letters or epistles: papyri, 209; Seneca, 995; Cicero, 295; Pauline epistles, 2495. See Richards 2004: 163.
3. Campbell 1969: back cover.

The function one assigns to Paul's autobiographical remarks affects not only the interpretation of these sections of the letters but profoundly influences the generic conception of, and thus the interpretation of the letters as a whole... The consensus approach to Paul's autobiographical remarks, the hypotheses which sponsor it, and the generally accepted interpretive technique, 'mirror reading', as applied to Galatians and 1 Thessalonians is clearly a failure...

Since we have only Paul's autobiographical remarks and not his opponents' accusations, which the consensus assumes provoked them, it is necessary to exercise restraint in asserting too confidently that specific charges actually existed, much less what they may have been. Even the existence of 'opponents' in the usual sense of the word is far from certain... What he says is determined by his rhetorical approach and not by his opponents' reproaches...

Proper recognition of the rhetorical elements in Paul's autobiographical remarks provides a further challenge to existing approaches, which characteristically reach historical conclusions before the question of literary function has been adequately addressed.

(4) *References about readers/communities.* What is true of Paul's pictures of himself is true also of his pictures of his reader or communities, including his opponents; they are pedagogical rather than historical. For Jean-Noel Aletti (1996: 49), the Pauline letters construct their readers, make them up, from beginning to end: *'Les lettres pauliniennes construissent leur lecteurs, du praescriptum au postscriptum'.*

(5) *References to receiving traditions.* Paul's pictures of himself as receiving various traditions (for instance in 1 Cor. 7.10-16; 11.2, 23; and especially 15.1-8) blend well with conventional pictures about the reception of formal transmission, and at first sight seem to provide evidence of a solidly historical process of transmission. But, as just mentioned, several key historical-looking aspects of the Pauline epistles are not in fact historical: especially the presentation of Paul as author of thirteen epistles; the presentation of the Pauline documents as essentially spontaneous occasional letters; the presentation of Paul's autobiography; and the presentation of Paul's communities and readers. So, given this context, given this widespread imitating of history, it seems appropriate that the references to transmission should be read accordingly: not as historically factual but as imitating history, as history-like. This view is corroborated by close examination of the transmission regarding the appearances of the risen Jesus (1 Cor. 15.1-8). The account of the appearances has such closely studied dependence on the Old Testament, particularly on God's appearance at Sinai (Exod. 19.3b-11) and on the various climactic appearances of Numbers (Num. 11.25; 12.5; 14.10; 16.19; 17.7), that it is best seen not as the spontaneous listing of an eyewitness but as a very careful literary synthesis of older texts.

(6) *References to writings from himself and his readers.* As well as constructing a world of background readers, the Pauline letters also construct a world of background writers or writings. Paul speaks, for instance, of letters or writings to and from the Corinthians (1 Cor. 5.9; 7.1; 16.3; 2 Cor. 2.4; 7.8; 10.10-11). These references expand the drama, but they do not necessarily refer to actual documents. The procedure of referring to such background documents fits into the larger practice whereby ancient writings, including the Hebrew Bible, sometimes referred to other documents for rhetorical purposes, to achieve a certain effect, even if these documents did not exist (Stott 2008: 122, 136).

(7) *Travels.* The travels of Paul are described in ways that reflect older travel accounts—for instance, the bringing of money to Jerusalem (1 Cor. 16.1-4; cf. Bar. 1.6-7), the shipwreck (Acts 27) (see Praeder 1980; Robbins 2010); and the culminating journey, as a prisoner, to the great city (Acts 28 to Rome; cf. 2 Kgs 25 to Babylon). The full extent of how Paul's travels reflect older travel accounts has yet to be investigated.

(8) *Occupation as tent-maker.* The reference to Paul as a tent-maker (Acts 18.3) seems to point to solid history, but, before taking the description at face value, it is necessary first to investigate the literary relationship of the tent-making image to the Septuagint image of the tent and to the image of Paul as architect (1 Cor. 3.10-11). In particular it needs to be taken in conjunction with other references to tents: God spreads out the earth like a tent (Isa. 40.22); tents are given a central role among the people in the desert; and there is also John's later image of the Word as having 'tented among us' (Jn 1.14).

* * *

Paul as a Literary Figure: Circumstantial Evidence, from Biblical Studies as a Whole
(1) *The slow retreat away from historical claims and towards recognizing history-like writing.* As mentioned earlier, in 1909 the Pontifical Biblical Commission effectively held for the historicity of Adam and Eve; it would not accept the strength of the evidence that questioned the literal historical sense of Genesis 1–3 (*RSS*: 122), but in 1943 a papal encyclical (*Divino Afflante spiritu*) emphasized the need to recognize the Bible's literary forms, thus clearing the way for some researchers to express a clearer perception of biblical writings. As late as the 1960s many scholars held for the historical reality of the patriarchs in Genesis, but the work of Thompson (1974) and Van Seters (1975) provided evidence that the account of the patriarchs originated in a later time than had been thought, evidence that the account could not be regarded as historically reliable.

While much biblical narrative may not be historical, it has a powerful history-related aspect; the fiction has been historicized; it has been written in such a way that it resonates with the realities of history and of human experience. It is *like* history, or, as is sometimes said, history-like.

(2) *The slow acceptance of attributed authorship.* It was presumed for centuries that diverse bodies of Old Testament writing had been composed by one author (Moses, Solomon, David, Isaiah), and that these authors were all solidly historical. But gradual research has revealed serious problems about accepting such unity of authorship, and has shown difficulties about establishing their historical reality, especially that of Moses.

(3) *Growing awareness of the literary nature of the Hebrew Bible.* Around 1970 study of the literary nature of the Bible began to flourish, and a variety of scholars were increasingly able to discern the characteristics of the Bible's foundational narratives, especially of much of the long narrative that runs from creation to the fall of Jerusalem (Genesis–Kings, 'the Primary Narrative'). One of these characteristics was historicized fiction.

(4) *Growing awareness of the literary nature of the New Testament.* In recent decades, awareness of the literary features of the New Testament also began to develop, first through redaction criticism, then through the study of narrative and rhetoric. This has already brought a fresh sense of the nature of some New Testament writings. Mark, for instance, has gone from being regarded as unliterary, clumsy, to being recognized as literary, as carefully composed.

(5) *Incipient awareness of the continuity between the Old Testament and the New Testament.* The sense of continuity between the Old Testament and the New Testament is as old as Christianity, but it suffered a severe setback in the twentieth century—Bultmann, for instance, had little time for it—and it was only towards the end of the century that it began to recover, as it did for instance through increased awareness of the role of the Septuagint, of Paul's adaptation of Old Testament theological narrative, and of the systematic detailed use of specific Old Testament texts. Once the awareness of the deep affinity between the Testaments begins to develop, it is just a matter of time before the link between the two, instead of seeping through slowly, comes flooding in. And with it comes the question of whether, like Hebrew narrative, the thirteen Pauline epistles are historicized fiction—except that, whereas Alter spoke of historicized *prose* fiction (1981: 23-46, esp. 24), we are now faced with historicized *epistolary* fiction.

The idea seems valid, but it needs prolonged testing, by someone else. It particularly needs a systematic comparison between the elements of Hebrew narrative artistry—as listed by Alter and others—and the art of the Pauline epistles.

* * *

Outline of a Working Hypothesis

The production of the thirteen epistles bearing Paul's name may, perhaps, have drawn special inspiration from one individual, but, if so, that individual's name and history are probably irretrievable, and the available evidence indicates rather that the thirteen epistles came not from one person but from some form of group or school. This accords partly with occasional suggestions about a possible Pauline school and with the view that 'Paul's letters were not an individual enterprise'—E.E. Ellis.[4] The attribution of authorship to someone other than the actual author follows a practice of pseudonymity that was particularly common in antiquity and that has ample biblical precedent, especially in the attribution of diverse bodies of writing to Moses, David and Solomon.

A key purpose in composing the epistles with Paul's name was to build a new Moses, a figure who, like Moses of old, would bring God's word to the people, in Paul's case to *all* the people, and would do so in a form that showed God's word as continuing creation into a new phase, into a new creation. In doing this they followed ancient methods of composition. They reshaped existing writings, especially the scriptures—with which they saw themselves in continuity—and particularly the scriptures pertaining to Moses. But instead of using prose narrative, they used letter writing (epistolography), and in doing so brought the composition of epistles to a new level. Yet they

---

4. See Ellis 1993: 183 and 188-89: 'In Acts and the Pauline letters some one hundred individuals, under a score of titles and activities, are associated with the apostle at one time or another during his ministry. They are participants in his preaching and teaching and in his writing, and they define the apostle's work as a "collaborative ministry"...'

'The total number of Paul's co-workers has been placed at ninety-five...or eighty-one...depending on how broadly one defines the term. When the names mentioned only in Acts and those with unspecified or general relationships to Paul are eliminated, thirty-six coworkers under nine designations can be identified with considerable probability' (opening paragraphs, p. 183). 'Given the numerous and varied contributions of Paul's fellow ministers to his mission, it is clear that they were an essential factor in its accomplishments and that even *Paul's letters were not an individual enterprise*. These missioners indeed deserve the considered attention of students of Paul. For it does not detract from his greatness to bring into greater prominence those with whom he served, those he was glad to praise and call his co-workers' (concluding paragraph, p. 188, emphasis added).

did not lose the force of ancient narrative; the epistles were written in such a way that they told powerful narratives concerning God and concerning the new Moses—Paul.

Moses is not the only Old Testament character reflected in Paul. So, for instance, are much later characters such as Tobit and Daniel.[5] In fact Paul has been called 'a Danielic figure'.[6] But Moses is central. And Ezra, a second Moses, provides a framing role.[7]

The tone for the epistles' rewriting process would seem to have been set by the *Logia*, the brief arrangement of sayings, now found within Matthew 5 and 11, which consisted largely of a distillation of Deuteronomy, the last great book of Moses, but which also included a systematic reflecting of Ben Sirach.[8]

First Corinthians played a key foundational role. The writers of the epistles were aware of one another, and in diverse ways, while each built something new, they also built on one another.

The figure of Paul was built up not only by the epistle writers, but also by Luke. And in a striking addition, Paul's name was connected to further places, monuments and events—a variation on the process by which the Roman Empire used architecture and iconography to communicate its message, a message that included the foundational epic in Virgil's *Aeneid*.[9]

5. Brodie 2004: 595-604.
6. Gladd 2008: 268.
7. Initial research indicates that Ezra–Nehemiah, originally one book, has been distilled to form a frame for 1 Corinthians. This research is taking place within the SBL Seminar on the Transformation and Weaving of Scripture in Paul.
8. Brodie 2004: 109-24.
9. Palmer Bonz 2000: 62-64. See Geiger 2009.

Chapter 17

A MARGINAL JEW: RETHINKING THE HISTORICAL JESUS—
THE MONUMENTAL WORK OF JOHN P. MEIER

During the simmering years surrounding the American Revolution, between the publishing of the French *Encyclopédie* (1751–72) and the outbreak of the Revolution in France, an author in Germany drip-fed to the public some 'fragments' from the unpublished work of a cautious scholar, designated '*An Anonymous Writer*', who had died a few years earlier. The work turned out to be that of Hermann Samuel Reimarus, a noted philosopher, and a professor of Hebrew and Oriental languages, who had died in Hamburg, on 1 March 1768.

The *Fragmente* may have been limited and late, but, once arrived, they stayed. Reimarus maintained that the original historical Jesus was a failed revolutionary, and from Reimarus developed the classic 'quest for the historical Jesus', a project that reached a crescendo in 1906 when, as we saw already, Albert Schweitzer reviewed the entire undertaking and effectively concluded that it was mission impossible.

The project seemed to have petered out, yet as the twentieth century went on, and especially during the 1950s, the fire reignited ('the Second Quest') and has now been building to a further crescendo ('the Third Quest'), above all in the work of John P. Meier, of Notre Dame University, Indiana. Meier's work is not one volume, but several, appearing in 1991, 1994 and 2001, and when he was asked at the Fordham meeting when the next volume would be out, he replied 2009.

And after that?

'Five books were enough for Moses', he said lightly, 'so they should be enough for me'.

Since then the 2009 volume has duly appeared, another mighty tome. The fifth volume will focus on Jesus' final days.

The essential purpose of this present book is not to engage in polemic but simply to try to communicate the truth as I see it. However, if I am to maintain that the figure of Christ needs to be radically reinterpreted, then I need to address the work of great scholars such as John Meier, N.T. Wright,

James Dunn, A.-J. Levine, Sean Freyne, John Dominic Crossan, Gerd Theissen, and many others, who in varying degrees still seek to rebuild the biblical figure of Christ into a specific historical individual. So, when I focus on John Meier it is in acknowledgment both of Meier himself and of the many others. It seems right to highlight Meier because his work on the historical Jesus is among the most well known, and it is the most voluminous.

If the first four volumes of John Meier's *Marginal Jew* are a reliable indication of the final fifth volume, then regardless of what Meier may claim, the ultimate judgment on his quest will have to be the same as that of Albert Schweitzer: mission impossible. The impossibility of the quest does not mean that the five volumes will lack value. They contain huge information and commentary on biblical-related matters of the first century—an achievement far greater than I could do. But on the central issue of reconstructing one individual life, they try to do what cannot be done.

* * *

Marginal Jew has two key problems. First, like many other studies, it uses an unreal compass—oral tradition. By relying unduly on form critics of the 1920s and later, it assumes that the Gospels are something that they are not, namely, that they reflect oral traditions that go back to Jesus, back to about the year 30 CE (*Marginal Jew*: I, 41). At no stage, despite several references to oral tradition, does *Marginal Jew* stand back and examine closely how we know such tradition existed. Rather, backed by Josephus, it starts with an early claim that Jesus existed (I, 68), and with the essential answer to the whole inquiry thus in place, it needs something to fill the gap of about forty years between Jesus and the Gospels. And since oral communication is basic to humans—even more so in antiquity—it seems wonderfully plausible to fill the gap with oral communication, which is then turned into the idea of oral tradition. As we saw already, it is an idea that badly needs a funeral.

The second fundamental problem in *Marginal Jew* is that it largely bypasses Rule One of historical investigation, the priority of the literary aspect, and as a result misreads the origin and nature of its main sources—the Gospels. It does not do justice either to where the Gospel text came from (especially its traceable literary sources), nor to what it is and where it is going (to how the sources—the raw materials—have been shaped into sophisticated literary writings). And the reality is that the shaping of those sources is guided by considerations of literary and theological artistry that do not need the figure of Jesus to be historical; in themselves they are independent of the life of Jesus.

At first sight *Marginal Jew* does seem alert to the literary aspect of the task. It quickly acknowledges the principle of incorporating contemporary literary criticism (I, 12), and it sometimes traces links between texts. But the

engagement is brief. At no stage does it stand back and consider systematically the possible lessons that might be learned from the way in which the
great writers of the ancient world composed—how they rewrote existing
texts, and how they chiselled their own works into powerful art. There are
over three hundred pages on Jesus' competitors (III, 289-613), but not one
complete paragraph on Homer or Virgil, the two mountains who dominated
the world's literary landscape, including the Gospels. Without a clear handle
on the Gospels, it is impossible to get a handle on Jesus.

Imagining Connections: *Unreliable Criteria*

The two key problems in *Marginal Jew*—reliance on oral tradition, and
inadequate engagement with literary features—lead to further problems, first
concerning criteria.

The presumption that the gospels are based on oral tradition with all its
possible unreliability leads to a delicate operation of trying to decide what is
historical, and so, especially from the 1950s onwards, some form critics
sought to formulate criteria of historicity. *A Marginal Jew* relies on such
criteria, and despite its judicious approach, these criteria are problematic.

Two such criteria, for instance, include 'contradiction' and 'discontinuity:'
if something in the Gospel is seriously out of line with what is said elsewhere
in the Gospels or Epistles, then the reason for including it must be very
strong, must be due to its reality in history, in the life of Jesus. But there is a
problem here. Contradiction and discontinuity are integral parts of a biblical
literary artistry that, from Genesis to the epistles, is pervaded by multiple
forms of dialogue and dialectic. In Genesis 1–2, for instance, humankind is
shown first as image of God, then as made of clay (Gen. 1.26; 2.7); first as
ruling the earth, then as serving it (Gen. 1.28; 2.5, *abad* in Hebrew, literally
'serve', rather than 'till').

A further criterion ('multiple attestation') is the occurrence of some
features in several diverse documents of the New Testament (e.g. Mark,
John, Paul). If these documents are independent of one another, then the
points on which they agree would seem to be historically reliable. But again
there is a problem. Despite the huge differences between them, the documents are not independent of one another. They were written within the
context of a world of rewriting and transformation, and, as I have partly
indicated elsewhere (especially in *Birthing of the New Testament*), detailed
comparison shows that they built on one another. Other suggested criteria are
equally vulnerable.

* * *

Did Jesus Model Himself on Elijah?

Unawareness of the nature of the literary connections between texts causes particular confusion when *Marginal Jew* deals with the similarities between the gospels and the Elijah–Elisha narrative. The similarities are sufficiently strong that *Marginal Jew* concludes that Jesus understood himself as standing in the line of Elijah and Elisha. However, when the full detail of the links between the texts are examined, the essential conclusion is about a relationship between two texts: the evangelists, especially Luke and Mark, used the Elijah–Elisha Narrative as one component of their Gospels. This is the explanation that accounts for the data. To claim that Jesus modelled his life on Elijah or Elisha may be a very welcome idea, but it goes beyond the evidence. It is not reliable history.

The problem is seen more closely in the claim that Jesus' way of calling disciples reflects a historical trait. The reasons for this claim are that the call involves a distinctively sharp command, such as 'Follow me', and it is backed by texts that are independent of one another—independent witnesses (Mk 1.16-20; Mt. 8.21-22; and Lk. 9.61-62; *Marginal Jew*: III, 48-54). But the claim to the independence of the texts depends on a particular theory of the relationship between the Gospels, a theory featuring documents called Q and L. An alternative theory, more complex but more solidly grounded, shows that these texts depend on one another (Brodie 2004: esp. 162, 198), and once the links are traced, the independence disappears.

As for the distinctively authoritative command, it not only reflects Elijah's authoritative call of Elisha (1 Kgs 19.19-21; cf. *Marginal Jew*: III, 48); it is also a variation on the command-and-compliance pattern at the beginning of the Elijah account (1 Kgs 17.1-16). 'This "command and compliance" pattern is common not only in the Elijah stories but elsewhere in the Hebrew Bible as well' (Walsh 1996: 228). In fact, it adapts the pattern of command-and compliance that occurs both at creation (Gen. 1) and in the call of Abraham (Gen. 12.1-5; cf. Brodie 2000: 31-46). So, Jesus' style of calling disciples, his calm authoritative command, is patterned as a continuation of God's way of creating the world. What the Gospels show is continuity in the portrayals of the Creator, Elijah and Jesus. The conclusion that accounts for the data is literary: the portrait of Jesus is modelled ultimately on that of the Creator. To claim an individual history behind the text goes beyond the data. Elsewhere, Meier expresses the principle (*Marginal Jew*: I, 67):

> A basic rule of method is that, all things being equal, the simplest explanation that also covers the largest amount of data is to be preferred.

In this instance, the simplest explanation that accounts for the data is that the evangelists adapted the biblical figure of Elijah to draw the picture of Jesus.

Explaining the data does not require invoking the historical existence of Jesus. The explanation that suffices without invoking Jesus' historical existence is the simplest, therefore, in respect for a basic rule of method, it is to be preferred.

* * *

Was Jesus a Carpenter?
Sceptics See Only the Carpenter/Woodcutter

The Markan picture of Jesus' visit to Nazareth (Mk 6.1-6) provides another example of the need to take account of the literary background. The scene portrays a stark failure of recognition; the people do not recognize Jesus for who he truly is, but their disparaging reference to him as a *tektōn*, 'carpenter' or 'woodcutter' (Mk 6.3; cf. Mt. 13.55), may seem to provide solid historical information that 'Jesus spent…years…plying the trade of a woodworker' (*Marginal Jew*: I, 278-85, esp. 284).

However, the visit to Nazareth occurs in the context of Jesus' miracles, miracles related to creation, life and death (Mk 4.35–5.43), and this whole section of Mark has significant literary dependence on the (Septuagintal) book of Wisdom. Beginning in Wisdom 10, several chapters of the book of Wisdom speak of both God's role as creator and life-giver and of the failure of many people to recognize God as the true *technités*, the supreme craftsman (Wis. 13.1; cf. Wis. 13.22, wisdom is *technités panton*, 'the worker of all things'). Instead these people's vision is limited to the kind of vision found in the woodcutter (the *tektōn*, Wis. 13.11); that is all they can see.

In other words, the mindless people in Wis. 13.1-9 do not recognize the *technités*, the supreme craftsman, and turn their minds instead to lifeless things such as the *tektōn* produces (Wis. 13.10–14.4). And the audience at Nazareth do not recognize the presence of the Creator in Jesus the miracle-worker but can focus only on the world of woodcutting, and so they call him a *tektōn*.

Wisdom 13, particularly its account of people failing to discern the Creator and of seeing only the works of a *tektōn*, provides an adequate explanation for Mark's use of *tektōn*; it accounts fully for Mark's data. In essence: once the literary connection is seen, the historical explanation is unnecessary; it goes beyond what is needed to explain the data.

These two examples of historical claims concerning Jesus—that he was like Elijah, and that he was a woodcutter—show the perils of not taking adequate account of the literary background. What follows from the evidence is that the Gospel texts that portray Jesus as like Elijah and as a woodcutter were based systematically on texts from the Greek scriptures. To claim more than that is to go beyond the evidence.

The same phenomenon of dependence on the Old Testament pervades all the Gospels and Acts. It will take decades to spell out all the details, but sufficient evidence is already in place that it is no longer plausible to base claims to the historical Jesus on the Gospels or Acts.

* * *

Josephus (37–c. 100): What Did he Say, and Where Did he Get it?

Even if the Gospels or Acts do not provide a reliable claim to the historical Jesus, perhaps some other document does. Perhaps there are independent witnesses, people who, without relying on the biblical texts, bear witness to the existence and life of Jesus.

In the case of Joseph, for instance, the biblical account of his life in Pharaoh's Egypt is extraordinary, but outside the Bible he is never mentioned. Likewise, Moses. Is Jesus different?

There are in fact a number of extra-biblical writers, one Jewish and four Greco-Roman, who refer in diverse ways to Jesus, and who do not say that they get their information from the Gospels or Acts. So do we have five independent witnesses? The four Greco-Romans do not write until the second century, but the Jewish writer, Josephus, is earlier and belongs to the first. For John Meier (*Marginal Jew*: I, 68) the testimony of Josephus is 'of monumental importance':

> In my conversations with newspaper writers and book editors who have asked at various times to write about the historical Jesus, almost invariably the first question that arises is: But can you prove he existed? If I may reformulate that sweeping question into a more focused one, 'Is there extra-biblical evidence in the first century A.D. for Jesus' existence?' then I believe, thanks to Josephus, that the answer is yes.

This conclusion is indeed important. An independent witness—independent of Christians and the New Testament—would be invaluable. So in assessing this conclusion it is good to pause in some way. Therefore, with a prayer to heaven, along with many saints and scholars, and also to Agatha Christie, Hercule Poirot, Sherlock Holmes, and Watson, it is appropriate to turn aside as it were, and sit out in the evening with a leisurely drink to see how the conclusion was reached. This presentation will be brief, but the discussion can continue afterwards.

References to the first volume of *A Marginal Jew* are hereafter abbreviated to *MJ* plus page number(s).

It is good to begin at the beginning. Apart from the New Testament, the clearest statements concerning the existence of Jesus come from Flavius Josephus, generally referred to as Josephus. He was born within the heart of institutional Judaism, into the family of high priests and kings descended from the legendary Mattathias, defender of the temple, inspirer and father of the revolutionary Maccabees. By birthright a priest, well-educated in Jerusalem, his full name was Joseph ben Mattathias, and, having led a Jewish delegation to Rome at age twenty-seven to try to negotiate with Nero, he later became a general in Galilee during the revolt against Rome—the disastrous Jewish War that destroyed the temple (70 CE). But he was captured, received patronage from the emperors who bore the general name of Flavius, and so changed his name to Flavius Josephus, was given imperial quarters in Rome, and there, for about thirty years (c. 70–100), he lived and wrote. He wrote, first all, about that deadly war and his own role in it, *The Jewish War*; and having got that out of his system, he then settled down for about fifteen years to writing an encyclopaedic 20-volume history of the Jewish people, from the beginning—*Antiquities* (completed 94 CE). Both books refer to Jesus, the *War* once, the *Antiquities* twice.

Josephus's references to Jesus have two problems: first, authenticity—do they really come from Josephus or were they inserted in his text by some later Christian writer(s)? And second, even if the references are authentic Josephus, where did he get the information? Is he an independent witness, or is his information derived directly or indirectly from Christians or from some of the New Testament writings?

Did Josephus Write the Three References to Jesus?

The reference in the first work, *The Jewish War*, is missing in most manuscripts, and is a mixture of passages from the Gospels and from material of the kind found in the later apocrypha. Virtually all researchers agree that it does not come from Josephus.

The two references in *Antiquities* occur towards the end of the 20-volume work, in Books 18 and 20, about two hundred pages apart. *Antiquities* 18.63-64 has a distinctive paragraph—sometimes called Josephus's *Testimonium*, 'Witness' (or *Testimonium Flavianum*)—that first summarizes the character and work of Jesus, and then tells that he was accused, crucified under Pilate, and that he still has a following, the Christians. In the course of this summary it refers at diverse points to at least three extraordinary features of Jesus: he should perhaps be called more than a man; he was the Christ; and he reappeared on the third day as the prophets had foretold.

The further reference in *Antiquities* (20.200) is very brief, when, in order to identify a certain James, Josephus adds that he was 'the brother of Jesus who was called the Christ'.

Regarding the first reference, the distinctive *Testimonium*, there are three opinions: it is all original, all written by Josephus; it is all an insertion, placed there by a later Christian writer; and, it is a mixture of original and insertion.

MJ excludes the first two options: it cannot all be from Josephus; the statement that Jesus was the Christ, the Messiah, was 'something Josephus the Jew could never affirm' (*MJ*: 60); nor can it all be a Christian insertion, because the later passing reference (in Book 20) to 'Jesus who was called Christ' seems to presuppose an earlier reference; 'some earlier reference to Jesus becomes a priori likely' (*MJ*: 62). For *MJ*, the best explanation is the mixture theory: Josephus did indeed write a distinctive paragraph on Jesus, but it did not contain the three most extraordinary features: Jesus was perhaps more than a man; he was the Christ; and he appeared after his death. *MJ* suggests that if these three features are omitted, the paragraph is a very pragmatic summary of Jesus, such as a Jewish historian might write, and it flows well; 'the flow of thought is clear' (*MJ*: 60).

MJ's conclusion may not be the last word, but it forms a reasonable working hypothesis that Josephus did write some of the distinctive paragraph about Jesus now found in copies of *Antiquities*, and it permits us to move on to the next question.

Is the Witness of Josephus Independent?

MJ (67-68) lists five possible sources Josephus may have used in composing his *Testimonium* about Jesus:

1. Christians, especially Jewish Christians, encountered in Palestine or Rome.
2. Some New Testament writings, especially the Gospels.
3. Imperial archives, which could have been available to Josephus in Rome.
4. Educated Judeans within Josephus's partly Romanized world.
5. Information obtained in Palestine before the Jewish war.

The challenge for the investigator is to establish with as much certainty as possible which one(s) of these five provided information to Josephus. In practice, this means trying to match Josephus' information with one or more of the five. The more the information matches a source, the more likely it is that that is the source Josephus used.

There is no perfect match. The ideal would have been a verbatim quotation, with an explicit reference to a specific source, preferably a verifiable written source. Josephus did not give that, so rather than establish complete certainty, the aim is to get something approaching certainly, or at least a strong degree of probability.

Given the lack of absolute certainty, *MJ*'s initial conclusion (68) is that 'all opinions on the question of Josephus' source remain equally possible because they remain equally unverifiable'—a judgment that seems to refer to all five. So, all are 'equally possible'. The process by which *MJ* moves from that initial conclusion to a final conclusion is essentially as follows:

In seeking to match Josephus with the five possible sources, *MJ* focuses on two basic features—language and content. What do these tell us about the likelihood that Josephus used one or other of the five sources?

Did Josephus get information from some New Testament writings? *MJ*'s discussion is minimal: New Testament *language is different* from that of Josephus, and so, concludes *MJ*: Josephus did not draw on a New Testament writing (*MJ* 67).

Did Josephus get information from Christians? *MJ*'s basic argument is clear: Christian belief is defined by the resurrection, but Josephus' account of Jesus omits the resurrection, therefore Josephus did not get his account of Jesus from Christians. Under scrutiny, this argument becomes elusive. To begin with, insofar as Josephus tells of Jesus reappearing on the third day, he *does* in fact mention the resurrection, and it is *MJ*'s reconstruction of Josephus' text that omits it. However, it is probably not necessary to become entangled in the details of this aspect of the debate.[1]

Once Christians and New Testament writings are out of the running, the way is clear for saying that Josephus's evidence is independent of Christian sources. And so, as *MJ* sees it, Josephus emerges as an independent witness for the existence and life of Jesus (*MJ*: 68-69). Since *MJ* has already declared that 'all [five] opinions on the question of Josephus' source remain equally possible' there is no problem in assuming that Josephus drew his independent witness from one or more of the three remaining possible sources—Roman

---

1. *MJ* 67-68 gives three statements: (1) 'It is possible that Josephus had known some Christian Jews in Palestine before the Jewish War; it is even more likely that Josephus had met or heard about Christians after taking up residence in Rome'.

(2) Since Josephus's text does not mention Christians' defining belief, the resurrection, it is 'doubtful [that there was] any direct oral Christian source for the *Testimonium*'.

(3) While Jesus was 'a marginal Jew...[Josephus was] a more prominent Jew...in no way connected with this marginal Jew's followers'.

The separation of Josephus from Christians becomes more difficult because Josephus's text *does* mention the defining belief, but, in reconstructing the *Testimonium*, *MJ* includes the reference to the resurrection as among the three phrases that 'strike one as obviously Christian' and so they are removed (*MJ*, 60). Thus, distinctively Christian features are removed from the text, and then a conclusion is drawn that the text is not from any Christian source. This puts *MJ*'s hypothesis about the original shape of the *Testimonium* under strain. It is dangerously close to removing the peacock's feathers and then conclud-ing that the resulting creature is not a peacock. However, *MJ* also argues from the *flow* of the reconstructed text. Flow is often a matter of style, and assessment of style can be very personal, subjective. Whoever first assembled the present text of the *Testimonium* must have thought it flowed reasonably well. Still, it is useful to stay with *MJ*'s reconstruction of Josephus's words as a working hypothesis.

archives, educated Judeans from the Romanized world, and pre-war Palestine. These three sources sound rich—they sound varied and potentially deep—so the idea that they supply independent evidence seems plausible.

While granting in principle that these three sources (or similar sources) may be independent, it is appropriate to look carefully at what they tell us. Independent witnesses generally add *something* new to what is already known. In speaking of Pilate, for instance, Josephus adds considerably to what is otherwise known. Historians of Jesus yearn to hear what he was like before Christians started seeing him through resurrection-tinted spectacles, and before the evangelists started writing accounts directed to building faith. The likelihood of gaining new information is all the greater because the matter under investigation is not one incident but a person's entire life, and because, like Jesus, Josephus at one stage was particularly associated with Galilee. So what do these sources tell us that is not already in the Gospels or Acts? What do they tell us that bears out independence?

Nothing.

Josephus's account of Jesus mentions no new person or place or significant episode, nor even an insignificant episode, not even one line or angle or detail about some episode already known, nor any saying about anything. Everything that *Antiquities* says about Jesus is found in some form in the Gospels and Acts. The only thing that is new is the presentation—Josephus's own distinctive vocabulary and style.

The failure of these non-Christian sources to provide information that is new does not completely exclude them as witnesses. It may have just happened that what they say is not new. But it makes their claims sufficiently fragile that it is appropriate to come back to the factor that *MJ* skims over— the possible dependence of Josephus on one or more of the evangelists.

As already mentioned, the main reason for deciding that Josephus did not have access to any New Testament writing is language: 'The language of the *Testimonium* is not markedly that of the New Testament' (*MJ* 67). This is very true. Like many authors, Josephus had his own distinct language, and no matter what sources he uses—and in the course of writing *Antiquities* he used dozens of diverse sources—he almost invariably adapted them to his own style and his own language. Besides, in the wider ancient practice of rewriting sources, verbatim quotation was an exception. And so, the variation in language proves precisely nothing.

Thus the question still stands whether Josephus might have known about the work of the evangelists. It is easy to imagine that he did not:

> [Jesus was] a marginal Jew in a marginal province of the Roman Empire, [but Josephus was] a prominent Jew of the 1st century in no way connected with this marginal Jew's followers. (*MJ*: 68)

This could leave the impression that Josephus was separated from both Jesus and his followers by the breadth and depth of the Roman Empire. However, three factors suggest a certain closeness of Josephus to some of the evangelists or their works.

(1) *General literary context.* First and most obviously, Josephus and the evangelists were writers. They belonged to the small percentage of the population that were literate, and to the much smaller group that engaged seriously in writing significant works and in having their works read by others. They were not enclosed in small worlds. Josephus drew widely on all kinds of writings. *Antiquities* absorbed everything from Homer, Hesiod and Herodotus to tragedy, philosophy and romantic motifs from Xenophon and Hellenistic novels. And, like most other writers of his day, he presented these materials through the medium of his own distinctive language and style.

Furthermore, Josephus and the evangelists were both engaged not only in writings and publishing, but essentially in the same field of writing—in diverse modifications and updatings of the Jewish scriptures. Thus while *Antiquities* uses many sources, it particularly builds on the traditional Jewish scriptures. And Luke–Acts is written as a continuation of the ancient Jewish scriptures (Sterling 1992: 363). And like Josephus, Luke too was a form of wide-ranging historian who went back to the beginning of things. Curiously, the *Testimonium* has affinities to some of the speeches concerning Jesus in the first half of Acts. In fact, the overall affinities between Josephus and Luke–Acts are so strong that researchers claim that one depends on the other, and, while the direction of dependence is debated, the two literary works do seem somehow intertwined.[2] Luke in turn had access to Mark, and Mark also was in continuity with the ancient scriptures (see esp. Winn 2010). In others words, given the link of older scriptures with New Testament narrative, it makes sense that the *Antiquities* that built so carefully on the older scriptures should also acknowledge New Testament narrative.

(2) *Specific content.* Josephus is significantly close to the content of some New Testament writings. What Josephus' *Antiquities* says about Jesus is like a summary of aspects of Mark and of some of Luke–Acts. The idea of summarizing a scripture-related text would not be new to Josephus. Much of the first half of *Antiquities* is 'a paraphrase of the Bible' (Mason 2000: 737), so summarizing a lesser, scripture-related, source would make sense. Mark's clear statements that Jesus was the brother of James (Mk 6.3) and was recognized as Christ (Mk 1.1; 8.30; 14.62) would provide the basic elements

---

2. Mason 2003: 251-95, reviews the evidence and concludes that Luke–Acts uses Josephus. Mason does not discuss the possible role of Proto-Luke.

for the reference to James as 'the brother of Jesus who was called the Christ' (*Ant.* 20.200). The main difference is one of language and adaptation to his own vocabulary, style and purposes.

(3) *Location and time.* Even if Josephus never acquired copies of the Gospels or Acts, he lived in Rome for about thirty years within walking distance of a Christian community that, by most estimates, had the works of at least some of the evangelists. And even if Josephus never saw the actual texts—though he was given to texts—it would seem that he could easily have discussed their contents with the Christians, many of whom, like himself, were Judeans living in Rome, far from their original homeland.

To look at the situation more closely, it is often reckoned, for instance, that Mark's Gospel was written in Rome around 70 CE, and *Antiquities* was composed in the decade or two preceding 94 CE, also in Rome. And regardless of when and where Mark was written, it had not been kept in seclusion. Copies of Mark were available to Matthew and Luke, wherever they lived, and so under normal circumstances they should also have been available to Josephus, who had the habit and means for consulting books, especially those related to the ancient Jewish scripture. The heart of the matter is that, as far as we know, he lived for years in the same city as Mark, within walking distance.

It is not necessary to insist that, like Matthew or Luke, Josephus had a copy of Mark. And it is not necessary to say exactly what form of access, if any, he may have had to Mark. Maybe Mark was written elsewhere, at another time. Nor is it necessary to disentangle his relationship to Acts.

What is important in the present context is the availability of a relatively simple working hypothesis: Josephus the writer, in accord with his general practice of adapting sources, especially scripture and scripture-related sources, knew enough about the writings of at least two specific New Testament authors, authors to whom in various ways he seems to have been close, that he could adapt and summarize what they had said, and so could make reference to Jesus.

This hypothesis may not be as detailed as one would like, but it is at least as strong as the hypothesis that appeals to an undefined mix of three sources that are vague—Jesus-related imperial records that may never have existed; unspecified educated Judeans; and a pre-war career in Palestine—sources that, as well as being vague, do not provide one solitary item of fresh information about Jesus.

What is certain is that it is extremely risky to conclude that Josephus did not have access, direct or indirect, either to serious discussion with some Christians or to some of the work of the evangelists, so it is not possible, *in any reliable way*, to invoke Josephus as an independent witness to Jesus. Unreliable witness cannot be used to condemn someone to death. And neither can it be used to assert that someone lived.

* * *

References to Jesus in Greco-Roman Sources

References to Jesus occur in four Greco-Roman authors writing in the second century:

- Tacitus (writing c. 115 CE)
- Suetonius (shortly before 120)
- Pliny the Younger (c. 112)
- Lucian of Samosata (c. 115–200, date of writing unknown).

Among these, the strongest reference occurs in Tacitus (*Annals* 15.44):

> Nero…punished with…cruelty, a class of men, loathed for their vices, whom the common people [the *vulgus*] styled Christians. Christus, the founder of the name, had undergone the death penalty in the reign of Tiberius, by sentence of the procurator Pontius Pilate (Loeb translation).

The information is minimal and negative: the Christians' founder was Christ, executed by Pilate, in the time of Tiberius—the kind of information that would have been commonplace, or that could have been distilled or inferred from the work of Josephus, written twenty years earlier. One of Tacitus's general methods was to use older writings, and while doing so, to adapt them to his own style; 'he rarely quotes verbatim'.[3] At a time when some of the Gospels were decades old, basic contact with Christians would have yielded such information.

As for Suetonius, Pliny and Lucian, they 'are often quoted in this regard, but in effect they are simply reporting something about what early Christians say or do; they cannot be said to supply us with independent witness to Jesus himself' (*Marginal Jew*: I, 91).

Conclusion Regarding the Five Non-Christian Authors

Of the five writers frequently cited as independent witnesses to Jesus, none ever met him; none said they met anyone who had met him; or said they met anyone who had known someone who had met him. None gives a piece of information that is not already found in some form in the Gospels or Acts. And Josephus, the only one who may have given a significant amount of such

---

3. Charlesworth and Townsend 1970: 1035.

overlapping information, lived for decades in Rome within walking distance of a Christian community that in all probability had access to material from the evangelists. Consequently, none of these five provides reliably independent witness to the existence of Jesus.

General Conclusion Regarding A Marginal Jew

Meier's *Marginal Jew* provides valuable background information for New Testament times and for several features of the New Testament itself. Yet, while his work is vastly different from that of Renan's fabled *Life of Jesus* (1863), it shares with Renan a key problem: it can leave the impression that knowledge of background provides knowledge of Jesus.[4] But background knowledge, whether of Renan's kind or of John Meier's kind, does not constitute information about Jesus. And neither do other forms of background knowledge—for instance, about the history, sociology, economy, and archaeology of the Holy Land and of burial sites. Nothing can compensate for inadequate examination of the basic literary features of the primary written sources.

The root problem underlying *A Marginal Jew* is reflected on page one. The fantasy scholarly conclave that is to deal with the historicity of Jesus, 'a Catholic, a Protestant, a Jew, and an agnostic—all honest historians cognizant of first-century religious movements—[are]…locked up in the bowels of the Harvard Divinity School library'. The Harvard Divinity School library is a very fine place, but if you are locked into it, you never reach some of the surrounding libraries that would provide a wider truer picture, particularly concerning first-century literature, of which the New Testament is a part, as is Josephus.

General Conclusion Regarding the Nature of the
Gospels, Acts and Epistles

The main New Testament documents look historical but are not. Most Epistles appear to be spontaneous letters, responses to specific historical occasions by one main figure. However, detailed examination of these epistles reveals a degree of complexity and precision, both in their sources and final shape, that places them in the category or genre not of spontaneous letters but of *formal epistles* which, partly as a way of reaching people, have been dressed in the clothing of spontaneous letters to specific historical communities and occasions.

---

4. See Neill and Wright 1988: 207-208.

The gospels and Acts likewise are dressed partly to be history-like; they imitate history. As with any writing they do indeed reflect something of their historical background, and especially something of early Christianity, but a mass of literary data—about their use of sources, and about their art, including their form/genre—indicates that they are not history.

The history-like way of presenting the New Testament documents is not simply to reach people. It is an expression of the conviction that God is in human life, in the fiercely specific reality of history, even in events as horrendous as the crucifixion. But rather than present history as it sometimes appears on the outside, as one damn thing after another, the New Testament writers, like great artists, went for the heart of the matter, and then, having secured the centre, presented it to historical people in a historical way.

This conclusion—that the Epistles and Gospels are history-like but not historical—is the simplest explanation that accounts for the data, and again to quote Meier (*Marginal Jew*: I, 67): 'A basic rule of method is that, all things being equal, the simplest explanation that also covers the largest amount of data is to be preferred'.

Part V

GLIMMERS OF SHADOWED BEAUTY

Some steps towards clarifying
Christianity's origin and meaning

Chapter 18

BACKGROUNDS OF CHRISTIANITY:
RELIGIONS, EMPIRES, AND JUDAISM

Luke's account of Christian origins is vivid—a clear strong line from Jerusalem to Rome, from the opening description of how, 'in the days of Herod king of Judea', an aged priest called Zechariah was worshipping in the temple, in the centre of traditional Judaism (Lk. 1.5), to the closing report that 'Paul spent...two years...proclaiming the kingdom of God' in the capital city of the great new empire (Acts 28.30-31). The account is *so* vivid that when it begins to fade, and for me it faded dramatically in the 1970s, it is difficult to put something in its place. Yet, the question is insistent: How did Christianity begin? To answer, it seems best to step back first and look at the larger picture.

1. *Religions: The Elusiveness of Ancient Religious Origins*

The origins of most religions as old as Christianity are obscure. Hinduism proper is generally said to have developed in India around 1500 BCE, but to a degree that is unknown it may have drawn on the residue of the older Indus Valley civilization which began about a thousand years earlier and which in turn was engaged in trade with the civilizations of Egypt and especially of Mesopotamia. Hindu scriptures are reckoned to have first flourished between 1400 and 400 BCE, but amid the complex history there is no clear evidence of an individual founder.

Buddhism owes much to Hinduism and in addition claims an individual founder, Siddharta Gautama, known as the One who is Enlightened (or Awakened, 'the Buddha'), said to have lived in northeast India. However, the documents recounting the narrative of Siddharta's life are late, and while his birth is often dated to around 560 BCE, the actual calculations concerning his dates vary by sixty years or more.[1] There is an unresolved tension:

---

1. See Bechert 2004: esp. 82: 'Traditional dates of the...decease of the Buddha... range widely from 2420 B.C.E. to 290 B.C.E.'

Most scholars working in the field at present are convinced of the existence of the historical Gautama. The general consensus was well expressed by the great Belgian Buddhologist, Etienne Lamotte, who noted that 'Buddhism would remain inexplicable if one did not place at its beginning a strong personality who was its founder'... But at the same time scholars are aware that the available tests provide little information about the details of Gautama's life...

Can we go beyond [a] very generalized portrait of the historical Buddha towards a fuller biography? Lamotte has advised caution, observing...that writing the life of the historical Gautama is a 'hopeless enterprise'.[2]

The problems around Moses are equally great, and becoming greater. The broad problems are not just about Moses himself but about the history that surrounds him:

Forty years ago...a history of Israel began either with the Patriarchs (Abraham, Isaac, and Jacob) or with the coming into being of Israel as a tribal confederacy in ancient Palestine in the thirteenth century BCE...

Today...the burning question has become whether it is possible to proceed by following the biblical outline. The main reason is that recent archaeological work has indicated that the kingdoms of Israel, Moab, Ammon, and Edom did not become established until the ninth century BCE, with Judah following suit a century later (Rogerson 2006: 268-69).

As for Moses himself:

We can say little for certain about the historical Moses—not even when he lived. Biblical chronology places his birth ca. 1520 BCE (Exod 7.7; 1 Kings 6.1), but few critical scholars would endorse so early a date. Moreover, Moses' life story consists largely of stereotypical narrative widely paralleled in world literature....

More than one scholar has observed that, were there no tradition of a Moses, we would have to posit his existence anyway. Israelite religion...seems a deliberate innovation not a natural outgrowth. As there was a Muhammed, a Paul, a Jesus, a Zoroaster, and a Buddha, so there must have been a Moses. But because our written traditions are so much later, it is impossible to distinguish his teachings from those of his followers (Propp 2000: 921).

A major difficulty in identifying individuals in antiquity was the tendency among authors to remain anonymous, or use a pseudonym. This was particularly strong in Jewish writing. We have no idea, for instance, who wrote Genesis, one of the most foundational books in history, and opinions have varied hugely—from the ancient attribution to Moses, to the proposal by Harold Bloom, the impish Yale literary critic, that the main author was an unknown woman. It is possible that Hinduism, Buddhism, Judaism and Christianity each had one decisive guiding historical figure at its founding, but these are not the figures that the religions highlight. The founders,

---

2. Reynolds and Hallisley 2005: esp. 1061-62.

whether one or many, would have known the religions they were founding were incomparably bigger than themselves. And so, in the biblical case, what they put forward was not themselves but the figures of Moses, Paul and Jesus, figures who best encapsulated the truth that they, the historical founders, had experienced. As with the authorship of Genesis, it may well remain impossible to identify the historical founder(s) of Christianity. Certainly for the moment it does not seem possible. The names of the authors of the New Testament writings are largely hidden, and perhaps other leaders were similarly reticent about revealing their identity. It may indeed seem easy to move from clear New Testament statements about various people to making strong historical claims, but the problems surrounding the hypothesis of an historical Paul are very sobering.

Yet, whatever the difficulty of pinning down individual founders of Christianity, it is possible at least to clarify aspects of the larger picture.

* * *

2. *Empires and Threads of Unity*

The Mediterranean Sea…stretching from the Atlantic Ocean on the west to Asia on the east, separates Europe from Africa. It has often been called the incubator of Western civilization (Weigend 2003: 307).

Long before Christianity began, the known world of the biblical writers had experienced factors that tended to bring people towards unity. The Stoics, for instance, founded in Athens around 300 BCE, preached the essential unity of humankind (Bikerman 1972: 215). Stoics had not gone away in the first century, and were not some marginal club. They were greatly influenced by prestigious Socrates, their world-view was of a universe permeated by God's Reason (*Logos*), and they included central figures of the Roman regime, among them Cicero and Seneca, both of whom had written epistles (Spencer 2000: 1252). Paul is pictured as meeting Stoics in Athens (Acts 17.18), and if he had arrived in Rome in 61 CE, as is often suggested, he would have found Seneca trying to manage both young Nero and the Empire.

Furthermore, some sense of unity was implicit in three great political and cultural waves. The first was the Persian Empire (c. 550–330)—so vast it encompassed all the old empires of Mesopotamia, and all the other lands from northern Greece and Egypt to the River Indus; so co-ordinated, especially through its Aramaic-speaking civil service, it brought communication to a new level; and so humane that it also achieved a new degree of respect for diverse peoples. The Persians, ancestors of today's Iranians, helped the Judeans rebuild Jerusalem; and they also helped the Greeks rebuild Athens— though Athens was outside the Persian Empire and had fought them.

The second wave was the Greek cultural blossoming, an advance so great, proportionately, on so many fronts—philosophy, mathematics, art, architecture, natural science, literature, drama, medicine—that the like has almost never been equalled. The Greeks, with their god, Zeus, and his son Hercules (Heracles), were scattered far and wide, and they dominated the culture of the known world—first during the days of the Persian Empire, effectively the Greco-Persian Empire; and then again, with political and military backing, during what is called the Greek or 'Hellenistic' Era—the three-century period (around 330 to 31 BCE) inaugurated by all-conquering Alexander, the man who 'Greeced' the world.

The third wave was the Roman Empire, the power which absorbed and transformed the culture and religion of the Greeks and of the Near East, and which included effective means of travel and communication, plus the widespread use of a plain form of Greek, *koine*, 'common'—a language not as imposing as older Classical Greek, but very effective.

For a while it was not clear whether the Roman impetus towards conquest and unity would continue. On the day Julius Caesar was assassinated (15 March, 44 BCE)—part of a growing tendency to internal feuding—it may have seemed that the Roman Republic could not hold together. But Caesar's last will and testament revealed that he had adopted his eighteen-year-old grandnephew, Octavian, who then received the name Caesar and later the title Augustus, 'revered one'—the Caesar Augustus from whom, according to Luke, 'a decree went forth that the whole world be enrolled' (Lk. 2.1). 'Whole world' may be overstated, yet one thing is sure; Octavian meant business. He eliminated people with apparent ease, including eloquent Cicero, and young Ptolemy Caesar—born of Cleopatra and Julius Caesar—whom he had persuaded to return from his place of refuge in India. But he also steadied Rome, first as a general in the civil war that followed the assassination and in the decisive battle that ended the post-Alexander Hellenistic Age as a political and military force (Actium, 31 BCE), and later as commander, *imperator*. While keeping many of the trappings of the old Roman republic, Octavian centralized power, *imperator* became emperor, and in this new empire Caesar Augustus ruled for 45 years (31 BCE–14 CE). Furthermore, the Empire continued in his dynasty, first with his stepson, Tiberius (14–37), and then with Caligula, Claudius and Nero, until, following a year of turmoil, a second strong dynasty emerged, the three Flavians (69–96), two of them battle-hardened—Vespasian and his son, Titus, plus a further son, Domitian, who regarded himself as the new Augustus. When the Empire required it, Vespasian, still a soldier, could be transferred without a problem from brutally suppressing opposition in Britain to addressing a rebellion in the Middle East. The third imperial dynasty, which lasted almost a century, was dominated by 'the five good emperors', among them Marcus Aurelius, a

Stoic philosopher and author of the classic *Meditations*, written while on campaign. But long before Marcus Aurelius, the Empire had surrounded the entire Mediterranean, the only time in history that the Mediterranean has been under one rule. Octavian had introduced the concept of the *Pax Romana*, and, in one way or another, for about two centuries, the idea stayed.

* * *

3. *Christianity's Immediate Background: Judaism—Diverse and Dispersed*

Christianity emerged from Judaism, but if Jesus and Paul are essentially literary or symbolic rather than historical, it is not clear how that emergence happened. One thing is certain: all had not been well within Judaism. In particular, the centre was in trouble. The organizational core of the priesthood, namely the high priesthood, had become meshed in the worldly Hasmonean dynasty—often one of the roughest games in town. Such a high-priesthood could not avoid being divided, and there was no Octavian-like figure to step into the centre and pull it all together. Yet the divisions within Judaism were not all negative:

> Whereas it was once thought that there was a single 'mainstream' or 'normative' Judaism, it is now clear that Judaism was richly pluriform. There were a variety of parties and a wide variety of views on any number of subjects, and no particular group held full authority in teaching or practice over the others though the Jerusalem priests probably held the strongest claim to the average people's loyalty (Ulrich 2000: 328).

The diversity included the shifting arrangements that ruled the home region and juggled the high-priesthood. It also included diverse groups or movements, including the Sadducees, Hasideans, Pharisees, and Essenes.[3]

---

3. *The Sadducees* formed the Jewish party that stayed closest to home, so to speak. Their name probably derived from the ancient priest Zadok (1 Kgs 2.35). They emerged around 100 BCE, and while associated with the priesthood they were not identified with it; they included members of the lay aristocracy. Conservative not only in politics but also in religion, their scripture consisted essentially of just five books, the Torah or Law of Moses with its cultic rules, and they rejected later ideas—especially the doctrines that were associated with the claim to an ancient oral tradition.

The Hasideans consisted of devout Judeans who were likewise dedicated to the Torah. But while they had first supported the idealism of the Maccabean revolt (1 Macc. 2.42), they changed their minds when the idealism turned to harsh politics (see Fitzmyer 1992a: 96).

The Pharisees were probably partly inspired and formed by the Hasideans, and, even more than the Hasideans, they put distance between themselves and some of the established centres of power. They deliberately stood out. Their name, Pharisees, means

The diversity was seen also in Herod (Herod the Great, c. 74–4 BCE), not an ethnic Judean originally, but descended from a noble Idumean/Edomite family that had converted to Judaism. At twenty-six he had been appointed governor of Galilee, and he proved effective. A few years later, not long after Caesar's assassination, he had gone to Rome to seek help, and at a meeting of Octavian, Antony, and the senate, he was nominated somewhat surprisingly as King of Judea. And when he left the senate he was flanked by Octavian and Antony, the two most powerful men in the known world, Octavian ruling the west, Antony the east.[4]

Later, in the war leading to Actium, Herod backed Antony against Octavian, but soon after Actium, when Antony and Cleopatra had committed suicide, Herod went boldly to victorious Octavian on the island of Rhodes,

---

the 'separated ones'. They too were dedicated to the Mosaic Torah, but they interpreted the Torah on the basis of an oral tradition that they claimed went back to 'the fathers' or 'elders'. The invoking of the oral tradition meant that the Law could be adapted in diverse ways—partly towards burdensome obligations, but also towards 'doctrines such as personal immortality, judgement after death, the resurrection, and the existence of angels' (Harrington 1965b: 21). In many ways they enabled Judaism and the Law to survive. The strength of their adherence to the Law gave them a clear profile, and they put distance between themselves and the Maccabee-based dynasty. They also put distance between themselves and the Sadducees: 'In general the Pharisees belonged to the middle classes, the Sadducees to the wealthy priestly aristocracy. The Pharisees claimed the authority of piety and learning, the Sadducees that of blood and position; the Pharisees were progressive, the Sadducees conservative; the Pharisees strove to raise the religious standards of the masses, the Sadducees were chiefly concerned with temple administration and ritual, and kept themselves aloof from the masses' (Pfeiffer 1963: 56). The Pharisees were no small group. They numbered 6000 according to Josephus and had a strong popular following, and their conflict with the Sadducees was not some side issue. 'It was due partly to the conflict of Sadducees and Pharisees that the Judeans eventually lost their political independence: the appeal of both parties to Rome led to Pompey's intervention in 63 BC' (Harrington 1965b: 22). Apparently both groups were strongly represented in Jewish councils. Luke depicts the two as forming an acrimonious Sanhedrin, divided on a number of issues, especially the resurrection of the dead (Acts 22.30–23.11). The Pharisees looked forward to the messiah and the coming of God's rule.

The Essenes may have overlapped with the Hasideans, and were like the Pharisees in that they believed it was necessary to put distance between themselves and the Jerusalem priesthood. But the Essenes also put physical distance between themselves and Jerusalem itself. It was they apparently who went into the desert near the Dead Sea and there, at Qumran, built a community that, like the Pharisees, was inspired strongly by the Jewish scriptures, including expectation of the messiah, and according to Josephus (*Ant.* 15.10.4 par. 371) followed 'a way of life taught to Greeks by Pythagoras' (cf. Fitzmyer 1992a: 53, 97). The Qumran community defined themselves as the New Covenant. For them, 'New' meant a community that was restricted to Judeans and faithful to the Mosaic Law.

For extensive discussion of Jewish groups, see Meier 2001: III, 289-613.

4.   Josephus, *Ant.* 14.379-88.

stood before him, and fully acknowledged his own former allegiance to Antony. Once again, as during Herod's Senate appearance in Rome, Octavian was impressed. He reinstated Herod as King of Judea, and later added to his territories.

Within the proportions of his own world, Herod was somewhat like Octavian; his long rule (effectively 37–4 BCE) brought stability and generated a form of dynasty. But unlike the case of Octavian, the challenge proved too much, especially for the dynasty that followed him.

Amid all the divisions, Herod tried to build bridges. He already had the Romans on his side, and to connect himself to the traditional Maccabee-related dynasty, the Hasmoneans, he divorced his first wife and married Mariamne, a Hasmonean princess.

He also built literally. Not even Solomon in all his glory reshaped the landscape as did Herod, building on an awesome scale, and in one famous instance, *rebuilding*. The most prestigious structure in the land, the temple, was already about five hundred years old in Herod's time, but, beginning around 20 BCE, Herod so rebuilt it that it became know as Herod's Temple. It was spectacular. It must have seemed that Herod's building plan would help to solve a problem. Many Judeans had suffered intense cultural pressure from the dominant Greeks, and to some degree from other Judeans who were Greek sympathizers. Even the temple had been through rough times, and had suffered the forcible installation of a statue of Zeus (167 BCE). Now the temple was being rebuilt as never before, and the rebuilding process was done sensitively, in cooperation with the priests, to ensure the full round of services was maintained. Somewhere in the reconstruction, as the new temple began to emerge, some people, priests and Levites must have been gaining fresh heart for the future.

But serious problems persisted. When Mariamne's teenage brother, the high priest, began to look popular, Herod had him drowned in a swimming pool. Some years later, Herod was manipulated by his own sister into executing Mariamne, whom he loved, and for months he lived in depression, often calling her name. Other executions were more calculated, including those of three of his sons.

Besides, the problem of relating well with the outside world would not go away. Herod might reassure the Roman authorities, and the new temple might reassure many Judeans, but the deeper issue was cultural and religious. Judaism's relationship to the larger world remained unresolved. The Maccabean ancestors of the Hasmonean dynasty had fought fiercely against Hellenization, yet in the experience of many Judeans, particularly those in the vast Jewish Diaspora across the Empire, the Greek-speakers were almost everywhere. Directly or indirectly some of them had heard of the Greek version of the Scriptures, and had become attentive to the Judeans and their God—had become 'god-fearers'. Some Judeans in turn had become aware that many Greek-speakers, at diverse levels of society, had effectively developed a form of faith. Besides, God's blessing at creation was for all people, and the call of Abraham was likewise to bring blessing to all (Gen. 1.28; 12.3). There had to be some openness to the Gentiles, 'the Greeks'.

Herod had been relaxed about these things. On the day in Rome when, as King of Judea, he had walked out of the Senate with Octavian on one side and Antony on the other, he kept on walking with an imposing procession to the Capitoline Hill to offer sacrifice to Jupiter (Jove), otherwise known as Zeus.

Philo of Alexandria (c. 20 BCE–50 CE) bridged the gap in a different way. He often used allegorical interpretation to blend Judaism with Greek philosophy, and he was supremely attentive to the spiritual journey of the human individual.[5] Philo was not some neglected recluse. As already mentioned, when the massive Judean community in Alexandria wanted someone to head a political delegation to Rome around 40 CE to complain to Caligula about hostile riots, Philo was their man. People knew Philo and what he stood for. He was thoroughly Hellenized, but he was also a loyal Judean.

Herod may have maintained a form of peace, and Philo may have bridged aspects of the gap between Judean and Gentile, but certain tensions remained, especially between the compromised priesthood and groups such as the Pharisees and Essenes that sought some kind of new beginning, and there was tension also between Roman government and Judean aspirations. The governorship of Pontius Pilate (26–36 CE), for instance, has been described by Philo and Josephus as offensive, cruel and corrupt.[6]

In the early summer of 66 CE a quarrel about a field ignited the tension between Judeans and Romans, and against all odds, the Judeans revolted. Eventually Nero assigned his most experienced general, Vespasian (Flavius Vespasianus), from Britain to Judea. Vespasian's progress was interrupted—as he was about to invade Judea he was acclaimed emperor—but the following year, 70 CE, his son, Titus (Flavius Titus), approached Jerusalem with four legions, and slowly and systematically overwhelmed the hungry city. Resistance continued for a few years in some places, last of all near the Dead Sea, in isolated Masada, but by then the issue was decided. On 9 August 70 CE, the Temple was overtaken and destroyed by fire. The remains of the Temple were used in later centuries to build palaces, a Temple of Jupiter, a Church, and—the project that finally flattened it—the Dome of the Rock (around 690). Meanwhile, even in 70, even as the Temple was being destroyed, Vespasian was planning a different kind of building—the Colosseum.

---

5. Hay 2000: 1052.
6. Cheney 2000: 1058.

The destroying of the temple meant that for Judaism the institutional centre was not merely in trouble; it was gone, and with it the traditional priesthood—a numbing moment for many, but for others a time to build something new. According to one opinion Judean sages and writers regrouped near the sea shore at Jamnia, a few miles south of Jaffa, and, with considerable help from the Pharisees, clarified which books were regarded as sacred, and they also initiated the process of building a further formulation for the future—the Mishnah (meaning both 'teaching' and 'recapitulation'), a collection of rabbinical traditions and interpretations. Completed around 200 CE, it was about twice as long as the New Testament, and was based not on history-like narratives and history-like epistles but on topics, somewhat like a systematic book of instruction. The Mishnah in turn was elaborated until about 600 CE into the Talmud (literally, 'study'), a multi-volume production which developed in two diverse forms—the Babylonian and the Palestinian—and which has inspired much subsequent Jewish thought, writing and poetry.

Chapter 19

CHRISTIAN ORIGINS: WRITING AS ONE KEY

Not all Judeans followed the writing tradition often associated with Jamnia. Instead, some developed and followed the tradition of a new Joshua, *Iēsous*— the way that eventually led to the New Testament. It is not clear what sparked this development—what inspired those at the origins of Christianity. A colleague has suggested that they too were responding to the fall of the temple. Certainly the temple's demise had a major effect: 'More than any other single action, it was the destruction of the Temple of Jerusalem…in 70 CE… that activated the slow…transformation of religion to which we owe, among other things, European culture' (Stroumsa 2009: 63). And Lloyd Gaston (1970), for instance, has long indicated the significance of the fall of the temple *for the Gospels*. But a theory that set the fall of the temple at the very origins of Christianity would have to deal with difficulties about dating, particularly the dating of the early epistles. So, while granting a role to the fall of the temple, it would seem a role should also be given to the inspirations and divisions that existed within Judaism prior to 70 CE.

One thing is certain: when the final story is told there will be a special role for the process of writing. Many reconstructions of Christian origins have pictured the process of writing the books of the New Testament as late and loose—decades after Jesus is said to have lived, and without direct links between the various writers and writings. And the process of tying the books together in what is now called the New Testament has been seen as not happening until considerably later.

However, in several human movements a process of writing comes early and is carefully developed. It would probably be worthwhile to check the nature and role of the process of writing in various events—the roles perhaps of the Magna Carta, Luther's theses, the Spanish *Salmanticences*, the French *Encyclopédie* in relation to the French Revolution, the US Constitution, the Communist Manifesto, the Irish 1916 Easter Proclamation of independence, plus, more recently, the role of tape recordings and the internet—but what is certain is that, while the Jewish people became known as the People of the Book, the Christians became de facto the primary developers of the codex, the bound book which replaced scrolls, and which, whatever its origin, emerged energetically about the same time as Christianity.

In any case, regardless of what may have happened around various other events and the codex, there is significant evidence that writing, coordinated writing, had an important role in the founding of Christianity. I will mention six points:

1. Christianity was founded significantly on a process of rewriting.
2. The rewriting indicates coordination—a group or school.
3. The existence of other schools gives support to the idea of a New Testament school/group.
4. The scholarly linking of biblical books with schools gives further support to the idea of a New Testament school.
5. The quest for the sequence of the books.
6. The truth of writing.

Christianity as Founded Significantly on a Process of Rewriting

In Christianity, as in any religion, two of most central elements are its story (the narrative or *mythos* that links it to the divine) and its institutions (how it organizes itself from day to day around specific people) (McGrath 2009: 23-25). The story revolves essentially around Christ Jesus, and to a lesser degree around other characters, especially Paul. The institutions include baptism, Sunday observance, Eucharist, a liturgical calendar that hinges especially on Easter, a human network that serves people, and the congregating of people in communities of various sizes and forms.

When Christianity began, these basic elements—the narrative and institutions—had a certain newness. But they were not fully new. To a large degree they were an adaptation of the narrative and institutions of Judaism.

First, the narrative. I will not labour the details. To some degree, the principle was already present in St Augustine: 'The New is latent in the Old and the Old is revealed in the New'. And along with many others, I have begun to show the increasing evidence that the New Testament portrayal of Paul is modelled significantly on the Old Testament picture of Moses, and that the portrayal of Jesus is largely a synthesis of the Old Testament account of God and of all that God does, often through people. The evidence is not complete, but it is already sufficient, and as each year of research now passes, the degree of continuity between the two becomes clearer, slowly.

Second, as regards the institutions:

> The central elements of Christianity in their entirety, including the eucharist, the cross and the system of excommunication, are directly derived from Jewish sects of the most traditional type claiming to represent the renewal of the true Covenant, especially in Galilee (Nodet and Taylor 1998: 437).

Such are the basic facts, along with the fact of the existence of Christians themselves and the evidence of their lives.

So the starting point for the history of Christianity is as follows. The story/narrative and institutions of Christianity are an adaptation of the story and institutions of Judaism. But the leading figures in the story, Jesus and Paul, were not the originators either of the story or institutions. Rather, the account of them is modelled on the old story in such a way—complete, complex, detailed, artistic—that they emerge as scriptural figures formed by others. So, who were the others? Who was the person or persons at the origin of Christianity? What event(s)?

* * *

The Rewriting Indicates Coordination—A Group or School

The first major evidence concerning the origin of Christianity comes not so much from what the New Testament says—otherwise we would begin Christianity with the angel Gabriel—but from what the New Testament is, and what it does. Essentially it consists of twenty-seven writings that, despite many differences, are all rooted, directly or indirectly, in the Old Testament, and are also variously *rooted in one another.* The connection to the Old Testament is important and is being increasingly acknowledged, but, in tracing the origin of Christianity, the connection *between the New Testament documents themselves* is particularly decisive.

The central fact is as follows: the connections of the writings to one another are so many and so deep that as they were being written, the writers generally must have had access to those already written. They built on one another. Most researchers, for instance, would now say there is solid evidence that Matthew and Luke used Mark, and that there is some form of borrowing, direct or indirect, between Matthew and Luke. That is the easy part—rewriting that calls out for investigation. But given the growing awareness of the complex ways in which ancient texts were often transformed, and given calm and clear patience on the part of researchers in applying tested criteria for establishing literary transformation and dependence, the connections begin to emerge. The evidence is not as precise as in scientific connections—for example, connections made through DNA—but overall a critical portion of it is already traceable.

As the pattern of connection becomes clearer so does a basic conclusion: Christianity was founded not just by one or two people but by a whole group. It is possible that the group drew much of its inspiration from one or two key figures, but, contrary to most modern practice, ancient biblical writers often maintained anonymity or a pseudonym, and it seems unlikely that we will ever know much about individual leaders. What we can do, however, is try to get a sense of the nature of the group.

The evidence indicates that the group formed or contained some kind of school or writing community, diverse people who were in communication with one another. This seems to be the only explanation that accounts for both the diversity and coordination of the twenty-seven documents. The easiest explanation is that the group was centred in one place, but the group could also have been scattered. Communications were good, and ancient books could be produced and circulated efficiently (Alexander 1998: 71-105).

The same group or school must also have been involved in the transformation of the institutions. As a general principle, in the composition of a religion, narrative and institutions are inextricably connected, and the narrative has a certain precedence at one level over the institutions. In fact, the reshaping of the Old Testament institutions is in line with the reshaping of the Old Testament scriptural narrative, and to some degree is best seen as following from it.

Conclusion: Christianity, insofar as it was a new religion, was founded by a school of writers, or more likely by a religious community many of whose members were writers.[1] The process of writing was probably interwoven with specific events and/or religious experiences—a matter that needs urgent research.[2]

This emphasis on writing is not new. Others have already reached similar conclusions. 'Scribes are the main figures behind biblical tradition. In fact, we owe them the Bible, the entire Bible' (Lipiński 1988: 157). 'Written prophecy is not secondary [to spoken prophecy]... The Old Testament had writers who were genuinely prophetic' (Utzschneider 1989: 17). Furthermore, the emphasis on writings is also indicated briefly by Australia's John N. Collins. As partly indicated earlier, when Collins is explaining Luke's preface, and the meaning of the reference to those involved with the word (the *autoptai*—often translated as eyewitnesses—and *hypēretai*, ministers, of the *logos*, Lk. 1.2), he reads Luke as referring to a literary process and to writers sanctioned by the community:

> Literary compositions have prompted Luke to plan and compose another one, which now lies before Theophilus.
> The subject matter of the earlier writings constitutes the tradition which is central to the community out of which Luke is writing. He projects a keen awareness of the communal dimension of the activity, 'us' occurring twice,

---

1. Richard Bauckham (1998: 44) arguing from a different basis, reaches a somewhat similar conclusion: 'The early Christian movement was a network of communities in constant communication with each other, by messengers, letters, and movements of leaders and teachers—moreover, a network around which Christian literature circulated easily, quickly, and widely'.

2. See Johnson 1998; Schneiders 1998; note the critical assessment of Larry Hurtado's hypothesis in Fletcher-Louis 2009.

and all the activity being in-house. Two stages are apparent, which implies a considerable number of years: the writing of the narrative about the affairs of the community (1.1) and the reception of the narratives within the community through the agency of the *autoptai* and *hypēretai* of the *logos* (1.2). The reception of the narratives is an extension of the literary activity which produces them, and was itself literary: the narratives had to be read aloud to the community...

Luke...opens and closes the narrative by explicitly engaging the literary tradition of Judaism... This web is by no means of Luke's own contriving. Long before Luke, Paul had evidenced his own need to draw upon the literary treasures of Israel for an understanding of the new dispensation... [In addition,] the *autoptai*...and *hypēretai*...have responsibility for the library of the community, receiving and authenticating documents of the tradition. They are highly literate and have received their appointments from the community. They fill precisely the role Bauckham selected for his 'specially authorized guarantors of the traditions' (Collins 2010: 451-52).

The idea that a specific school of writers underlies a group of biblical books is not new. However, before speaking of it, it is good to look at the larger picture, namely, the presence in the ancient world of several such schools, of several communities with a writing component.

* * *

The Existence of Other Schools Gives Support to the Idea of a New Testament School/Group

The lands of the Bible were at the crossroads of where writing was invented, and were next to the place that later invented the alphabet. It is no accident that in time the Jewish people became known as the People of the Book. They were never far from the world of writing. And writers generally were not far from other writers; they did not work in isolation.[3] The process of learning was so slow and the technology so specialized and cumbersome—finding manuscripts and materials, copying manuscripts one by one—that writers worked best in situations of cooperation such as libraries or schools.

As archaeologists have long realized, some of the libraries were remarkable. Even the oldest libraries, containing cuneiform scripts, were far-seeing:

These libraries [in Babylonia, Nineveh, Ebla, Ugarit, etc.] tried to collect most of the technical, legal, and literary texts known in their times (history, astronomy, religion, myths, etc.) so that they could be easily consulted; eventually catalogues of the titles of the texts were compiled to make consultation easier (Lemaire 1992: 1004).

---

3.   On schools and communication in antiquity, see Brodie 2004: xxxi, 63-75.

Ancient Egyptian libraries, with writing in hieroglyphic script, were sometimes located near temples, though of course the most famous Egyptian library, at Alexandria, was on the sea shore. Jewish libraries have not survived, apart from Qumran, which—despite its closeness to Masada, further down the coast of the Dead Sea—escaped the attention of the Romans (Lemaire 1992: 1004-1005).

Regarding schools, the best documented are those of the widespread Hellenistic system. Much of the research on this system has been done by Alan Culpepper, and, in Sheffield, by Loveday Alexander (Culpepper 1975; Alexander 1992: 1001-1005). She distinguishes four main structures: individual tuition; individual teacher with many students; multi-teacher; and multi-centre (Alexander 1992: 1005):

Individual tuition was the basis of the whole system. Schooling on any kind of a mass scale would not come until the late Roman Empire, when the state began to take some responsibility for education.

Individual teachers sometimes attracted several students in such a way that together they would form a kind of school community and would often follow the ideals of imitation, emulation and friendship. The emulation (or rivalry) was sometimes between students of other teachers.

The *multi-teacher* school was a place where several teachers worked together in pursuit of a common goal. 'A wide degree of variation is possible here, from the high-powered research organizations of the Theophrastus or the Alexandrian Museum to the religiously committed brotherhood of Pythagoras or Epicurus' (Alexander 1992: 1005).

In the *multi-centred* school 'a number of small groups in different localities [were]...conscious of belonging to the same sect or movement: the "school" here means an agglomeration of geographically scattered groups professing adherence to the same ideals and teaching tradition. This kind of grouping is mainly associated with certain philosophical schools, particularly that of Epicurus' (Alexander 1992: 1005).

The one-teacher schools were especially dedicated to mainstream literary education, in other words to rhetoric, the core of public discourse. This Greece-based rhetoric was not something specialized or localized. After 400 BCE it was 'the central component in the higher education of the free-born...[and] Athens was the educational Mecca for the whole Mediterranean world' (Alexander 1992: 1007). So, when someone as gifted as Isocrates (436–338) taught rhetoric, large numbers came, and together they formed their own distinctive school.

The more complex schools, whether multi-teacher or multi-centred, were generally interested not so much in rhetoric (frequently career-oriented) as in mature research and reflection, often with an emphasis on philosophy, religion, and morality. Plato, in fact, resisted concentration on rhetoric, at least at the level of higher education. Rhetoric was taken for granted, and Plato's goal was philosophy (Alexander 1992: 1007). Some schools were well known:[4]

- In southern Italy, towards 500 BCE, Pythagoras established a group that combined two aspects—religious community and a scientific school.[5]
- In 387, Plato bought land near Athens and there built a school, *The Academy*, which would last a thousand years, and which, somewhat like the Pythagoreans, emphasized philosophy and frugal life.
- *The Academy* might indeed last a millennium, but within fifty-two years it had a rival, right in Athens. In a grove given to him by the Athenians, Aristotle established the formidable *Lyceum*, similar in some ways to the Academy.
- Less than thirty years later, in 306, Epicurus in turn bought a house and garden in Athens. His school was more withdrawn and more monastic than *The Academy* or *The Lyceum*, but it was outgoing insofar as it sent members to establish groups in many other places, and eventually formed a worldwide network of communities (Culpepper 1975: 117-21).

The Epicureans' journeying did not occur is a vacuum. The whole Mediterranean was a crossroads. In the fourth century BCE, the Mediterranean saw a proliferation of small schools and a tradition of mobility. Later, when there was a 'tendency for teachers to congregate in certain cultural centres, notably Athens, Alexandria and Tarsus, mobility...became characteristic of students as much as teachers' (Alexander 1992: 1007).

This brief survey of some schools gives an idea of the ethos in which much writing took place. It was in schools that two of the greatest writers in antiquity, Aristotle and Plato, carried out their work. And schooling, including writing, was not a world of narrow intellectualism or self-centred curiosity. In varying degrees, the schools were involved with multiple centres, with the wide world, and with a whole lifestyle. Imitation was a guiding principle. In Plato's school, the students imitated even his stoop (Culpepper 1975: 67).

Schools were also well established in Judaism, though their age and origin is elusive. A type of school or centre began to flourish at some time during or after the exile—the synagogue—a thoroughly Greek word, meaning a bringing together or assembly. And while the Hellenistic world witnessed

---

4.   See especially Culpepper 1975.
5.   Alexander 1992: 1007; Culpepper 1975: 48-54.

a proliferation of small rhetorical schools, the Jewish people experienced a proliferation of synagogues. It is not clear whether the two phenomena—rhetorical schools and synagogues—are in any way connected. Synagogues were found not only in the diaspora but also in Galilee and Judea. Jerusalem alone is said to have had hundreds of them: 365 in the late post-exilic period, and 480 in the time of Vespasian (69–79 CE) (Meyers 1992: 252). Some sense of an individual synagogue emerges from an inscription (first century CE) referring to a certain Theodotus:

> Theodotus, son of Vettenos, the priest and archisynagogos, son of a archisynagogos and grandson of a archisynagogos, who built the synagogue for purposes of reciting the Law and studying the commandments, and as a hotel with chambers and waters installations, to provide for the needs of itinerants from abroad... (Meyers 1992: 252).

This echoes aspects found more broadly around writings and schools: the transmission from father to son, and the fact of itinerancy or mobility. But the primary purpose of the synagogue is its connection with something written: the Law. Josephus echoes the same emphasis—the synagogue's focus on Scripture reading and study (Meyers 1992: 252).

If writings were central to the synagogue and if synagogues proliferated as apparently they did, then, even if literate people were a small minority within Judaism, that minority was engaged, and the process or reading and writing was a widespread phenomenon. To some degree, the situation is reflected in the case of Philo and his great literary output. The details of how Philo wrote are not clear, whether, for instance, he spent his time in the great library, or in the synagogue, or at home, or in some other type of school or library. It may be, for instance, that his writings were used 'in a synagogue-school where Philo taught the higher vision of scripture to a select group' (Culpepper 1975: 211). What is certain is that, in his exposition of scripture, he did not live in isolation. He worked among writings and students of writing. Even if all the work attributed to him is his own—rather than the work of a school (as was once suggested)—it nonetheless comes from within the context of schools, or at least from within the schooling tradition of the synagogue. In Loveday Alexander's words: 'Philo himself located the bulk of his scholastic activity within the sabbath-day teaching of the synagogues, which he describes (in an intentional comparison with the Greek philosophical schools) as "schools of Moses"' (Alexander 1992: 1010). It is not only the two greatest Greek philosophers therefore who wrote in schools; so did Philo in his own way. Thus, among both Greeks and Judeans, some of the greatest writing was done in schools.

* * *

The Scholarly Linking of Biblical Books with Schools Gives Further
Support to the Idea of a New Testament School

In the course of research into individual biblical books or groups of books, several claims have been made that these writings reflect the work not just of individuals but of a series of writers in some form of school or community. Very briefly:

- M. Weinfeld, faced with the rhetorical continuity between Deuteronomy and other biblical books, especially Joshua to 2 Kings, used the title, 'Deuteronomy and the Deuteronomic School'. The quality of the changes in the Deuteronomic material 'points to a continuous ideological and literary development…and attests to the dynamism of the school' (Weinfeld 1972: 4).
- P. Davies, speaking of the Hebrew scriptures, goes further. The logic that led Weinfeld to invoke a distinct group, a school, for the Deuteronomic work, applies to '*all* of the biblical literature' (Davies 1992: 109). For Davies (1992: 106), the origin of literature goes back to a literate class, and 'in the case of the biblical literature a class which exercises its profession through an institution, namely a scribal school'. What causes Davies (1992: 107) to invoke a school is the complexity of the work of composition: 'The production of scrolls containing histories, cultic poems, wise sayings and oracles is not an individual hobby. Such work requires a professional class with time, resources and motivation to write. In some cases, it implies access to official archives.'
- In New Testament studies, K. Stendahl spoke of 'the school of St. Matthew and its use of the Old Testament' (1954). Stendahl claimed a school both because the form-critical account of Matthew, as found for instance in M. Dibelius's emphasis on preaching, does not fit the data in Matthew (1954: 13-19), and also because Matthew's use of the Old Testament resembles that of a particular school, namely Qumran, with its Habakkuk commentary (1954: 31). Furthermore, a scribe does not work in isolation: 'How does a Christian scribe fit into the context of his church?... If we owe the gospel to a converted rabbi, we must suppose that he was not working entirely alone, but that he took an active part in the life of the church where he lived and served. That is tantamount to saying that there was a school at work in the church of Matthew' (Stendahl 1954: 30).
- In the view of D.E. Orton (1989: 38, 175), Matthew's sense of the scribe is essentially positive, and he sees himself as standing in the tradition not only of the prophets but also of the apocalyptic scribes. Matthew evokes both Ben Sirach and Qumran, and his work falls within a tradition of creative 'charismatic' exegesis.

- Luke has long been acknowledged as a writer in the Greco-Roman mold, trained in rhetoric and an imitator of several aspects of the Greek Old Testament. His background, therefore, is that of rhetorical schooling. Furthermore, while Luke imitated the Old Testament, he also appears to reflect various aspects of Greco-Roman historiography and biography, especially the kind of intellectual biography which was associated with the schools and with the recounting of the life of Socrates. In the words of Loveday Alexander, 'The school traditions lying behind the literary texts are of great significance for Acts' (Alexander 1993: 31). This does not prove that Luke worked with a school, but it shows that the experiences and traditions of schools were not alien to him. On the contrary, he seems to have been very much at home in them. And as already seen in this chapter, Australia's J.N. Collins sets Luke within a literary line.
- The Johannine writings have often been attributed to a school. R. A. Culpepper (1975: 4) traces the actual phrase 'school of John' back to Renan (1863) but shows also that the idea of Johannine disciples or of a Johannine circle had been suggested even before that (Culpepper 1975: 4). After Renan the idea recurs in several scholars, among them Lightfoot (1875–76), Martineau (1891), Bartlett (1899), von Weizsäcker (1899), Schmiedel (who spoke of a community of writers, 1908), Scott (who visualized writers working together in the same neighbourhood, 1908), Jackson (who distinguished an inner circle of writers from a larger school, 1918), Charles (who said diverse writers were 'master and pupil, or...pupils of the same master, or...members of the same school', 1920) (Culpepper 1975: 4-13).

In subsequent Johannine studies (1976–88), the search for the old idea of a school was overtaken by the search for a distinct community (see Brodie 1993: 15-20). This hypothesis of a distinct community derived from a different starting-point and it turned into the process that, in the words of J.L. Martyn (SBL Meeting, Anaheim, CA, 19 November 1989), became like a genie out of control.

Yet the original arguments for a school remain. Among these arguments, the following are particularly significant (see Culpepper 1975: xvii-xviii, 264-90):

1. The Johannine writings show such a curious relationship of similarities and dissimilarities that it seems reasonable to assume that the writers worked together in communication or in community—and so, in some form of school.

2. John's use of the Old Testament suggests a use of writings such as might be found in a school.

   3.   The ethos of the Johannine writings, especially the central
        and exemplary role of the leading figure (the Beloved
        Disciple), corresponds to the ethos of actual schools.
  •   With regard to Paul, the epistles bearing his name present a puzzle
      that in some ways is similar to that of the Johannine writings: a
      series of works seems to come from one person but those works
      sometimes shows such dissimilarities that it may be better, in some
      instances, to think of a school. Such, for instance, is the conclusion
      of P. Müller (1988) concerning 2 Thessalonians and Colossians.[6]
      This idea of Paul's association with some kind of school is rein-
      forced by his use of the Old Testament. Analysis of Paul's use of the
      Scripture by scholars such as R.B. Hays (1989) and especially by
      D.A. Koch (1986) indicates that Paul engaged whole books and that
      he was in the presence of elaborate manuscripts.[7] Furthermore,
      recent research has begun to speak of Paul as someone surrounded
      by co-workers, and even co-writers.
  •   The traditional account of how the Hebrew Bible was translated into
      Greek—the colourful *Letter of Aristeas*—contains the image of a
      community of about seventy writers who, working independently,
      all produced the same translation. The details of the account are
      overdrawn but the underlying image of a community of writers
      seems to have been completely acceptable to all concerned.

The preceding views hold that, where diverse books show an obvious
mixture of similarity and difference—the Deuteronomic history, the Johannine writings, the Pauline corpus—the explanation lies in some form of
school. As evidence now emerges that all twenty-seven New Testament
books are linked not only by a pattern of similarity and difference but also by
systematic literary connections, the case for some form of school becomes
compelling. In some sense the origin of Christianity is linked to one key
community that contained writers who built on one another and interpreted
one another.

* * *

The Quest for the Sequence of the Books

Determining the who, where and when of that writing-oriented community
does not seem possible, at least not now. Perhaps it never will. Aspects of
their work and organization may have had affinities with the Pharisees, with

---

6.   Müller 1988, concerning 2 Thessalonians and Colossians.
7.   Hays 1989: 14-21, esp. 16; Koch 1986: 92-104, 284.

Qumran, with the Pythagoreans (who apparently were represented in some way at Qumran), with the Epicureans, and no doubt with other schools or groups, but, whatever their links to other groups, those who followed the name of Jesus Christ had a very clear identity and energy of their own. Mason (2003: 290) maintains that 'in Luke's portrayal the Christians take the place of the Essenes'.

The problem of identifying the school and its place of origin is illustrated by Luke's portrayal of Paul. Luke seems to provide a spontaneous open account of Paul, but he completely omits Paul's connection with writing—with epistles. In fact, he portrays Paul's only connection to epistles (*epistolae*), those of the high priest, as deathly (Acts 9.1-2). If Luke makes such a major deliberate omission or reversal, then what else has been omitted or changed? Some major person, place, event, or date?

Progress may seem elusive, but one approach is particularly promising. If, instead of trying to trace the whole history of Christianity, we try first to trace the process of writing the New Testament, then we have a starting point for further discussion. More specifically, if we can establish the sequence in which the New Testament documents were written, and if, in doing so, we can trace how they relate to one another, then we have an outline of how the picture of Jesus Christ emerged.

The basic idea of tracing the sequence of the New Testament writings is not new. During the 1860s, a Liverpool-born professor of New Testament at Cambridge, Joseph Barber Lightfoot, 'chaplain to the Prince Consort and honorary chaplain in ordinary to *Queen Victoria*',[8] but a solid man apparently, and future bishop of Durham—this man highlighted the long-term value of trying to establish the sequence of the Pauline epistles, and in recent times the idea has received fresh support (Tatum 2006: esp. 13-14).

Instead of emphasizing a pre-established framework of dates within which to fit the epistles, Lightfoot proposed concentrating on the epistles' own contents, so that by a process of comparison, especially comparison of unusual language, it would be possible to discern the sequence or order in which they had been written.

Needless to say, the insights of such a pioneer almost inevitably need refinement (Tatum 2006: 15), but the principle is more valid than ever: detailed comparison of the epistles will probably reveal their essential sequence, and that sequence should give insight into the process by which the various epistles emerged. Furthermore, what is true of the epistles is true of the New Testament documents as a whole: patient comparison of the twenty-seven documents should eventually reveal the essential sequence in which they were written. The task is a little like that of tracing the human gene map.

---

8.   'Joseph Barber Lightfoot', *Wikipedia*, on the Internet (accessed 30 April 2010).

Yet it may seem impossible. The human gene map is a matter of science, something that despite its complexity is open to clear verification. Tracing the sequence between the documents is a matter of art, and therefore more elusive.

Art is indeed elusive, but not completely. The sequence between Matthew and Mark seemed elusive for a long time, but eventually, by repeated testing, it has come to be widely accepted that Mark preceded Matthew. And the priority of Mark casts light on a whole scenario surrounding the Gospel of Matthew. As we saw earlier, in discussing Rule One of history writing (Chapter 13): 'Write the history of the literature, and then the [wider] history...can be written' (Gunn 2001: 182). Some of the work is already done. Earlier, in Chapter 5, I gave an overall framework that ran from Matthew's initial Sayings and some Epistles to Proto-Luke, and then on to Mark, Matthew, John and Luke–Acts. As for the Epistles, when first attempting to indicate their sequence in 1975, I proposed the following: 1 Corinthians, 1 Thessalonians, 2 Thessalonians, Galatians, Romans, 2 Corinthians, 1 Peter, Colossians, Ephesians, Philippians, Philemon, but obviously any such proposal needs testing. The view of 1 Thessalonians as involving a distilling, adapting and reshaping of 1 Corinthians is summarized at the end of *Birthing of the New Testament*. Second Thessalonians may not necessarily precede Galatians and several other epistles, but it is later than 1 Thessalonians and adapts it. Since Matthew's Sayings include systematic use not only of Deuteronomy but also of Sirach, it is not surprising that, from the beginning of the New Testament writings, Wisdom was central at some level, including the revelation of personified Wisdom as found for instance in Sirach 24, a chapter that, in its content and its central role within Sirach, is akin to the dramatic revelation of primal Rebekah at the centre of Genesis (Gen. 24).[9]

Eventually, when the essential sequence of the New Testament documents has been reasonably well established, there will be a backbone concerning the history of writing, and around that backbone it should be possible to build further history.

In the meantime it is appropriate first to pause for a moment to consider the general role of writing, and then to come back to the heart of the matter.

* * *

The Truth of Writing

People have mixed feelings about art, writing, libraries and librarians, and that is true also of religious people. Christians through the centuries have

---

9.   On Rebekah, see Brodie 2001b: 201, 277-82, 303-307, esp. 281, 306.

struggled to understand God and Jesus and atonement, and it is has also been a struggle to know where schools and writers fit within God's active presence. The idea that Christianity was founded by a community that was significantly oriented towards writing may seem strange or dissonant. Christianity is sometimes wary that emphasis on writing will exalt the cleverness of literacy and of superficial intellect (including legalism) above the supreme values of love and justice. As the New Testament tells it, Jesus never put pen to paper. The Sanhedrin regard the troublesome disciples as unlettered (Acts 4.13). And, as already mentioned, Luke never mentions that Paul wrote a word. The only time Luke connects Paul to the process of writing is to say he was carrying letters (*epistolae*) from the high priest— letters related to death (Acts 9.2). Writers can mean trouble. Some people despise librarians. Plato banned poets from his ideal Republic. It has been said Pancho Villa built his revolution on the solid rock of ignorance. The images of the carpenter, the fishermen, and the tentmaker suggest a ruggedness far from writing's rhetoric but close to honest living, close to the ruggedness of the cross.[10]

Yet writing has its place. If Christianity is about the good in things, including the presence of God in human bodies, then God and good are also present in other human things, including writing—which, next to language, is almost a defining feature of humanity; it is language in another form. Though bodies can abuse, they remain essentially good, and so do language and writing. It is not surprising then that, despite its caution, Christianity treasures writing. It realizes that words and pages can carry or revive a message, even a message that helps to bring one into the realm of God. And Christianity has been deeply involved in the development of writing—from the blossoming of the codex, to illustrating the Book of Kells, to promoting literacy in distant parts of the world (Gamble 1995; Stroumsa 1998). While the inflating of intellect and writing is always a hazard, the healthy growth of intellect and writing is a blessing, and, as seen for instance in the role it played in the Jesuit community of the University of El Salvador around the time of the killings (December 1980), study and writing form a beacon of hope.

On balance, therefore, the action of a community in taking their old heritage, their old narrative, and transforming it, through writing, into a new heritage, a new covenant, may have been audacious, may have pushed creativity to new limits, but the central role of writing is not itself something negative. The issue is not whether writing was central, but whether the message of that writing was true.

Writing at its best conveys truth, even if it is through a story. One day, not long after David had committed adultery and effectively murdered the

10. On factors related to the Gospels' rusticity, see Brodie 2004: 61.

woman's husband, Nathan the prophet came and told him a distant-sounding story about two men and some animals. David listened, and in listening he was finally faced with the truth of his own life (2 Sam. 12.1-15). And when a lawyer asked Jesus about the identity of his neighbour, Jesus told him a story (Lk. 10.29-37).

The point is well known; stories can carry truth, and often do so far more effectively than the facts of history. Facts may indeed be facts, but they are often so disjointed and threadbare that they communicate almost nothing. Yet, as my sister recently reminded me—the same sister whose childhood reading was once such an object of wonder to me—great writing, even if is a work of the imagination, can reach the core.[11]

Like the word 'fiction', 'imagination' is ambiguous; it can suggest what is unreal, like imagining that the moon is made of green cheese. But, as parables show, imagination can also be a guide to truth. It can choose images and image-filled stories that get to the heart of the truth. It is often more effective than abstract or factual analysis, and it can work through diverse forms of writing, especially through imaginative poetry, imaginative prose, and imaginative letter writing.

Images and words that emerge from the deepest level of experience are not just signs. They bring reality into being. In the words of Catherine Hilkert, they 'embody' reality:

> Human words spoken from the center of ourselves...allow a deeper dimension of reality to emerge. These...words are not merely signs that point to a reality that exists independently of the naming. Rather, in a public, conscious, histori-cal way, these words 'embody' the deeper spiritual reality from which they emerge. Primordial words become sacraments—they function as symbols that allow a deeper mystery, the offer of grace, to become more concretely present and available in human life (Hilkert 1997: 33).

This process whereby words bring reality into being is connected some-how to the very beginning of the Bible: words brought the world into being (Gen. 1).

The essential point is basic. 'Art', 'fiction', and 'imagination' may at first suggest something unreal, but in fact they can be the surest guides to the deepest truth. The accounts of Jesus may in one sense be fiction, and may be shaped by many older accounts, including for instance the account of the death of Socrates. But art at its best can reach to the core of the truth, and symbols do likewise. The word 'fiction' is ambiguous. It can indicate what is untrue; but it can also refer to a writing which, though not historical, is a searing depiction of reality, of radical truth, and the Gospels are a supreme example of such writing.

11.　On the Bible's relationship to fiction, see Brant 2005.

Chapter 20

IS IT POSSIBLE TO REDISCOVER
THE MEANING OF CHRIST?

Is it possible for a believing Christian to accept that Jesus Christ never existed as a specific historical individual? At first sight it may seem not. The sense of Jesus as an historical individual is not just in the brain. For many it is in the bone and in the soul. Most Christians feel connected *somehow* to Jesus and to history. And in the Christian creed, Jesus 'suffered under Pontius Pilate'.

But perhaps the Christianity to which we are accustomed is not the last word. Abraham Lincoln once said that what we have had are small doses of Christianity—enough to be inoculated against it. Apart from 1 Timothy (6.13), generally dated late, the twenty-one New Testament epistles never mention Pontius Pilate, and Nazareth not at all.

Besides, given the pervasive evidence for how the New Testament was composed—how it built on a reweaving of the Old Testament, a weaving so dense and artistic that specific events in the life of Jesus are neither traceable nor necessary—it is still a fair question to ask what is meant by the reality of Jesus. And, even granting how the New Testament was composed, is there still some sense in which he may be said to be historical?

In September 1972, when I was first struck by the deep similarities between the Gospels and the Old Testament, I immediately had two responses: 'This is strange stuff that may have radical implications'; and, 'It's OK'. Rightly or wrongly, my sense of God's presence at the time reassured me that whatever was happening would be alright.

The first person to become alarmed at what I was doing was Pierre Benoit when, early in 1973, he read about the degree to which Jesus' words and actions, as recounted in Matthew, seemed to originate in Deuteronomy. Yet, such examples of dependence did not worry me, not even when the dependence of Luke–Acts on the Elijah–Elisha narrative began to indicate a key role for an earlier document, Proto-Luke, a document that was hypothetical. I would have preferred not to invoke a hypothetical document, but at least the document in question was modelled directly, often in detail, on a climactic prophetic narrative from the Primary History, and so it was much more solidly grounded than the hypothetical Q, and more useful, *brauchbar* as the Germans say.

It was only in May–July 1974, when I slowly realized what 1 Corinthians had done—synthesize several sources, especially from the Old Testament, thus composing the very figure of Christ and laying that figure down as a foundation for others—it was only then that my own foundations felt the full impact.

Still it seemed that, in some way I did not understand, things would be OK. God was still God, and eventually things would work out, they would become clear. However, while I kept trying, as usual, to be faithful to the practices of the Catholic faith, I often wondered what that faith really meant. When I told my old friend Miceál O'Regan where I had reached, he said after a while, 'That must be a lonely place'. The thought had not struck me explicitly.

At one stage during the late 1980s, in St Louis, I found myself asking with ever more insistence, 'What do I believe? What do I really believe?' And eventually I concluded that I was really sure of the Abraham story, not of its history, but of its meaning. Somehow Abraham would get me by. And without fully understanding why, I held on to the Mass (Eucharist).

In July 1995, while in South Africa, I had to give a retreat to a community of Augustinian nuns. They lived in Botha's Hill, in KwaZulu-Natal, and were roughly half elderly French, and half young Zulu. All things considered, it seemed good to base the whole retreat largely on Genesis, with a sprinkling of John's Gospel.

Afterwards, someone asked one of the old French nuns what she thought of a retreat based on Genesis.

'A lot better than poverty, chastity and obedience.'

A key problem in speaking and writing was that I could never give the full story, I could never say, in crude terms, that Jesus Christ never existed. When I first gave my hand-written manuscript to be typed, in March/April 1975, I made the crucial paragraph on Jesus' existence illegible and typed it in later myself. I could not say it, partly because I would not be believed and would effectively be shut out, and partly because the crude statement of non-existence seemed grossly inadequate. It may be true, but it is so far from the whole truth that it is a radical distortion.

As we were developing the biblical institute in Limerick, a few of us went to Ennis to talk to Dr Willie Walsh, the bishop of Killaloe diocese, about what we were doing—the bishop in Limerick already knew—and, as we spoke of the importance of the Bible, he said (almost verbatim), 'Yes, any renewal of the church must begin with a renewed sense of Christ'. A momentary chill went through me. I knew he was essentially right, and I was glad for him, but I had no idea how we would get from where I was to the ultimate truth of what he was saying.

When I eventually managed in 2004 to publish *Birthing of the New Testament*, the basic thesis about how the New Testament was formed—formed largely by rewriting and rethinking the Old—the General Conclusion (Chapter 26) still did not state clearly that Jesus was not a historical figure. Essentially I simply appealed to historians to do more literary homework—to seek out patiently the nature of the key documents—before attempting to draw historical conclusions. As far as I know, no historian took any notice.

A few years later, in writing the reflection requested by Tom Thatcher, I was able to see a little further, and, while still being somewhat reserved in stating a conclusion about the historicity of Christ, I indicated somewhat more clearly the importance of both imagination and mysticism, in other words, the role of imaginative literature in communicating truth, and the role of spiritual experience, including mysticism, in understanding the Gospels and Christ (Thatcher 2007: 77-80).

Then, in 2008, I decided to just tell the whole story to a journalist whom I knew to be competent and responsible, Áine de Paor, who worked with the *Limerick Leader*. She started coming to my library office in the mornings. But I could not do it. I began to realize very soon that I had no idea what effect my conclusion would have on her, and I was unsure of my ability to explain things in a way that would ultimately be positive for all concerned.

Finally, in 2009, as the age of Copernicus approached—seventy—I decided that I would write the story as directly as I could, along the lines of the Thatcher book. Regarding Copernicus, I was not engaged with his work, but only with his decision, regardless of the consequences, of trying to publish his work before he would die, and of doing so at seventy. And so, when I mentioned Copernicus in the opening line of the Preface—and I drafted the Preface at the very beginning of the process of writing—I did not expect to refer to him again.

However, in giving the account of historical criticism ('the first revolution'), it seemed right to mention Copernicus as contributing to the questioning of the Bible. And there was another factor. At the centre of Genesis, the beauty and generosity of Rebekah is a sign of God's faithful love. I had become aware that a biblical centre that wanted to speak to people could not focus on the Bible alone. Account would have to be taken of the world's other great stories, especially those of literature and particularly that of science. Popular communication would be greatly helped by some form of religion-and-science exhibit, and so I began reading about science and talking to some scientists, and was thinking again about Copernicus and Galileo.

Then on Saturday 16 May 2009 a simple thought emerged: the rethinking of the role of the earth (by Copernicus and Galileo) provides a precedent for the rethinking of the role of Christ. The cosmos and Christ are like the two great outpourings of God and God's Word. Within the Bible, the earth was the heart of God's creation, and Christ brought a new creation. And just as the role of the earth within the cosmos had to be rethought, so also the role of Christ has to be rethought. Rethinking the earth was not easy. It was only in 1984, through Pope John Paul II, that the Catholic Church officially made peace with Galileo, and it will take some time to accept the rethinking of the role of Christ. What is essential is that the slow process of rethinking God's creation provides a precedent for rethinking God's Christ. The prospect of being removed from the familiar historical Jesus may seem dark and challenging, but the earth has not gone away, and neither has the true meaning of the presence of Jesus Christ. On the contrary, at a time when the portrayal of Jesus is often constricted—whether in film, story, or research—there is a chance to come closer to the true meaning of Jesus.

Some may say that there is little connection between God's creation and God's Christ, that rethinking one in no way provides a precedent for the other. In comparison to creation, the figure of Christ may seem much closer to the core of Christian teaching. Surely there is no space in Christian teaching for such a radical rethinking.

Yet the link between understanding Christ and understanding creation goes back to early Christianity (Young 2000), and the idea of some form of present-day radical rethinking is not altogether new. On 8 April 1979, at an academic convocation in Cambridge, Massachusetts, Karl Rahner gave a talk that was brief but extraordinary—perhaps the nearest Karl Rahner ever got to a Gettysburg Address. But while Abraham Lincoln's speech looked across recent history ('Fourscore and seven years ago...') and also to 'the unfinished work' ahead, Rahner, in assessing the meaning of the Second Vatican Council, looked across the entire history of the Church, and into future work that seems even more unfinished (Rahner 1979). For him Vatican II meant that the Church was being asked not just in principle, but in practice, to become a world Church. This would require a radical transition—leaving a Europe-based culture, and genuinely engaging the culture of the world, a transition for which Christianity had only one precedent—namely the transition of the early church from being Jewish-based to engaging the European/ Roman world:

> We are experiencing a break such as occurred only once before, that is in the transition from Jewish to Gentile Christianity....Such transitions happen for the most part...unreflectively.... (1979: 723).

For Rahner, then, the present transition is as great as that of the first centuries, and regarding its content he made three observations (1979: 724):

> The second break, towards a world church, naturally has or must acquire a completely different content than the first break.

> It is an open...question whether and to what extent the Church... still has the creative powers and authority that she had in the period of her first becoming. The open question is whether, during such historical breaks as the one we are discussing, the Church can legitimately perceive possibilities of which she never made use during her second major epoch...because these possibilities would have been meaningless in that epoch and consequently illegitimate.

> No one can correctly predict the...future to which the Church must do justice in the new interpretation of her faith and of her essence as world Church...

Rahner does not try to spell out how this transition will affect the formulation of Christian teaching. In fact, as he saw it, the reformulation of the message seemed distant and difficult:

> None of us can say exactly how, with what conceptuality, under what new aspects the old message of Christianity must in the future be proclaimed...if this message is really to be present everywhere in the world... It will be necessary to appeal to the hierarchy of truths...and to return to the final and fundamental substance of the Christian message. This reduction or return...is not easy (1979: 725).

We are faced, then, with a situation where radical transition has come or is coming to our understanding of both Creation (the Cosmos) and the Church—two entities interwoven with Christ. If they can change, then can the understanding of Christ do likewise?

Here we return to Timothy Radcliffe, someone who explicitly refers to the idea of rethinking the meaning of Jesus Christ. As I already mentioned, the youthful Radcliffe—later head of the Dominican Order—experienced 'as a student the dizzy excitement of discovering that the Council of Chacedon was not the end of our search to understand the mystery of Christ but another beginning, exploding all the tiny coherent little solutions in which we had tried to box him'.[1]

No question, then—our understanding of Christ can indeed change. The only issue is how far? Far enough to see Christ not as an individual human, but as a symbol of God among us, God within us? It is a challenging change. It is disturbing. But perhaps it is not greater or more disturbing than the re-imagining of Creation and the Church? And it calls once again for 'a conversion of the imagination' (see Hays 2005). It would seem that it is time—adapting Radcliffe's image—it is time that Jesus Christ emerged from our tiny boxes.

---

1. Radcliffe 1999: 60, emphasis added. See the Preface to the present study.

Chapter 21

GLIMMERS OF SHADOWED BEAUTY:
SYMBOL OF THE INVISIBLE GOD

For the moment I do not have a clear sense of what Jesus Christ means. I only have glimmers of it, and it is tempting to want to be in my twenties again, so as to have the possibility of starting afresh to explore the meaning of the New Testament. As a student, I sometimes thought of trying to specialize in the systematic study of knowledge about God, 'systematic theology', but I could never muster the conviction for it, because I felt that in talking about God, and especially about Christ, I would always be looking over my shoulder at the Bible, wondering about its origin and nature. The ideal was to go back to the Bible, find out quickly how it originated, at least roughly, and then move immediately to a more systematic exploration of the meaning of God and Christ, and the implications of that meaning for people's lives.

I did indeed find out something about the Bible fairly quickly but I was unable to move immediately to a more mature exploration, and consigning the 1975 manuscript to the archives of the Divinity School library in New Haven in 1983 was like taking out insurance lest my immobility become permanent. I was not even sure of the insurance. Maybe the Divinity School had dumped the blessed stuff. As it turned out, 1983 became the year when some progress began, at least in a narrow academic way, and decades later, at the end of the Summer of 2010, a message came to Limerick from Martha Smalley, who was about to retire as Special Collections Librarian at the Yale Divinity School, and who asked if I could be contacted concerning 'some writings he left with us for safekeeping'. After a brief exchange of messages, the material was then graciously assigned to the Miscellaneous Personal Papers Collection with a dated restriction of 2015.

Meanwhile, I had gone another course. What is given in this chapter is far from being a systematic account of the meaning of Christ. It is not even the outline of such an account. It is essentially a brief report on part of where I have landed.

The first finding is that, as a simple literary fact, within the Greek Bible the names of Jesus and Moses' successor, Joshua, are identical (*Iésous*). So the name given to Jesus suits him perfectly to be Moses' successor. And the larger depiction of Jesus, as Lord Jesus Christ, involves an innovative synthesis of aspects of older figures, especially of *kyrios* (the 'Lord'), Moses, Elijah—and also 'Christ' (the 'Anointed'), the one who would come to inaugurate a final kingdom (an 'eschatological' kingdom; see esp. Dan. 9.24-27), someone to set the world aright.[1]

From its beginning this new synthesis maintains continuity between the Lord Jesus of the New Testament and the Lord God (Yahweh) of the Old Testament, but it gathers much that was said more obscurely about the Lord God, particularly about the Lord God's involvement in human suffering, and expresses it with a vividness that constitutes a new stage of revelation.[2]

This process of portraying Jesus was not a petty literary exercise. It was laying forth a vision of all time, a vision that was born of a long process of experience and reflection—*somewhat* as St Teresa of Avila's *Interior Castle* set forth her vision of the soul as an interior castle containing seven dwelling places, which she saw as seven stages of faith on the way to union with God. In one sense there was no castle, yet in another sense nothing is closer to the truth. When Edith Stein, as a brilliant young philosopher of about thirty, was looking not only for truth but for *the Truth*, for a long time she looked in vain. Then one night, when visiting friends, she was left alone and chanced on Teresa's autobiography. She started reading, and read relentlessly until finally, as she finished it, she knew her conclusion:

'*Das ist die Wahrheit*', 'That is the truth'.

In the case of the New Testament, the vision was not just that of one person. It was shared among several people, and those who contributed to putting it in writing had the freedom to give their own particular insight to the vision, so that the New Testament is not just one vision but different views of that vision—with different views of the meaning of Christ, different 'Christologies'.

Amid all these diverse views of Christ, some aspects stand out, aspects that tell of Jesus as symbol of: (1) the heart of reality; (2) the measure of reality; and (3) the enigmatic form of reality—shadowed beauty.

---

1. In Dan. 9.24-27 the idea of the kingdom is implicit rather than explicit: this 'piece of apocalyptic writing has otherwise no mention of the Davidic dynasty. This lack of mention, however, does not mean that the author has no hope for the restoration of that monarchy...' (Fitzmyer 2007: 62). And the context of Dan. 7 highlights the setting up of God's throne (7.9) and is explicit in speaking of a coming kingdom (7.17, 18, 23, 27), imagery that helps to prepare the way for speaking of the inauguration of a final eschatological kingdom.

2. The continuity of Jesus with the God of the Old Testament has already been highlighted by Richard Bauckham (2008).

Jesus as Symbol of the Heart of Reality

One of the key features of Christ was that *he died for our sins and rose to save us*. The words are so simple that it can be difficult to think that there is a problem with them. Yet, in another sense, nobody knows what they mean; nobody knows fully. Christian thinkers have never been able to establish a clear meaning for how somebody's death redeems from sins, or makes atonement for sin; they do not understand how reconciliation works. Even a single Epistle, Romans, gives two diverse explanations (Rom. 3.24-25; 6.1-4).[3]

What is generally agreed is that the New Testament sets out a vision of reconciliation with fresh strength and clarity, so fresh that the revealing of the figure of Christ brings creation to a new level and inaugurates a new covenant. The new vividness plays a role like that of a great insight in the life of an individual. It brings that life to a new level.

Despite this newness, the basic idea of reconciliation is old; it builds on the Old Testament. In the Old Testament God is often angry at sin, but God also shows heartfelt involvement. The account of the sin that precedes the Deluge describes God as regretting having made the world, and as grieving at heart (Gen. 6.6), but afterwards God takes account of the whole human heart, and promises never to repeat the punishment (Gen. 8.21). As the *Jerusalem Bible* notes, the reference to God 'regretting' creation is a human way of speaking.[4]

* * *

A second key feature of the New Testament is that it seems to *link reconciliation with something radically new—God's son/Son* (Rom. 1.4). God gave his son/Son. The son/Son laid down his life. How could God, the one and only God, have a child? But in fact the linking of reconciliation with images of children or sons is not new. In the story of Joseph, who reconciles and saves his bitter brothers, the role of Joseph is inseparable from his role as a beloved son and from the role of God who is with him (Gen. 37.3; 39.21; 45.7). Elsewhere too, some sinful situations involve the image of a child who is related to God. In Isaiah's opening panorama of sin, of how awful things are (Isa. 1–12), the gloom is lifted increasingly by references to light and children, especially Emmanuel—the child who is a sign and bears God's name, a child who in the Greek version is born of a virgin (Isa. 7.10-25; 8.21–9.6; 11.1-10), and who is in continuity with the later Suffering Servant who was crushed for our sins (Isa. 52.13–53.12; see esp., 'root', 11.1, 10; 53.2). And for the prophet Hosea, God is like a parent who loves a child from

---

3. On Rom. 3.24-25 and 6.1-4, see, for instance, Horrell 2006: 62.
4. *Jerusalem Bible*, Gen. 6.6, note d.

its infancy, a parent whose heart, whose whole being, recoils at the idea of punishment, and who will not act according to the fury of his anger (Hos. 11). These too are human ways of speaking.

So, long before the New Testament, the Bible recounts that God suppresses fury, has a heart that is deeply involved with a sinful people, gives the sign of a God-related child who shines out amid a panorama of sin, and sends a beloved son (Joseph) to Egypt to save the lives of his sinful brothers. In light of these images, and in light of the many transformations that occur within biblical writing, it is not too far to speak of God as giving his son—in other words of saying that God is so involved that God gives of God's own self, gives of what is deep within. And this too is a human way of speaking.

The greater vividness of the New Testament accords with the New Testament's overall approach, and also with aspects of contemporary rhetoric (Brodie 2004: 15-17). The ultimate implication is that within God and God's creation there exists a dynamism that absorbs the world's forces of sin and death—an idea which overlaps with that of Buddhism that the heart of reality is compassion. It also overlaps with Muslim tradition, where Allah is known, above all, as 'Allah, the Merciful, the Compassionate'.

This status of Christ as Son is interwoven with the Christian way of picturing God, as three-dimensional—Father, Son and Spirit. This image of a trinity is insightful, but it can sometimes be a disaster. In the words of Samuel Ruiz, the fearless peace-loving Bishop of Chiapas, southern Mexico, addressing an assembly of catechists in Mexico City in 1976, 'I lay my hand on my heart, I do believe we are teaching three Gods'. He wanted the catechists to remember the age-old vision that the three are completely one, just as one person can be spouse, parent and care-taker. Or one person can be Dr Gonzalez in public, Beth to her husband, and Mom to her child. The three titles are simply *three aspects* of one person. Unfortunately the Latin word used for aspect or face was *persona*, and so the three aspects sound like three persons! But God is one, as much as the aged beloved face across the morning coffee is one with the simmering teenager you met sixty years ago. Six decades have shown diverse aspects or faces, but the person is still one.

On the other hand, the diversity is to be treasured. The face across the morning coffee is not the face of sixty years ago, but something of that former face is still there, and, given grace, something still simmers. Likewise, regarding God, but more so. The three faces or aspects are still there—Father, Son, Spirit: Father, like the face of a loving parent; Son, like the face of a close friend; and Spirit, like the face of someone closer even than yourself to your own deepest spirit. The complexity of the old face across the table is a richness, and so is the complexity of the one God, an extraordinary blessing.

But sometimes religious talk about God becomes *unduly* complex, and so does religious practice. To some degree, the New Testament was a response to complexity. While maintaining the older Scriptures, it also provided stories and guidelines that seemed easier to manage than the old, and in a sense it made God clearer. But in time Christianity too sometimes seemed desperately complex—everything from difficult debates about Christ to selling indulgences. The two greatest religious revolts affecting the history of Christianity, namely, Islam and Protestantism, were both trying in their different ways to reclaim the heart of the matter—a sense of God's sovereignty, a sense of the one God. In Islam, the new formulation centred on God as Merciful and Compassionate. In Protestantism, it centred, under Luther, on God's graciousness (God's gift of grace) through Jesus.

Explaining this graciousness, explaining how Jesus' grace saves those who believe in him from sin and death, can in turn become obscure, complicated, even strange—as though Jesus were constantly trying to hold God at bay, and as though church services, especially the Eucharist/Mass, were doing likewise—paying protection, constantly having to use Jesus to ward off a predatory God. But the essential meaning of this graciousness goes back to a sense of something within God: despite crimes, catastrophes and unspeakable tragedies, God's basic presence and action towards creation and people are as generous and all-embracing as is imaginable, even to giving what is absolutely dearest to God's own self. Ultimately the picture of God giving his Son is a vivid way of saying that God gives God's own self, so that within God reconciliation is already established. This is the dynamic that is pictured in the New Testament account of Jesus: 'Every particular right (and wrong) is already harboured in the comprehensiveness of that which is [universal]'.[5]

---

5.   Explanations of the meaning of reconciliation have varied over the centuries, and some variations go back to the New Testament. As already mentioned, even within Romans there are diverse ways of expressing what is going on between Jesus Christ and God. First, Christ's death is seen as a sacrifice—something unselfish that as it were *makes up for our selfish sins* (Rom. 3.24-25). Then his death is seen as a form of breakthrough into a new relationship with God, and, *within the new space created by that breakthrough, we can all participate* (Rom. 6.1-4; see Horrell 2006: 62). If I may risk a crude approximate summary: in the first case, someone pays for you to get it on your behalf; in the second, someone has created an open space for you, so you can just walk in and participate. The diversity of views is sobering, and warns against oversimplification.

Romans goes on to speak of a much larger process, one going on within all of God's creation: from the beginning until now the whole of creation has been groaning in one great act of giving birth, and we too groan within us as we wait for the future (Rom. 8.22-23).

The prodigious Swiss theologian, Hans Urs Von Balthasar—the man who declined to be made a cardinal when Pope John Paul II nominated him, and who, when the Pope later insisted, died in June 1988, two days before he was due to go to Rome for the red hat—this man too went back to creation: '[Balthasar] only hints at the traditional answer that, by means of the cross, Jesus has paid penance for our guilt and has reconciled us with God. For Balthasar, something else seems to be of greater importance in this context: light can be shed upon the outrage of the cross by the fact that God created

The challenge for humans is to tune in to this space where reconciliation already exists.

It may seem that no such place exists. Evil can seem so powerful that the idea of a good God makes no sense. But while God and evil are distinct, and are not to be confused, they are not separate. In a fierce challenge to our tendency to simplify and to oversimplify, God in some sense is at the heart of evil, at the heart even of the crucifixion. Only something as horrendous as the crucifixion can communicate the full complexity of God's presence, and so the crucifixion became central to Christianity. The horror, of course, is part of something larger, something involving a form of resurrection, of greater life. Childbirth captures the apparent contradiction, often mixing pain and life.

human beings as "persons with their own proper freedom" and that "these free beings collide with each other and confine each other even before this can be called guilt or sin". This not only requires an appeal to a conciliatory attitude i.e. to morality. There is also need for a definitive possibility of being, for a "status…, in which every particular point of view with its absolute particular right (and wrong) *is already harboured* in the comprehensiveness of that which is [universal]". As history since Christ tells us, it is not so much a question of abolishing confrontation, but of *the reconciliation of contradictory viewpoints through that which is [universal]*, as allowed purely through the possibility created by the cross' (Körner 2000: 422-23, emphasis added). If I understand correctly that final comment about the cross, Von Balthasar saw the cross as symbolizing such a synthesizing of opposites that it includes and reconciles all conflict and sin. What is pivotal is the vision of God's universality as 'harbouring' every particular point of view with its absolute particular right (and wrong).

In any case, it would seem as if there is sufficient space within God to encompass everything, including sin. Such an idea of space within God makes more sense if the one God has diverse aspects—the kind of diversity envisaged by the idea of a trinity within God. The dynamic between Father, Son and Spirit—the process of mutual self-giving and of a giving that is outward—provides gracious space for forgiveness. The doctrine of the Trinity may not have been formulated until the Christian era, but the reality of God's comprehensive richness already existed long before the formulation.

Again it is useful to go back to creation. The rich complexity within God is seen not only in the carefully crafted unity of the two-part creation account (Gen 1.1–2.24) but especially in the tumultuous crisis surrounding the world's sin (the Deluge account, Gen. 6.1–9.17). At one level God is so aware of human sinfulness that God decides to destroy humankind (6.5-7), yet at a later stage, after Noah offers a burnt offering, God decides never again to strike humankind, even though God is now even more aware of the full depth of evil in the heart (8.21-22). It is as though, through the flood, God's in-built capacity for reconciliation is revealed.

Incidentally, the role of the Deluge within Genesis provides a partial precedent for the role of the account of the world's sinfulness within Romans (Rom. 2.18-32).

Whatever the details, the idea of making peace with God is not new to the New Testament. It is already in the Old, but the symbol of the cross gives it new clarity and strength.

Such mixes are hard to take. As are other aspects of God. The mind cannot solve them. Jean-Paul Sartre was brilliant in ways, but 'Sartre's idea of God was surprisingly simplistic', and so he rejected God, declared himself an atheist, and became for many 'the ultimate atheist philosopher' (Wang 2010). However, another Frenchman was able to hold opposites together. For Peguy, 'The sinner is at the heart of Christianity'.

* * *

A third key feature is Jesus' *rising from the dead*. The idea of life after death occurs in diverse forms throughout the Old Testament/Septuagint, including the dry bones (Ezek. 37.1-14), Enoch (Gen. 5.24), Elijah (2 Kgs 2), Moses (Deut. 34), the intensifying pictures of raising someone dead in three episodes of the Elijah-Elisha Narrative (1 Kgs 17.17-24; 2 Kgs 4.8-37 and 13.14-21), and in later texts (Dan. 12.1-4; 2 Macc. 7; Wis. 4.7-19). But, as with reconciliation, this idea also, of life after death, becomes much more vivid in the New Testament through the resurrection of Jesus. And this vividness too is a human form of speaking, but the essential message stands on its own merits: there is something in humans, some inherent capacity, that calls for remaining with the divine, even after death.

Obviously from one point of view the idea of life after death sounds like nonsense. Yet, it does not seem possible to make definitive pronouncements about the non-evolution of life without knowing more about the larger context, about life itself. And, despite science's remarkable advances, we are still a long way from knowing. We do not know what underlies the smallest units of matter—whether it be a particle or a wave or a wavicle, whatever a wavicle may be. The smallest elements are 'comprehension-defying'; and in one way of measuring these elements 'atoms [by comparison] appear bigger than entire galaxies' (Matthews 2012: 38-39). And we do not know what underlies the largest unit—the Big Bang. For A.N. Wilson, 'The Resurrection, which proclaims that matter and spirit are mysteriously conjoined, is the ultimate key to who we are' (see Wilson 2009a, 2009b). John Moriarty (1999: 255) implies that resurrection is about the extra dimension of everything. The original Old Testament sense of miracle was something that evoked wonder, including the wonder of ordinary things (Brown 1968: 78, para. 112), and creation is strewn with wondrous stuff. It seems right to allow the element of wonder due space. In the Christian vision, the God who made first light shine out of darkness can make light shine out of death. And whatever one makes of the resurrection account, it is difficult to avoid the idea of an all-encompassing spirit that is mind-surpassing. Again, mind-surpassing seems to apply even to the physical universe. According to Lord Rees, president of the Royal Society of London, 'A "true" fundamental theory of the universe may exist but could be just too hard for human brains to grasp'.[6] The account of Jesus' resurrection emerges as a human way of speaking, and it need not be taken literally, but it is still a symbol of truth—of an extraordinary mystery of life and of the renewal of life.

* * *

These three features—God's Son, dying for sin, rising for life—encapsulate a drama that beats words. It may seem a cop out to say we are talking about something that beats words, but neither do we have adequate language for the smallest particles of matter or for the entire cosmos. The language of God's Son dying for sin and rising for life synthesizes a wide range of human experience and culture, including that of the Old Testament, and despite its limitations it says something significant about the heart of reality.

It also says something significant about every human being. If God can be truly pictured as within a human body, then every human body, of woman and man, has a dignity and capacity for enshrining God, for being Christ, and while this presence escapes words, and often escapes clear awareness, in some way it remains, not as a kill-joy but as a source of life, possibility and togetherness, and ultimately of peace.

God remains God, retaining self-possession. God does not lose it, so to speak, and the Deluge episode, despite God's upset, ultimately confirms God's reliability. This self-possession is reassuring, like that of a wise leader, or calm parent.

At the same time, lest the self-possession suggests indifference, the Bible uses diverse images to portray God's down-to-earth involvement in history and human lives, and in the New Testament these changing images reach a fresh level, including that of God as not only within human lives, but in a special way as being within a specific individual, Jesus Christ the Son of God who died for our sins. The image of God's compassion in Jesus need not be taken literally—just as, in its own way the image of God's compassion in the book of Jonah need not be taken literally—but the image of Jesus clarifies something important about God. God may be self-possessed, but God's whole being is churning within and outwards towards people, so that even as sin and death happen, God is processing them, constantly offering forgiveness, a process of healing, and various forms of life. In the words of Gerald Manley Hopkins,

> I think that we are bound
> By mercy round and round.

6. Quoted in Leake 2010.

The drama within God, within God's three aspects or personae, is somewhat like the complexity within an orchestra conductor. The conductor first of all maintains self-possession; second, because of involvement with the orchestra, conductors may cut loose, pouring out their guts so to speak, so that the conducting body is being offered up to the orchestra; and third, through a combination of both self-possession and cutting loose, the conductor sends a particular spirit over the orchestra:

> And the orchestra plays on:
> 'I think that we are bound
> By mercy round and round'.

This divine drama is indeed beyond words, and if we want to be sure of not saying a wrong word about God we will say nothing. But one of our distinctive gifts is that of words, so we try to use them about God, even if in doing so we have to follow Beckett's motto: 'Fail, fail again…' and to keep on failing in the hope that somehow we can '…fail better'. Yet, though all our words are failures, as are all our ceremonies and signs or sacraments, they are not useless. They can fail better, and so it is still appropriate that the classic language and symbols derived from the New Testament be used, especially in the celebration of baptism, and the Eucharist:

> Before he was given up to death…,
> he took bread and gave you thanks…
> and said…This is my body…

But, as one's life goes on, these classic formulations need reflection. What is learned and treasured in childhood must be allowed, like the rest of the body and mind, to mature and to blend with other insights, to other ways of viewing the world. The full history of the Eucharist/Mass is immensely complex, and apparently involves both the Jewish Passover meal and Greco-Roman meals,[7] but, despite this richness, modern celebrations of the Mass can sometimes seem as boring as the crackling of an old radio. Yet for whoever is tuned in, it is like pausing for breath, like reconnecting batteries with their source of life, or like Moses turning aside to see the burning bush. It is also like the two young astronomers, Arno Penzias and Robert Wilson, who, in 1965, having struggled month after month with an inveterate noise as they tried to use a large radio antenna in Holmdel, New Jersey, were eventually brought to realize that they had stumbled on something that some scientists thought should exist and were trying to find—residual cosmic radiation resulting from the Big Bang. In the noise, Penzias and Wilson had connected to the origin of the universe.

---

7. See Smith 2002; and Daly 2005.

When dramas are beyond words, it is not clear what to say or do. The response to the stumbling discovery of Penzias and Wilson included bestowing a Nobel Prize. The Eucharist/Mass is a small drama, usually much less elaborate than the granting of a Nobel Prize, but in principle it seeks to reflect a drama beyond words—an opportunity to take in something of the totality of creation, with all its crucifixions, catastrophes and blessings, something of the ultimate puzzle. The writer Annie Dillard says we should wear crash-helmets in church.

It is possible, then, to maintain essentially the same gospel accounts, rituals and devotions as before, not because they reflect specific events of the past, but because they use life-like stories set in ancient times to evoke the deepest truth about past, present and future. The old narratives may be read as if they were true, because they are true, but not literally. In fact, freedom from fretting about history provides an opportunity to appreciate the depth of what the stories are saying. It also gives new space for the ancient practice of spiritual reading (*lectio divina*)—reading the biblical text for what it says to one's own situation. To repeat what Albert Schweitzer said in his conclusion, in 1906, before setting off to work in Africa: 'To those who obey him, whether they be wise of simple, he will reveal Himself in the toils, the conflicts, and sufferings which they shall pass through in His Fellowship, and as an ineffable mystery, they shall learn in their own experience Who he is'.

Insofar as the enigmatic figure of Christ engages sin, death and resurrection, it is a reminder, first of all, that reality challenges every human being to face squarely into suffering and death. There is no easy road. Life has more suffering not only than we want but often even than we imagine. Yet the figure of Christ is also a reminder, amid all the world's pains, that the heart of reality is a compassion that knows us through and through, and that there is more life in heaven and on earth than many of us ever dream of. The figure of Christ is not to be reduced. It opens out hearts and minds and souls to life's full scope, its full depth. At some level, deep inside us, it gives us space.

2. *Jesus as Symbol of the Measure of Reality*

Part of the challenge as one grows up is to expand the image of Christ, the symbol of God, so that it encompasses more of its full capacity. At times the New Testament does this in ways that are surprising or disconcerting. It presents Christ not just as a specific individual but as the rock in the desert (1 Cor. 10.4), or the one through whom all things were created (Col. 1.16).

What does this mean—the one through whom all things were created? All things? To get some sense of the implications it is useful to glance at two realities—the universe, and the human mind. The universe is beyond us in many senses. In Sean O'Casey's *Juno and the Paycock*, Captain Boyle says 'I ofen looked up at the sky an' assed meself the question—what is the moon, what is the stars?' Today more is known but less gets through. More is stashed in books and data-banks and perhaps in brains, but on a cloudless night, when we step outside our front door, our skies are so clogged by smog and light that we see less than the cavemen.

For myself, I find it difficult to get my mind around a simple thing like the speed of light. I know the figures, but I cannot grasp the reality. The nearest I came to it was in Germany during the Cold War, when NATO planes, practicing for possible war with the Soviet Union and its Warsaw Pact allies, would fly low over the city, screaming from horizon to horizon in seconds. You could scarcely turn your head fast enough to keep them in sight. But to see a plane setting off in the direction of Australia, flying low around the entire earth, and to turn around and see it coming back from the other side, with residues of Australian dust or whatever, and to see it again set off and come back, back seven times in one second, with seven layers of residue— that is beyond me. It leaves me speechless, breathless. And then to think that even if you could get a plane, a spaceship, that would travel at that speechless speed, and you decided, now that you had some serious wings, to have a look at the local galaxy, the Milky Way, crossing all the way from one side of it to the other, coast to coast as it were, and to get an early start, you set out two thousand years ago—how would that be? By now you would be one-fiftieth of the way across.

As for other galaxies, it's not just that we cannot cross them. We cannot even count them.

It gets worse. The unawareness of the outside universe is balanced by an unawareness of the universe that is within ourselves—the universe that is our brain/mind/soul. Much modern psychology was dominated first by the doctrinaire pronouncements of Freud. Then, in reaction to Freud's sweeping dogmas, psychology became much more careful and painstaking, but in its care and pains, in its prolonged experimentation, it focused considerably on rats.

Psychology now has generally moved beyond both Freud and rats, but the over-simplifications of those years still colour today's views, and they have found new energy in writers such as Richard Dawkins who, in a peculiar adaptation of Darwin, reduces everything in humans to the mechanics of selfish genes, mechanics that know nothing about altruism. Altruism may indeed be tainted at times, but the evidence for its existence is solid, and Dawkins' refusal to allow such features to human beings means that his picture of the human mind is fiercely reduced.[8] The mind is rendered absent; inwardness has been dispelled from the modern story of the self.[9] To a

8.   Robinson 2010: 31-75.
9.   Robinson 2010.

significant degree we literally do not know what is going on inside. We are unaware. In a phrase sometimes attributed to Elie Wiesel, survivor of a Nazi death-camp, 'We have reached the moon and lost sight of our souls'.

The general unawareness regarding the mind is matched or mirrored in unawareness regarding individuals. To take a simple example, I remember in the build-up to an American football final—perhaps the 1987 Super Bowl in Pasadena, or a college final—the name of each player was called out before he ran on to the field, and for one particular name the crowd gave an exceptional cheer; and the TV commentator said something like, 'Everybody knows his name'. However, afterwards the player said, 'Yes, everybody knows my name, but nobody knows who I am'.

The name of Jesus Christ is often like that—well known but often without having a sense of what is behind the name. Sometimes it is just a swear word, or a name that makes people uncomfortable. It seems easy to picture some Gospel scenes—a couple with a baby seeking safety in a foreign land; fisherman mending nets; brothers seeking top jobs—but when you take the figure of Jesus in full dimensions, as 'Lord, Son of God, image of the invisible God, the Word through whom all things were made', then there is a problem. How do you get a sense of this reality?

One of the first steps is to avoid reducing things. At times it is indeed right to reduce things, to cut them down to size, for instance, to shrink inflated problems. But it is also necessary to allow things to be as expansive and as complex as they really are. Fundamentalism in its broadest sense is a refusal to accept genuine complexity—whether the complexity of people, especially opponents, or of greater realities, especially the ultimate realities of creation, the creator, and the creator's ongoing role—the role that is depicted through the figure of Jesus.

But again the figure of Jesus is not to be reduced. The tragedy with the quest for the historical Jesus is not just that it is seeking something impossible, but that—*somewhat* as Dawkins reduces the mind—the historical reconstructions present forms of Jesus that are desperately reduced. It is hardly an accident that the kind of science underlying Dawkins's flattening of the mind coincided in time with the kind of scientific history that flattened Jesus. The quest for the historical Jesus installs the flicker of a matchstick in place of the aurora borealis. And many forms of talking about Jesus, instead of expanding people's lives, makes them constricted.

We need more than a matchstick Jesus. From the very beginning of Christianity and through the ages, people of all levels of life have sought to spell out the reality of the creator's presence. Some of the names used by the early Epistles—Son of God, Lord, and image of the unseen God (Col. 1.15)—place Jesus in the realm of the eternal and divine. And the beginning of John's Gospel's goes further, into the *Logos*, the Word—meaning 'the very Reason and Mind of God' (Young 2000: 198), something so close to God that, like God, it is the source of truth and goodness. Again to quote Young:

> Wherever there was truth and goodness,
> it ultimately came from the immanent *Logos* of God,
> and anticipated the full revelation of the *Logos* in Jesus Christ (Young 2000: 198).

This is hard to absorb: 'Wherever there was truth and goodness'. Wherever.

Jesus as Symbol of Shadowed Beauty

The 'wherever' concerning truth is not only hard to absorb. It comes with something else—beauty. The full revelation of God's *Logos* or Word, moving through truth and goodness, inevitably involves beauty. The grouping of truth, goodness and beauty is found also in ancient philosophers.

Beauty is a key theme in the Bible—from the drum-beat of the goodness of creation (Gen. 1) to the resounding emergence of the beauty of the new Jerusalem at the end of the book of Revelation (Rev. 21–22, esp. 21.1-2). In the Bible's opening chapters (Gen. 1.4; 6.2) the word for 'good', *tov*, seems interchangeable with 'beautiful':

> God saw that the light was *tov*.
> The sons of God saw that the daughters of men were *tov*.

The Bible's emphasis on beauty appears in many ways. For instance, the very form of many biblical books, their construction, shows beauty. There is beauty for example in the architectonic symmetry and multi-faceted variation of texts such as Genesis, Judges, the Elijah–Elisha narrative, Mark and John—a beauty that in modern times was often bypassed, until quite recently.

The beauty is found also in creation, in the goodness that seems to flow through all creatures—from light and stars, to land, animals and humans. Beauty occurs yet again in the various images of God or of the Lord God: taking clay to form a human; providing companionship; walking in the garden; making clothes; showing concern for the victim, Abel; and concern for the killer, Cain; moving from anger with the world to an understanding of the world; setting the rainbow in the clouds—a sign that, with its evoking of the deathly deluge, encompassed evil and good.

The presence of beauty continues in Christ, especially in giving him names and titles. Like ardent lovers, ancient writers sometimes gave Christ several names, and even the cool-headed Thomas Aquinas

> in [commenting on] the book of Isaiah…identifies about ninety names as names of Christ. These are the result either of a spiritual reading of Scripture or of the application of prophecy to the person of Christ. Of these ninety names over forty are not mentioned in the New Testament, e.g., Flower, Stream, Mountain, Fruit of the Earth, Covenant (Schoot 2000: 337).

In a more formal discussion of Christ, in his *Summa theologiae*, Aquinas mentions over one hundred names, mostly biblical (Schoot 2000: 335-43, esp. 335). Something or someone with over a hundred names is beyond names, or as they say in Spanish, *'una cosa que no tiene nombre'*, a thing that has no name. Again, 'I ofen looked up at the sky an' assed meself... what is the stars?' The figure of Christ is about the heart of reality—far away, close at hand, and deep inside. Christ is like another dimension of reality. To return to Lord Rees:

> In theory, there could be another entire universe less than a millimetre away from us, but we are oblivious to it because that millimetre is measured in a fourth spatial dimension and we are imprisoned in just three.[10]

This is indeed just theory, but it may reflect something of the complexity of the physical world, and in doing so suggests the complexity of the world of the spirit and particularly the world of Christ, who is like a bridge between spirit and matter.

In Islam, Jesus is regarded as one of the prophets, but the extraordinary reverence that traditional Christianity gives to Jesus Christ, goes instead to the Holy Koran, and the book is revered and beautified accordingly. However, though the Bible is inspired and sometimes beautified, the biblical tradition keeps a greater distance between God's revelation and books. God alone is good (Lk. 18.19), and in that sense, is the ultimate beauty.

But the beauty is shadowed. At first it may seem otherwise. In the Bible's opening scene, God leads the earth on to the stage as it were, and the procession of creatures is splendid and sure-footed. Amid the steady march of creation's six days, the drum-beat seems solid:

'it was good',
'it was good',
'it was good',
'it was good',
'it was good',
'it was good',
'it was very good'.

In such a scene, where the declarations of goodness outnumber the six days, it may seem that the goodness will always last, and the beauty will never be shaken. But, amid all the solemn splendour, one of the days misses a beat. There is no 'it was good' on day two.

Then, from among the wild beasts, beasts 'that the Lord God made' and that originally were seen as good, one emerges that lures the woman into something that does indeed look good, but when she and her man fall for the luring words, the goodness and beauty begin to unravel. In a few scenes the

10. Rees, quoted in Leake 2010.

action moves on to fratricide, seventy-seven fold vengeance, and eventually to a deluge that engulfs the world.

The beauty has an ambiguity. The beauty of the daughters of men leads to the chaos that triggers the deluge. The beauty of Sarah brings a threat of death to Abraham and leads to lies, then to the takeover of Sarah by Pharaoh's officials, and finally to the subsequent infliction of plagues on Pharaoh and his household. Beauty is combustible.

Yet when Genesis asks the most crucial question of all, whether God has steadfast love for Abraham, a question that dominates the book's longest and most central episode (Gen. 24), the answer comes in the person of a woman who is like an incarnation of God's steadfast love—the 'very beautiful' Rebecca, the woman whose entrance and energy stand out (Gen. 24.15-21).

Yet even here, even when Rebecca appears and lights up the stage, even when she effectively puts the exotic camels in the shade—ten of them!— even then the magnificence of her beauty does not come across fully to Abraham's emissary. He is slow in seeing clearly what is in front of him. Somewhere a shadow hovers.

And so it is through the Bible. Whether the focus is on Rebecca at the well, or the Beloved in the Song of Songs, or Jesus on the road to Emmaus, the realm of God is elusive, the beauty is shadowed. In Isaiah (Isa. 53.2) the Suffering Servant—someone inseparable from Christ—is 'without beauty'. Not to mention the planet's non-stop procession of numbing losses and deformities of mind and body. And in crucifixion, beauty gives way to horror.

But the figure of Jesus, instead of hiding the horror, places it centre stage. Somehow, it is by taking in the horror, by facing it squarely, that the divine figure will be encountered, and that the underlying beauty will be seen. The beauty—or glimmers. Even at the end, as Jesus dies and all seems bitter and final, there are suggestions of a further reality.[11]

The interweaving of beauty and shadow is probably at its sharpest, at its most sustained, in the Song of Songs. The Song of Songs is sometimes read as standard love poetry, just as Genesis–Kings has sometimes been read as standard history. But Genesis–Kings has a whole other layer of meaning, and has traditionally been classed as Mosaic or prophetic; and the Song of Songs is likewise open to a whole other level of meaning, and traditionally has also been interpreted by both Judeans and Christians as a drama of the encounter between God and the human soul, or God and a human community. In the context of the overall prophetic nature of the Bible, the deeper meaning of the Song of Songs is completely at home. According to Jewish tradition, Rabbi Akiva declared:

11.   Brodie 1993a: 551-52.

The whole world is not worth the day
on which the Song of Songs was given to Israel
for all the writings are holy
but the Song of Songs is the holiest of the holy.

The Song of Songs has long needed a study that sets its interweaving of beauty and shadow within the larger context of similar interweavings in the Bible as a whole. This need now finds some answer in Edmée Kingsmill's *Song of Songs* (2010).

The vividness of the biblical images, including those of the Song of Songs, is partly mirrored by the vividness of a mystical writer such as Meister Eckhart (c. 1260–1327). The purpose of Eckhart's imagery is to lead people to an awareness of what is beyond image—a beauty beyond words.

In love, in the zone, in Christ. The idea of union with the living Jesus, or of being 'in Christ' may sound trite, but like being 'in love' or 'in the zone' it refers to something real. When someone falls 'in love' their circumstances may remain largely the same, but, without any change of address, they have moved to a new space, and their life has changed.

Likewise when, in the course of play, a sportsperson is 'in the zone'— when through an enigmatic process, often associated with long practice but ultimately unquantifiable, their play switches into a gear where they do everything right—they still look essentially the same, and they are still on the same field of play, but again they have moved to a new space, and for a while their life has changed.

Likewise too amid the rough and tumult of life, when, instead of caving in to despair or bitterness, a person keeps their sights on something true and good and genuinely beautiful (no matter how shadowed), then—particularly if they open their heart and mind to the source of that truth, goodness and beauty, and to its presence in the people and world about them—then they move into another kind of zone, the zone that Paul calls 'in Christ'. It is hardly an accident that *chriō*, 'anoint', the word underlying 'Christ', is associated primarily with communicating dignity, beauty and well-being. Here too Jesus is not to be reduced. In John's Gospel there is no escaping the increasing shadows, especially as reflected in the three simple phrases, 'it was winter'; 'it was night'; 'it was cold' (Jn 10.22; 13.30; 18.18), but, against all odds, the advance of life is shown as also bringing an increasing joy; 'it is only when the abiding deepens that the joy really blossoms' (Brodie 1993a: 482). John's final chapter (ch. 21) 'is…evocative of profound beauty' (Brodie 1993a: 581).

Overall, the picture of Christ emerges not so much as God in God's own self but as God's presence in the cosmos, a presence that incorporates everything from stars to hearts and minds, a presence that is sufficiently attentive and self-giving not only to counter and absorb the weight of sin and death, but to stand by the searching heart and mind and to constantly offer a spirit of truth and goodness and beauty.

Jesus, in a sense historical, and also for all humans. This shadowed living beauty that we call Jesus Christ is not a specific human being. It is visualized as a Jewish-born carpenter, and at one level it is personal and history-related. Jesus Christ is historical insofar as he symbolizes the aspect of a personal God that is interwoven with the fierce particularity of history and with the bloodied beauty of individual lives.

But the full reality of Christ is a universal presence and is not owned by any religion, nation, class, colour or gender (the masculine 'he' is a temporary convention). Christians have played a central role in visualizing and naming this presence, but Jews had done so first—though without using the name Jesus Christ—and despite the variations in subsequent Jewish and Christian formulations, despite occasional better insights by one or the other, it is often the same Jesus who underlies both religions.

Likewise other religions. Formulations may vary, and from time to time one may be more insightful than another, but it is the same Jesus Christ who underlies all formulations, no matter what name we use. The blessed Mohammed may not have known of the divinity of Jesus—his account of Jesus came from a Christian monk who was an Arian and who therefore would not have included Jesus' divinity—but such was the Islamic emphasis on the sovereignty of Allah, known especially as the Merciful, the Compassionate, that, in the final analysis, Islam reveres much of what is otherwise signified by the name of the Lord Jesus Christ, Son of God, and so, despite important differences, Islam has a huge overlap with Christianity. It contains Jesus far more than its picture of Jesus as simply a prophet.

And likewise also further religions, especially Hinduism and Buddhism. Even if they have never heard of Jesus, and are not to be referred to as Christians, some of their truths and values overlap with those of the biblical tradition, especially some of the universal truths expressed by the figure of Jesus, and to that degree, they carry Jesus within them.

As for Christians, they may indeed carry Christ's name, but perhaps little more. Many do not necessarily reflect the deep reality of Jesus. Other Christians, however, bear not only something of the reality of Jesus but also some of the universal truths and values of other religious traditions, including Hinduism, Buddhism, Judaism or Islam.

What is important is that, while the loss of Jesus as a specific individual human may bring sadness, union with the living Jesus—the universal living figure of truth and goodness and shadowed beauty, the Gospel figure who touches the leper, embraces the children, and lays down his life for our sins— union with this Jesus brings new life.

Chapter 22

REASONING WITH BEAUTY

Late have I loved you, O Beauty ever ancient, ever new,
Late have I loved you…
—St Augustine of Hippo (*Confessions*, Book Ten)

Whatever the full meaning of the New Testament, a basic question remains: Can I believe it? Can I believe it in the same way that I believe a parable— not as an account of historical facts, but as a story that portrays the ultimate truth? Can I take the story of the Magi visiting the baby as seriously as I take the account of the Good Samaritan caring for the man who was left half-dead? Or the Resurrection as seriously as I take the father's welcome for the Prodigal Son?

Maybe I can so believe. Maybe I can take reassurance from those who already have believed—the cloud of witnesses and writings, down through the ages and now.

But the cloud is often dark. And in practice the view of beauty is not only shadowed—for many, the message about Jesus Christ is mired beneath layers of pain and anger, because, regardless of how you interpret the Christian vision, history is strewn with sickness, accidents and disasters; and the religious institution or its representatives have done harm: crusades; inquisitions; imperious use of authority; involvement with brutal regimes and conquests; mistreatment of people, of peoples, of women, of children, and of those who are different in some way; unduly black-and-white rulings on wrenching moral and medical issues; cover-ups; and thousands of diverse kinds of offences committed by members and ministers of the church. How could anyone believe the message given by such a messenger?

As in a quarrel between two people, at times even a single issue can block the entire process of communication—like a blockage in a thousand-mile pipeline that was meant to deliver clean water to those in the desert—and so there may be no sense of harmony with the institution, and, consequently, no sense of harmony with God and those formally associated with God.

To believe or not to believe, that is the question.

If this weight of evil is ever to be surmounted, it is necessary first to face it in all its awfulness—whether it be in a large institution, or in an individual or in one's own self. And then, when the evil has indeed been acknowledged, it is necessary to ask what else is there—whether in the large institution, or the individual, or oneself.

The struggle with believing has pushed me to look closely at what believing involves, particularly to ask whether it respects normal human intelligence—reason. This is something I should have learned years ago, and maybe I did, but the question then was not as pressing.

The essential facts seem fairly straightforward.

Reasoning and believing are obviously two quite distinct operations. Reasoning generally works things out methodically, step-by-step. Believing leaps across the details and just grasps the truth of the matter. This leaping process does not necessarily make believing wrong, any more than intuition need be wrong. It just means that its way of reaching the truth is different. Both capabilities—reasoning and believing—are important. They complement each other, *somewhat* as do seeing and hearing.

The eighteenth-century Enlightenment, partly in reaction to superstition and corruption, tried to base everything on reason. Reason would surely bring truth and justice. But, as is now becoming clearer, reason alone is insufficient. It does not catch some essential truths. 'The heart has its reasons that reason cannot know'—Blaise Paschal.

Yet reason is important in the process of believing. It provides clearance and confirmation. Clearance, because reason can open the way for believing, particularly if it allows that something is possible or probable, that maybe there is a higher power of some kind, and that Jesus is essentially a true symbol of that higher power, the Jesus who got crucified. On the other hand, if reason can prove that something is impossible, then that has to be respected. It does not make sense to believe what is definitely impossible. Reason can balance the probabilities. And some maintain that reason can prove the existence of a higher power, but, for diverse reasons, not all are convinced of this.

Reason can also give confirmation. *After* a person has believed, reason may find *indications or signs* that the belief is true, that, as symbolized in the figure of Jesus, the higher power—God in shorthand—did make humans for a purpose.

Two such signs are the physical world and the human mind. We have already mentioned the physical world and the mind simply as reminders of reality's complexity. The physical world is more vast and more miniscule than we can imagine; and the mind has a quality of inwardness and universality that we have not yet fathomed. In their complexity the physical world and the mind act as reminders not to simplify Christ, through whom they were made.

The focus here is not on their complexity but on their orientation. Put simply, the cosmos seems to be tuned for us; and there are indications that we are tuned for the cosmos—for all things and for the Presence underlying all things. And, for someone who already believes, these orientations of the cosmos and of the mind provide confirmation that believing has found the truth.

(1) *A cosmos tuned for us.* At first sight reality may seem to be based on the random distribution of chemicals—of endless millions of purposeless molecules. The universe is a chemical accident, and so are we. Even if some extraordinary explosion or power once set the universe in motion, that power has long abandoned the random process to its collisions and catastrophes. Even when plants and animals emerge from the accident, that too is a random process, natural selection, where the only law is a law of the jungle—survival of the fittest. And so Richard Dawkins, having studied the process of natural selection, proclaims that the notion of God is an illusion.

However, the process of natural selection is but a small part of a vast pattern which shows extraordinary evidence of design, a phenomenon of design that not only extends all the way from the Big Bang but that seems peculiarly oriented towards the development of the world and the emergence of human life—so much so that it provides strong confirmation to the belief that God made the world for the purpose of giving life and of inviting people to enter into the process and to engage the underlying multifaceted God with all one's heart, soul, mind and strength. Or quite simply: the universe functions as if it were made for *anthropoi*, for people—'the anthropic principle'.

For instance, if the force of gravity had been a tiny fraction weaker, the initial fragments of the universe would have continued to expand indefinitely and would never have been drawn together to make many stars or planets—and eventually plants or animals. But if the force of gravity had been a tiny fraction stronger, all the fragments would have been drawn right back to their point of origin with such force that the universe would have imploded into itself.[1]

(2) *A mind tuned for the cosmos, for everything.* There is reason to ask whether humans, especially humans' minds, are tuned for the cosmos. Even the role of the body is not to be overlooked. Without the chemical fallout from exploding stars our bodies could not exist, so the body too is somehow kindred to the cosmos. But the mind needs special attention.

In this discussion, this prolonged cup of coffee, the story of how humans see the mind can be summarized in three steps, three stages of history.

---

1. On the anthropic principle, see McGrath 2009: esp. 111-222.

First, in ancient times, philosopher-scientists such as Aristotle put huge energy not only into mapping the details of natural science but also into observing the working of the psyche, and concluded that there is a basic affinity between the human soul and everything: 'The soul (*psyche*) is in some way all things'.[2] Marilynne Robinson reviews the scene:

> Consider the notion of the human being as microcosm, as a small epitome of the universe. This idea persisted from the beginning of philosophical thought to the beginning of the modern period. In the thought of Heraclitus, we are of one substance with the fire that is the essence of the universe. Monads being for Leibniz the fundamental constituents of the cosmos, we are in his scheme a kind of monad whose special character is to mirror the universe. Through many variations, the idea of the microcosm asserted a profound kinship between humankind and the whole of being, which common sense must encourage us to believe does in fact exist. It would be more than miraculous, indeed an argument for something like a special creation, if we were in any sense set apart from being as a whole. Our energies can only derive from, and express, the larger phenomenon of energy. And there is the haunting compatibility of our means of knowing with the universe of things to be known (Robinson 2010: xiii).

Overlapping with this persistent thread in philosophy is the persistent experience of a long line of spiritual explorers and writers, including scriptural writers, who have spent much or most of their lives in meditation or in attentiveness to the deepest reality within us, and have concluded that we are built for connection with the supreme reality or presence underlying everything.

Second—the second stage in how humans have viewed the mind—*is the time of the emergence of 'modern science*, meaning the form of science that became dominant around 1900 and that is still dominant in much popular thinking and writing. This type of science tended to flatten the mind, to reduce it. Coming back to Freud and Dawkins, both reduce the mind, and they do so in ways that are mutually contradictory. For Freud, the human mind/spirit is grounded and governed by something universal—a repressed memory of killing a father, a memory which regardless of a society's sophistication, 'persists in every individual and all generations, as conscience, as religion, in repression and sublimation'; for Dawkins, the processes of the mind are powered by the selfishness of a gene, and the believing processes of the soul are a hangover, not from processes that may include sophistication, but from the primitiveness of ancient people; and Dawkins provides various theories about elusive distant events that first led primitive people to believe (Robinson 2010: 31-107, esp. 81, 91).

---

2. Aristotle, *De anima* III, 8, 431b, 21.

Third, present day science—as opposed to the brand associated with 1900—is giving new impetus to the study of the mind. To begin with, the larger world, with its quarks and photons, is emerging as much more mysterious than had been thought, and if we are part of that larger world, then it is not easy to reduce us to one dimension. Besides, present-day science is now uncovering a new picture of the brain, mind and soul. This is not going to be quick or easy. When one of my nieces, Caroline, showed me her thesis on the brain I could not digest even the first two pages. And when in June 2009, I went to Cambridge, England, to see John Polkinghorne about physics and the cosmos, he diverted my attention from physics to the emerging world of neuroscience and to the simple fact that the average brain has 100 billion cells and each cell has a thousand links to other cells. And he explained that in contrast to research on the universe, which has reached some maturity, research on the human mind is still in its infancy.

The complexity of neuroscience partly matches that of the universe, but neuroscience has not had the equivalent of a space programme. And even the space programme, despite all its successes, is only beginning to discern the reality of the cosmos. Some neuroscientists claim we are 'hardwired for God'. However, so far the scientific evidence is not clear. As neuroscientists remind us, there is a long way to go.

It does not seem possible to say how long it will be before the sense of the wonder inherent in much present-day science begins to pervade popular consciousness and to replace the 1900 sense of 'modern science' that, like late rumbling thunder, or like the Gunkel-related clinging fog of oral models of composition, still dominates much public discussion—science as woodenly sure, antagonistic to believing—but perhaps, when that time comes, science and religion, instead of being seen as enemies, will emerge as the allies that they are by nature.

Meanwhile, as we wait for further reports on how we are made and what we are capable of, it is already clear that from birth we are engaged in processes of believing, of trusting things, people, and groupings of people, and even if the trust is sometimes betrayed, we need to go on trusting/ believing to some degree.

Furthermore, the instinct to connect spontaneously with what is outside us goes beyond connections that are immediate and measurable. We also seem to be built for connecting with the heart of the universe. Obviously part of this connection is through our reason. Reason goes a limited and sometimes impressive way towards calculating and absorbing the entire universe.

But there is another capacity for connection that seems to go further, that can go right to the heart of things, and that in some sense connects with everything. For Augustine of Hippo the connection came slowly, 'You have made us for yourself, O Lord, and our hearts cannot rest until they rest in you' (*Confessions*, Book 1, Chapter 1). In recent times, this phenomenon of the human's inbuilt orientation towards the infinite, towards God, has been spelled out especially by Karl Rahner.[3]

Allowing that orientation to blossom is central to becoming a Christian: 'The Christian of the future will be a mystic or will not exist at all' (Rahner 1981: 149). The mystic's journey is not to the top of the Himalayas or to a distant planet, but, as Rahner goes on to say, to the core of our own being; it means 'a genuine experience of God emerging from the very heart of our existence'. This is down to earth stuff. Theology, reflection about God, can prepare the ground for such experience, but the experience is something else, and may be very low key.

This human orientation towards something greater may emerge in the part of us that wants something more, above all a greater love. There is a form of restlessness that would seem to be reflected, for instance, in a sentence from Edna O'Brien that runs something like: 'So many loves, so many loves, but never one true love'. The reference is to ideal romantic love, but it touches on wanting a love that meets a person's deepest desire, on having a place to lay one's head. Edna O'Brien is from Scariff, and Scariff was never a primitive place. So, Dawkins notwithstanding, the desire seems to come not from some undeveloped background but from the depths of the human heart.

What is important is that already there are significant indications that believing is not something that goes against the makeup of the mind or against reason. On the contrary, many serious contemplative explorers maintain that the mind is made for connecting to the source of all things. Connection can give energy, whether connection with one's body, feelings, reason, imagination—or capacity to believe. Believing brings a key capacity into play, and so brings something else to life within a person—more of what is human and deepest within us. It is somewhat like getting into the sea by jumping or diving from a height rather than by walking in. We become more alive. It is possible of course to get through life without much believing, as it is without much listening. But to do so is to miss out.

Again, Teresa of Avila saw believing as potentially developing through seven degrees of energy or vitality. Obviously, instead of developing positively, the energy of believing can be corrupted, and like the energy of a muscle, can be used to do harm. But in themselves, developed muscles are good, and so are other developed human capacities, including believing, whether it be the capacity to believe concerning people or concerning larger realities.

---

3. See, for instance, Rahner 1978: 31-35.

No one can tell what a specific believer will find. Contemplative people such as Eckhart and John of the Cross have lived with both insight and darkness. Matthew's Gospel tells of finding a treasure that becomes the most valuable thing in one's life (13.44). Albert Schweitzer (1906: 401) spoke of listening and becoming aware, even amid labours, conflicts and sufferings, of a truth beyond words. And in the end Augustine of Hippo was surprised:

> Late have I loved you, O Beauty ever ancient, ever new,
> Late have I loved you,
> You were within me, but I was outside
> And it was there that I searched for you...

Within me, and within every other human, and equally within 'the least... hungry...thirsty...a stranger...naked...sick...in prison...'

Bart Ehrman's 2012 book, *Did Jesus Exist?*, responds to a diverse group who recently have produced extensive literature questioning Jesus' existence. The book has three parts: (1) evidence for Jesus' existence; (2) counter claims; (3) who was Jesus? This epilogue first summarizes the essence of Bart Ehrman's study, especially the evidence in Part 1, and then responds to it.

Summary, Part 1: The Evidence for Jesus' Historical Existence

The Gospels (canonical and non-canonical) all tell of a historical Jesus, and despite some borrowing from one another (for example, from Mark), they are so varied, and each has so much distinct material that each is an independent witness to Jesus. Examination of the gospels indicates that they used many diverse written sources, sources now lost but sometimes seen as recoverable, and named in their absence as Q, M, L, a Signs Source, a Discourse Source, a core version of *Thomas*, and so on. These many texts too, the gospels' written sources, all speak of Jesus as historical; and their independence is so strong that 'we cannot think of the early Christian Gospels as going back to a solitary source... The view that Jesus existed is found in multiple independent sources that must have been circulating throughout various regions of the Roman Empire in the decades before the gospels that survive were produced' (82). And the gospels' written sources were quite old: 'A good number of scholars dated Q to the 50s' (81). And while we do not have absolute certainty that non-canonical gospels such as *Peter* and *Thomas* go back to written sources 'in both of these cases some scholars have mounted strenuous arguments that they do...[and a recent study, 2006] makes a strong... literary...argument that the core of...Thomas goes back to a Gospel in circulation prior to 50 CE' (82).

Underlying these many diverse written witnesses were oral traditions: 'Oral traditions...about Jesus circulated widely throughout the major urban areas of the Mediterranean from a very early time' (86). Evidence for oral traditions includes:

- Revised form criticism. While virtually 'no [scholars now] agree with the precise formulation of the form critics, Schmidt, Dibelius and Bultmann...the most basic idea behind their approach is still widely shared, namely that before the Gospels...and their sources [were written], oral traditions about Jesus circulated. [Apparently]... all our [written] sources for the historical Jesus...were entirely or partly...based on oral traditions' (85).
- Without oral traditions 'it is impossible to explain all the written sources that emerged in the middle and end of the first century' (86).
- Traces of Aramaic, especially in some gospels, must reflect a background in some oral traditions that began in Aramaic (87-92).

These oral traditions were old:

> If scholars are right that Q and the core of the Gospel of Thomas, to pick just two examples, do date from the 50s, and that they were based on oral traditions that had already been in circulation for a long time, how far back do these traditions go? [For] anyone who thinks that Jesus existed...they ultimately go back to Jesus...say, around the year 29 or 30. But even anyone who just wonders if Jesus existed has to assume that there were stories being told about him in the 30s and 40s. For one thing, as we will see [later]...how else would someone like Paul have known to persecute the Christians, if Christians didn't exist? And how could they exist if they did not know anything about Jesus? (85).

The role of oral tradition as a basis for all our written sources about Jesus is not something minor; it 'has significant implications for our quest to determine if Jesus actually lived' (85).

Other New Testament sources (non-Pauline letters and Paul) do not rely on the Gospels or on one another, but they too speak of a historical Jesus, and so they must have received it independently from the on-going oral tradition. Paul frequently spoke of Jesus as historical, and his meetings with two of Jesus' earliest and closest disciples, Peter and Jesus' brother James in Jerusalem and Antioch (Gal. 1.18-20; 2.11-14), ensured that he too had first-hand knowledge of the oldest oral traditions, and so he would have known for sure whether Jesus really existed. Early Church sources (Papias, Ignatius, 1 Clement) all speak of a historical Jesus, but they cannot be shown to depend on the gospels, so they must have drawn ultimately on the old oral tradition. Ignatius, for instance, as bishop of Antioch (around 110 CE), would have heard of the dramatic Antioch meeting involving Peter and Paul and so would have had an independent line to the oldest traditions. Besides—a key point—the message of a crucified messiah is so countercultural for a Jew that it can only be explained by a historical event, in this case the crucifixion of someone the disciples had thought was the messiah.

Overall then, the evidence shows a long line of sources, all independent—all with independent access to the oldest traditions—and all agreeing in diverse ways, that Jesus was historical. Such evidence is decisive.

Summary, Part 2: Contrary Claims

Writers who say Jesus was a myth exaggerate the similarity of myths with Jesus. Robert Price and Thomas Thompson say the gospels are essentially a paraphrase of the Old Testament, but such claims are to be classified under 'Weak and Irrelevant'. Using an Old Testament framework does not mean the event being described never happened. To say it does is like looking at a historical novel set in the French Revolution and saying, because of its novel framework, that the French Revolution never happened.

Summary, Part 3: Jesus' Life

Jesus, a Jewish *tektōn* ('carpenter'), became an apocalyptic prophet; he was not an Essene, yet somewhat like one, and he announced the imminent revelation/apocalypse of God's new kind of kingdom. But apparently he was misunderstood as claiming to be a self-appointed king, something Rome could not tolerate.

Response

At first this thesis seems plausible. The idea of Jesus as historical corresponds to age-old perception, and the three-phase picture of gospel development—oral tradition, adaptations, and gospel writing—corresponds largely with the picture developed early in the last century, first in form criticism, and, by the 1960s, in some church documents.

But the thesis has internal weaknesses. The key role attributed to oral tradition corresponds to no known model of oral tradition, and makes no reference to recent concerns about invoking oral tradition (see Chapter 12). Relying on Q and the *core* of *Thomas*, two hypothetical documents, to provide a bridge through the 50s is skating on thin ice. Ehrman's work refers to a recently published 'strong argument' for dating the *core* of *Thomas* to a date prior to 50 CE, but it does not attempt to summarize the logic of that argument. And the reader who tries to track down that logic by going back to the cited author will discover that the argument, which remains elusive, presupposes having read the author's yet earlier work.

But the bridge of thin ice is not necessary. Nor is oral tradition necessary to explain the New Testament books and their history-like picture of Jesus. Since around 1970 an alternative explanation of the New Testament and related texts has been emerging. Researchers are recognizing precise ways in which New Testament texts are explained as depending not on oral tradition but on older literature, especially older scripture. The New Testament books are Scripture reshaping Scripture to speak to a changed situation, and they may also reshape one another. Yet, whatever its source, each text is worked into something distinctive, and in that sense is independent. The dependence of the gospels on the Old Testament and on other extant texts is incomparably clearer and more verifiable than its dependence on any oral tradition—as seen, for instance, in the thorough dependence of Jesus' call to disciples (Lk. 9.57-62) on Elijah's call (1 Kgs 19). The sources supply not only a framework but a critical mass which pervades the later text.

The Old Testament, especially the Greek Septuagint, is being reborn in new books. God's down-to-earth word is finding new expression. N.T. Wright (2005: 7) speaks of recent Pauline research as taking place 'in a world with its eyes newly opened by contemporary literary study…and now all kinds of aspects of Paul are being tested for implicit and explicit [Old Testament] storylines'. Aspects of Paul, and equally aspects of the gospels.

But Ehrman's study does not take account of this new research. It does not concentrate on discerning the literary nature of the various documents and so breaks Rule One of historical investigation. It summarizes the criteria developed in the 1950s for tracing the historical Jesus, but makes no mention of the criteria developed since the 1980s for detecting literary dependence. So it cannot deal adequately with Price and Thompson, and shows little awareness that—whatever some of their opinions—their work has a place in a central new field of biblical research.

It is such studies that help to give an alternative explanation to many of the features in the New Testament. For instance: (1) occasional use of Aramaic fits the *literary* technique of archaism and the *biblical literary tradition* of inserting Aramaic into Hebrew (see Ezra–Nehemiah, later imitated in Daniel; Wesselius 2001: esp. 299-303); (2) the references to processes of going back to older material and handing it on (e.g. Lk. 1.1-4; 1 Cor. 11.2, 23; 15.1-5) are being recognized as referring to handing on a *literary* tradition (cf. J.N. Collins 2010), as being literally 'according to the scriptures'; (3) New Testament texts are independent in the sense that each one has a unique mix of sources and artistic shaping; (4) the Elijah–Elisha narrative provided a foundational literary model for the Gospels (Brown 1971; Winn 2010) and its contents were reshaped and interwoven with other texts; (5) the material attributed to the hypothetical gospel sources—Q, M, L, the Signs Source, etc—is being recognized slowly as a reshaping of extant texts; (6) as seen earlier (Chapters 15 and 16) Pauline letters construct features such as readers and opponents, and Paul's autobiographical texts (e.g. Gal. 1–2) are likewise a construct, not reliable history, so regardless of Paul's apparent assertiveness and intensity, the picture of Paul meeting Peter in Jerusalem and Antioch cannot be invoked as history, nor can it be used to explain the origin of Ignatius's information about Jesus; (7) if Ignatius did not get his information about Jesus from reports about Paul's visit, his dependence on the gospels becomes more likely. In any case, to claim in effect that neither Clement (c. 90), nor Ignatius (c. 110), nor Papias (c. 125) had ever learned directly or indirectly from any of the canonical gospels is high-risk history.[1]

The image of a crucified messiah is indeed countercultural, yet, given how biblical writers had long set narratives in opposition to one another and had refashioned older scriptures, it makes sense as part of a fresh synthesis of several Old Testament/Septuagintal texts (e.g. Isa. 52.13–53.12; cf. Acts 8.30-35; Lk. 24.25-27) that deal with the tension between suffering and God's hope. What is especially new about the crucified messiah is not just the seemingly radical contradiction of combining goodness and suffering, hope and despair, messiah and crucifixion, but also the stark image through which that contradiction is portrayed—Roman crucifixion. Yet such a process of adaptation is not new. When Luke was using the account of the death of Naboth to depict the death of Stephen, he replaced the picture of the old institutions, the monarchy and assembly, with Jewish institutions of the first century—the synagogue and Sanhedrin. And when he was using the account of the exemplary foreign commander, Naaman, he changed the nationality from Syrian to Roman, Roman centurion. So when there was a

---

1.   Details about all three are controverted, but the traditional picture is that they were bishops in three major cities (respectively Rome; Antioch; and Hierapolis), and that all three were very eager about their Christian heritage and were in contact with people in other cities.

Papias was head of the church at popular Hierapolis in 125 CE—now a UNESCO World Heritage Centre—and he was always on the look-out ('Whenever someone arrived...'), was always looking for someone who had been a companion of one of the elders who had known Andrew and Peter and the other disciples so that he could hear a living voice handing on the sayings of the Lord. Papias said he found more benefit from a living voice than from books, so it may seem credible that he had no interest in books, not even in the gospels. But the first thing said of him by the historian Eusebius—our main source on Papias—is that he 'was well known as bishop of Hierapolis, a man well skilled in all manner of learning and well-acquainted with the Scriptures', and Eusebius also recounts that Papias actually wrote books—'five books...which bear the title *Interpretation of Our Lord's Declarations*' (Eusebius, *History* 36.1; 37.1; trans., Cruse, 1998: 100, 102)—so the idea that he would not be interested in the gospels makes no sense.

Papias emerges as ambiguous. He emphasizes direct oral communication and decries books, but he has a huge interest in books, especially about the Lord. This ambiguity seems like a variation on the reference to tradition in 1 Corinthians (11.2, 23; 15.1-3) and Luke (1.1-4)—a tradition which at first looks oral, but, as already indicated, in fact is 'according to the scriptures', literary (J.N. Collins 2010), an ambiguity similar to Christianity's larger feeling about writing (as discussed in Chapter 19, esp. part 6).

need to express the ancient contradiction or paradox between God-based hope and life's inevitable sufferings it was appropriate to express those sufferings in a clear contemporary image—Roman crucifixion. It was doubly appropriate in the context of a rhetorical world that sought dramatic effect and *enargeia* (graphic presentation) (Walsh 1961: 188). Further issues of historical background belong to another discussion.[2]

Conclusion

Ehrman's book could seem to set up a false dilemma: stay with a claim to a historical Jesus, or lose Jesus and, with him, lose God. But there is a further option. Rediscover Jesus as a fresh scripture-based expression of suffering humanity's deepest strengths and hopes, and thereby rediscover a new sense of the reality we often refer to glibly as God.

Ehrman's book is to be welcomed. Despite its ill-founded version of history it helps bring the issue of Jesus' historical existence and other important issues about the nature of belief and religion to the centre of discussion.

2.   As already mentioned (Chapter 19), it is still not clear what historical situation led to setting up the image of the crucified messiah, but one of its components was a process that that was *writing-based*, and particularly *scripture-based.* Some form of crisis within Judaism apparently led a significant number of Jews to embark on a process of renewal that would require the development of their scriptures into a new narrative, involving a new covenant (or testament, 1 Cor. 11.25), a term that had precedent within the scriptures (Jer. 31.31-34); a fresh covenant had been seen as an addition, not a replacement (Deut. 28.69).

The undertaking contained the building of a story—narrative, historicized-fiction— especially about Jesus and Paul, and such story-building can be described with terms such as fiction, myth, invention, conspiracy and forgery (Ehrman 2012: 82, 114). The same terms can be used of the Torah, the Book of Moses, which was not written by Moses. At one level these terms are true, but used pejoratively they miss the heart of the matter, namely that, despite their use of story and their limitations, the Torah, Gospels and Epistles contain deepest wisdom.

BIBLIOGRAPHY

Aletti, Jean-Noel
    1996   'Paul et la rhetorique', in J. Schlosser (ed.), *Paul de Tarse* (LD, 165; Paris: Editions du Cerf): 27-50.

Alexander, L.C.A.
    1992   'Schools, Hellenistic', in *ABD*, V: 1005-11.
    1993   'Acts and the Ancient Intellectual Biography', in B.W. Winter and A.D. Clarke (eds.), *The Book of Acts in its Ancient Literary Setting* (Grand Rapids: Eerdmans): 31-63.
    1998   'Ancient Book Production and the Circulation of the Gospels', in Bauckham (ed.) 1998: 71-105.

Allison, D.C., Jr
    2000   *The Intertextual Jesus: Scripture in Q* (Harrisburg, PA: Trinity Press International).

Alonso Schökel, L.
    1961   'Erzahlkunst im Buch der Richter', *Bib* 42: 143-72.
    1985   'Of Methods and Models', in J.A. Emerton (ed.), *Congress Volume: Salamanca, 1983* (VTSup, 36; Leiden: E.J. Brill): 3-13.

Alter, R.
    1981   *The Art of Biblical Narrative* (New York: Basic Books).

Astruc, Jean
    1753   *Conjectures sur la Genèse. Conjectures sur les memoires originaux dont il paroit que Moyse s'est servi pour composer le Livre de la Genèse. Avec des remarques, qui appuient ou qui éclaircissent ces conjectures* (Brussels: Fricx).

Badiou, Alain
    2003   *Saint Paul: The Foundation of Universalism* (Stanford, CA: Stanford University Press).

Baird, W.
    1992   *History of New Testament Research*, I (Minneapolis: Fortress Press).

Bauckham, Richard
    1998   'For Whom Were the Gospels Written?', in Bauckham (ed.) 1998: 9-48.
    2006   *Jesus and the Eyewitnesses: The Gospels as Eyewitness Testimony* (Grand Rapids: Eerdmans).
    2007   *The Testimony of the Beloved Disciple: Narrative, History and Theology in the Gospel of John* (Grand Rapids: Baker Academic).
    2008   *Jesus and the God of Israel: 'God Crucified' and Other Studies on the New Testament's Christology of Divine Identity* (Milton Keynes: Paternoster Press).

Bauckham, Richard (ed.)
    1998   *The Gospels for All Christians: Rethinking the Gospel Audiences* (Grand
            Rapids: Eerdmans).
Bechert, Heinz
    2004   'Life of the Buddha', in *Encyclopedia of Buddhism*, I (New York:
            Thomson/Gale): 82-88.
Bikerman, E.J.
    1972   'The Augustan Empire', in J.A. Garraty and Peter Gay (eds.), *The
            Columbia History of the World* (New York: Harper & Row): 205-21.
Borgman, Paul Carlton
    2006   *The Way according to Luke: Hearing the Whole Story of Luke–Acts*
            (Grand Rapids: Eerdmans).
Brant, Jo-Ann A. *et al.* (eds.)
    2005   *Ancient Fiction: The Matrix of Early Christian and Jewish Narrative*
            (SBL Symposium Series; Atlanta: SBL).
Brien, Mary T.
    2012   '"Mercy and Righteousness have met": Literary Structure as Key to the
            Supremacy of Mercy in Romans' (unpublished diss., University of
            Limerick).
Brodie, Thomas L.
    1978   'Creative [Re]writing: Missing Link in Biblical Research', *BTB* 8: 34-39.
    1979   'A New Temple and a New Law: The Unity and Chronicler-based Nature
            of Luke 1:1–4:22a', *JSNT* 5: 21-45.
    1980   'Mark 10:1-45 as a Creative Rewriting of 1 Peter 2:18–3:17: An Abstract',
            PIBA 4: 98.
    1981   'Luke the Literary Interpreter: Luke–Acts as a Systematic Rewriting and
            Updating of the Elijah–Elisha Narrative in 1 and 2 Kings' (PhD diss.,
            Rome: Pontifical University of St Thomas, 1981).
    1981a   'Jesus as the New Elisha: Cracking the Code [John 9]', *ExpTim* 93: 39-42.
    1981b   'Jacob's Travail (Jer 30.1-13) and Jacob's Struggle (Gen 32.22-32): A Test
            Case for Measuring the Influence of the Book of Jeremiah on the Present
            Text of Genesis', *JSOT* 19: 31-60.
    1981c   'Galatians as Art', *The Bible Today* 19: 335-39.
    1983a   'The Accusing and Stoning of Naboth (1 Kgs 21:8-13) as One Component
            of the Stephen Text (Acts 6:9-14; 7:58a)', *CBQ* 45: 417-32.
    1983b   'Luke 7:36-50 as an Internalization of 2 Kings 4:1-37: A Study in Luke's
            Use of Rhetorical Imitation', *Bib* 64: 457-85.
    1984a   'Greco-Roman Imitation of Texts as a Partial Guide to Luke's Use of
            Sources', in C.H. Talbert (ed.), *Luke–Acts: New Perspectives from the
            Society of Biblical Literature* (New York: Crossroad): 7-46.
    1984b   Review of W.H. Kelber, *The Oral and Written Gospel*, *CBQ* 46: 574-75.
    1986a   'Towards Unravelling Luke's Use of the Old Testament: Luke 7.11-17 as
            an *Imitatio* of 1 Kings 17.17-24', *NTS* 32: 247-67.
    1986b   'Towards Unravelling the Rhetorical Imitation of Sources in Acts: 2 Kgs 5
            as One Component of Acts 8,9-40', *Bib* 67: 41-67.
    1989a   'The Departure for Jerusalem (Luke 9,51-56) as a Rhetorical Imitation of
            Elijah's Departure for the Jordan (2 Kgs 1,1–2,6)', *Bib* 70: 96-109.

1989b   'Luke 9:57-62: A Systematic Adaptation of the Divine Challenge to Elijah (1 Kings 19)', in D.J. Lull (ed.), *Society of Biblical Literature Seminar Papers 1989* (Atlanta: Scholars Press): 236-45.

1990   'Luke–Acts as an Imitation and Emulation of the Elijah–Elisha Narrative', in E. Richard (ed.), *New Views on Luke and Acts* (Wilmington, DE: Glazier): 78-85.

1992a   'Fish, Temple Tithe, and Remission: The God-based Generosity of Deuteronomy 14–15 as One Component of the Community Discourse (Matt 17:22–18:35)', *RB* 99: 697-718.

1992b   'Not Q but Elijah: The Saving of the Centurion's Servant (Luke 7:1-10) as an Internalization of the Saving of the Widow and her Child (1 Kgs 17:1-16)', *IBS* 14: 54-71.

1993a   *The Quest for the Origin of John's Gospel: A Source-Oriented Approach* (New York: Oxford University Press).

1993b   *The Gospel According to St. John. A Literary and Theological Commentary* (New York: Oxford University Press).

1993b   'Vivid, Positive, Practical: The Systematic Use of Romans in Matthew 1–7', *PIBA* 16: 36-55.

1994   'Again Not Q: Luke 7:18-35 as an Acts-oriented Transformation of the Vindication of the Prophet Micaiah (I Kings 22:1-38)', *IBS* 16: 2-30.

1995a   'Luke's Redesigning of Paul: Corinthian Division and Reconciliation (1 Corinthians 1–5) as One Component of Jerusalem Unity (Acts 1–5)', *IBS* 17: 98-128.

1995b   'Re-opening the Quest for Proto-Luke: The Systematic Use of Judges 6–12 in Luke 16:1–18:8', *Journal of Higher Criticism* 2: 68-101.

1996   'The Systematic Use of the Pentateuch in 1 Corinthians: An Exploratory Survey', in R. Bieringer (ed.), *The Corinthian Correspondence* (BETL, 125; Leuven: Leuven University/Peeters): 441-57.

1997   'Intertextuality and its Use in Tracing Q and Proto-Luke', in C.M. Tuckett (ed.), *The Scriptures in the Gospels* (BETL, 131; Leuven: Leuven University/Peeters): 469-77.

1999   'The Unity of Proto-Luke', in J. Verheyden (ed.), *The Unity of Luke–Acts* (BETL, 131; Leuven: Leuven University/Peeters): 627-38.

2000   *The Crucial Bridge: The Elijah–Elisha Narrative as an Interpretive Synthesis of Genesis–Kings and a Literary Model for the Gospels* (Collegeville, MN: Liturgical Press).

2001a   'An Alternative Q/Logia Hypothesis: Deuteronomy-based, Qumranlike, Verifiable', in A. Lindemann (ed.), *The Sayings Source Q and the Historical Jesus* (BETL, 158; Leuven: Leuven University/Peeters): 729-43.

2001b   *Genesis as Dialogue: A Literary, Theological and Historical Commentary* (New York: Oxford University Press).

2001c   'Genesis as Dialogue. Genesis' Twenty-Six Diptychs as a Key to Narrative Unity and Meaning', in A. Wénin (ed.), *Studies in the Book of Genesis: Literature, Redaction and History* (BETL, 155; Leuven: Leuven University/Peeters): 297-314.

2001d   'Towards Tracing the Gospels' Literary Indebtedness to the Epistles', in D.R. MacDonald (ed.), *Mimesis and Intertextuality in Antiquity and Christianity* (Harrisburg, PA: Trinity Press International): 104-16.

2004   *The Birthing of the New Testament: The Intertextual Development of the NT Writings* (NTM, 1; Sheffield: Sheffield Phoenix Press).

2008   'The Literary Unity of Numbers: Nineteen Atonement-Centered Diptychs as One Key Element', in Thomas Römer (ed.), *The Books of Leviticus and Numbers* (BETL, 215; Leuven: Peeters): 455-72.

2009   'Countering Romans: Matthew's Systematic Distillation and Transformation of Paul', in Udo Schnelle (ed.), *The Letter to the Romans* (BETL, 226; Leuven: Peeters): 521-42.

2011   *The Gospel of John: Jesus' Three Years as a Portrait of God's Spirit Working in Life* (The Bible as Dialogue, NT Series, 4; Limerick: Dominican Biblical Institute).

Brodie, T.L. (ed.)

2006   *Proto-Luke, the Oldest Gospel Account: A Christ-centered Synthesis of Old Testament History Modeled Especially on the Elijah–Elisha Narrative* (Limerick: Dominican Biblical Institute, distributed by Sheffield Phoenix Press).

Brodie, T.L., D.R. MacDonald and S.E. Porter (eds.)

2006   *The Intertextuality of the Epistles: Explorations of Theory and Practice* (NTM, 16; Sheffield: Sheffield Phoenix Press).

Brown, Raymond E.

1961   'Incidents That Are Units in the Synoptic Gospels but Dispersed in St. John', *CBQ* 23: 143-60.

1968a   'The Gospel Miracles', in R. E. Brown (ed.), 'Aspects of New Testament Thought', *JBC* 78:109-30.

1968b   'Hermeneutics', *JBC* 71.

1971   'Jesus and Elisha', *Perspective* 12: 86-104.

Bultmann, Rudolf

1931   *Die Geschichte der synoptischen Tradition* (Göttingen: Vandenhoeck & Ruprecht, 2nd edn [1st edn, 1921; 3rd edn with supplement, 1958]).

1963   *The History of the Synoptic Tradition* (New York: Harper & Row; Eng. trans. of 1958 edn of *Die Geschichte*).

Burkert, Walter

1992   *The Orientalizing Revolution: The Near Eastern Influence on Greek Culture in the Early Archaic Age* (Cambridge, MA: Harvard University Press; German original, 1984).

Byrskog, Samuel

2004   'A New Perspective on the Jesus Tradition: Reflections on James D.G. Dunn's *Jesus Remembered*', *JSNT* 26: 459-71.

Callebat, L.

1964   'L'archaïsme dans les Métamorphoses d'Apulée', *REL* 42: 346-61.

Campbell, Robin

1969   *Seneca: Letters from a Stoic* (Penguin Classics; Harmondsworth: Penguin Books).

Carmichael, Calum M.

1979   *Women, Law, and the Genesis Traditions* (Edinburgh: Edinburgh University Press).

Charlesworth, M.P., and G.B. Townsend
1970 'Tacitus', in *Oxford Classical Dictionary* (Oxford: Clarendon Press, 2nd edn): 1034-35.
Cheney, Emily
2000 'Pilate, Pontius', in *EDB*, 1058.
Collins, John N.
2010 'Rethinking "Eyewitnesses" in the Light of "Servants of the Word" (Luke 1:2)', *ExpTim* 121: 447-52.
Collins, T.A., and R.E. Brown
1968 'Church Pronouncements', *JBC* 72.
Congar, Yves
1964 *Power and Poverty in the Church* (London: Chapman).
Craig, J.D.
1927 'Archaism in Terence', *The Classical Quarterly* 21: 90-94.
Crawford, Barry
2009 Review of Brodie, MacDonald and Porter, eds., *Epistles*, *CBQ* 71: 220-21.
Cruse, C.F.
1998 *Eusebius' Ecclesiastical History* (Peabody, MA: Hendrickson).
Culpepper, R.A.
1975 *The Johannine School: An Evaluation of the Johannine School Hypothesis Based on an Investigation of the Nature of Ancient Schools* (SBLDS, 26; Missoula, MT: Scholars Press).
1983 *Anatomy of the Fourth Gospel* (Philadelphia: Fortress Press).
Daly, Robert J.
2005 'Eucharistic Origins: From the New Testament to the Liturgies of the Golden Age', *Theological Studies* 66: 3-22.
Davies, Philip R.
1992 *In Search of 'Ancient Israel'* (JSOTSup, 148; Sheffield: JSOT Press).
Dunn, James D.G.
2003 *Christianity in the Making*. I. *Jesus Remembered* (Grand Rapids: Eerdmans).
2004 'On History, Memory and Eyewitnesses: In Response to Bengt Holmberg and Samuel Byrskog', *JSNT* 26: 473-87.
2009 *Christianity in the Making*. II. *Beginning from Jerusalem* (Grand Rapids: Eerdmans).
Ehrman, Bart D.
2012 *Did Jesus Exist? The Historical Argument for Jesus of Nazareth* (New York: Harper One).
Eliot, T.S.
1944 *Four Quartets* (London: Faber & Faber).
Ellis, E.E.
1993 'Paul and his Co-workers', in Gerald F. Hawthorne and Ralph P. Martin (eds.), *Dictionary of Paul and his Letters* (Downers Grove, IL: InterVarsity Press).
Evans, C.F.
1955 'The Central Section of Luke's Gospel', in D.E. Nineham (ed.), *Studies in the Gospels* (Festschrift R.H. Lightfoot; Oxford: Blackwell): 37-53.

Fagels, Robert (trans.)
1996   *The Odyssey* (New York: Penguin).
Feine, Paul
1891   *Eine vorkanonische Überlieferung des Lukas im Evangelium und Apostelgeschichte* (Gotha: Friedrich Andreas Perthes).
Fischel, H.A.
1975   'The Transformation of Wisdom in the World of Midrash', in R.L. Wilken (ed.), *Aspects of Wisdom in Judaism and Early Christianity* (Notre Dame: University of Notre Dame Press): 67-101.
Fishbane, M.
1985   *Biblical Interpretation in Ancient Israel* (New York: Oxford University Press).
Fitzmyer, Joseph A.
1981   *The Gospel According to Luke I–IX* (AB, 28; Garden City, NY: Doubleday).
1985   *The Gospel according to Luke X–XXIV* (AB, 28; Garden City, NY: Doubleday).
1990   'Paul', in *NJBC* 79.
1992a   *Responses to 101 Questions on the Dead Sea Scrolls* (London: Chapman).
1992b   'A Palestinian Collection of Beatitudes', in van Segbroeck *et al.* (eds.) 1992: I, 509-15.
1992c   *Romans* (AB, 33; New York: Doubleday).
1995   *The Biblical Commission's Document 'The Interpretation of the Bible in the Church', Text and Commentary* (Subsidia biblica, 18; Rome: Pontificio Istituto Biblico).
2007   *The One Who Is to Come* (Grand Rapids: Eerdmans).
Fleddermann, Harry
2005   *Q: A Reconstruction and Commentary* (Biblical Texts and Tools, 1; Leuven: Peeters).
Fletcher-Louis, Crispin
2009   'A New Explanation of Christological Origins: A Review of the Work of Larry W. Hurtado', *Tyndale Bulletin* 60: 162-205.
2011   'The Influence of Q on the Formation of the Third Gospel' (paper delivered at the Annual SBL Meeting, San Francisco, 19 November).
Gamble, Harry Y.
1995   *Books and Readers in the Early Church: A History of Early Christian Texts* (New Haven: Yale University Press).
Gardner-Smith, Percy
1938   *Saint John and the Synoptic Gospels* (Cambridge: Cambridge University Press).
Gaston, Lloyd
1970   *No Stone on Another: Studies in the Significance of the Fall of Jerusalem in the Synoptic Gospels* (Leiden: E.J. Brill).
Geiger, Joseph
2008   *The First Hall of Fame: A Study of the Statues in the Forum Augustum* (Mnemosyne Supplements, 295; Leiden: E.J. Brill).

Gladd, Benjamin L.
  2008   *Revealing the Mysterion: The Use of Mystery in Daniel and Second Temple Judaism with its Bearing on First Corinthians* (BZNW, 160; Berlin: W. de Gruyter).
Grassi, Joseph A.
  1972   'The Wedding at Cana (John 2:1-11): A Pentecostal Meditation?', *Novum Testamentum* 14: 123-28.
Gunkel, H.
  1901   *Genesis, übersetzt und erklärt* (Göttingen: Vandenhoeck & Ruprecht; Eng. trans. *Genesis* [Macon, GA: Mercer University Press, 1997]).
  1926   *Die Psalmen* (Göttingen: Vandenhoeck & Ruprecht).
  1933   *Einleitung in die Psalmen* (Göttingen: Vandenhoeck & Ruprecht).
Gunn, David M.
  2001   'The Myth of Israel: Between Present and Past', in Lester L. Grabbe (ed.), *Did Moses Speak Attic? Jewish Historiography and Scripture in the Hellenistic Period* (JSOTSup, 317; Sheffield: Sheffield Academic Press): 182-99.
Habel, Norman
  1965   'The Call and Significance of the Call Narrative', *ZAW* 77: 297-323.
Haenchen, Ernst
  1971   *The Acts of the Apostles: A Commentary* (Philadelphia: Westminster Press).
Harrington, Daniel, and Maura P. Horgan
  1986   'Palestinian Adaptations of Biblical Narratives and Prophecies, I. The Bible Rewritten (Narratives)' and 'II. The Bible Explained (Prophecies)', in R.A. Kraft and W.E. Nickelsburg (eds.), *Early Judaism and its Modern Interpreters* (Atlanta: Scholars Press): 239-47, 247-53.
Harrington, Wilfrid J.
  1965a   *Record of the Fulfilment: The New Testament* (Chicago, IL: Priory Press).
  1965b   *Record of the Promise: The Old Testament* (Chicago, IL: Priory Press).
Hartley, L.P.
  1953   *The Go-Between* (London: Penguin Books).
Hassan, Ihab H.
  1977   'The Problem of Influence in Literary History: Notes Towards a Definition', in Ronald Primeau (ed.), *Influx: Essays on Literary Influence* (Port Washington, NY: Kennikat): 20-41.
Hay, David M.
  2000   'Philo of Alexandria', in *EDB*: 1052.
Hays, Richard B.
  1983   *The Faith of Jesus Christ: An Investigation of the Narrative Substructure of Galatians 3:1–4:11* (SBLDS, 56; Chico, CA: SBL; 2nd edn, Grand Rapids: Eerdmans, 2002).
  1989   *Echoes of Scripture in the Letters of Paul* (New Haven: Yale University Press).
  2005   *The Conversion of the Imagination: Paul as Interpreter of Israel's Scripture* (Grand Rapids: Eerdmans).
  2009a   'The Liberation of Israel in Luke–Acts: Intertextual Narration as Countercultural Practice', in Hays *et al.* (eds.) 2009: 101-18.
  2009b   Introduction to Hays *et al.* (eds.) 2009.

Hays, Richard B. *et al.* (eds.)
 2009 *Reading the Bible Intertextually* (Waco, TX: Baylor University Press).
Heffernan, Martin
 2009 'Acts 1–8 as a Component of John 1–4' (PhD diss., University of Limerick).
Hilkert, Mary Catherine
 1997 *Naming Grace: Preaching and the Sacramental Imagination* (New York: Continuum).
Holmberg, Bengt
 2004 'Questions of Method in James Dunn's *Jesus Remembered*', *JSNT* 26: 445-57.
Horrell, David
 2006 *Introduction to the Study of Paul* (London: Continuum).
Irish Dominican Chapter
 1996 *Acts, Provincial Chapter, 1996*, Part II (Tallaght, Dublin: St Mary's Dominican Priory).
Johnson, Luke Timothy
 1998 *Religious Experience in Earliest Christianity: A Missing Dimension in New Testament Studies* (Minneapolis: Fortress Press).
Joines, Karen, and Eric Mitchell
 2003 'Jericho', in C. Brand *et al.* (eds.), *Holman Illustrated Bible Dictionary* (Nashville, TN: Holman Reference): 885-88.
Kazantzakis, Nikos
 1965 *Report to Greco* (New York: Simon & Schuster).
Kingsmill, Edmée
 2010 *The Song of Songs and the Eros of God: A Study in Biblical Intertextuality* (Oxford: Oxford University Press).
Koch, D.A.
 1986 *Die Schrift als Zeuge des Evangeliums. Untersuchungen zur Verwendung und zum Verständnis der Schrift bei Paulus* (BHT, 69; Tübingen: Mohr).
Körner, Bernhard
 2000 'Jesus Must Be Catholic', in T. Merrigan and J. Haers (eds.), *The Myriad Christ: Plurality and the Quest for Unity in Contemporary Christology* (BETL, 152; Leuven: Peeters): 417-32.
Kowalski, Beate
 2004 *Die Rezeption des Propheten Ezekiel in der Offenbarung* (SBB, 52; Stuttgart: Katholisches Bibelwerk).
Kselman, John S.
 1968 'Modern New Testament', in *JBC*: 41.
Kuhn, Thomas S.
 1996 *The Structure of Scientific Revolutions* (Chicago: University of Chicago Press, 3rd edn).
Kümmel, W.G.
 1972 *The New Testament: The History of the Investigation of its Problems* (Nashville: Abingdon Press).
 1975 *Introduction to the New Testament* (Nashville: Abingdon Press).

Leake, Johathan
    2010   'D'oh, We May Never Decode the Universe', *The Sunday Times* (13 June): 5.
Lechte, J.
    1994   *Fifty Key Contemporary Thinkers: From Structuralism to Postmodernity* (London: Routledge).
Le Donne, Anthony
    2009   *The Historiographical Jesus: Memory, Typology, and Son of David* (Waco, TX: Baylor University Press).
Lemaire, André
    1992   *Les écoles et la formation de la Bible dans l'ancien Israël* (OBO, 39; Göttingen: Vandenhoeck & Ruprecht).
Levinson, Bernard
    1977   *Deuteronomy and the Hermeneutics of Legal Innovation* (Oxford: Oxford University Press).
Lipiński, E.
    1988   'Royal and State Scribes in Ancient Jerusalem', in J.A. Emerton (ed.), *Congress Volume: Jerusalem, 1986* (VTSup, 40; Leiden: E.J. Brill): 157-64.
Lyons, George
    1985   *Pauline Autobiography: Toward a New Understanding* (SBLDS, 73; Atlanta: SBL).
MacDonald, Dennis R.
    2000   *The Homeric Epics and the Gospel of Mark* (New Haven, CT: Yale University Press).
Mason, Steve
    2000   'Josephus', *EDB*: 736-37.
    2003   *Josephus and the New Testament* (Peabody, MA: Hendrickson, 2nd edn).
Martini, C.
    2008   *The Gospel according to St Paul: Meditations on his Life and Letters* (Ijamsville, MD: The Word Among Us Press).
Matthews, Robert
    2012   'Unravelling the Fabric of the Universe: What the Tiniest Details Tell Us about the Nature of Reality', *BBC Focus* 239 (March): 37-43.
McGrath, Alister
    2009   *A Fine-Tuned Universe: The Quest for God in Science in Theology* (Louisville, KY: Westminster/John Knox Press).
McIver, Robert K.
    2011   *Memory, Jesus and the Synoptic Gospels* (Atlanta: SBL).
McMullin, Ernan
    2010   'Galileo and the Church' (address to a Faraday Institute Course on Science and Religion, Dublin City University, 26 June).
Meier, John
    1991   *A Marginal Jew: Rethinking the Historical Jesus*. I. *The Roots of the Problem and the Person* (ABRL; New York: Doubleday).
    1994   *A Marginal Jew: Rethinking the Historical Jesus*. II. *Mentor, Message and Miracles* (ABRL; New York: Doubleday).

2001   *A Marginal Jew: Rethinking the Historical Jesus*. III. *Companions and Competitors* (ABRL; New York: Doubleday).

2009   *A Marginal Jew: Rethinking the Historical Jesus*. IV. *Law and Love* (ABRL; New Haven, CT: Yale University Press).

Meyers, Eric M.

1992   'Synagogue', in *ABD*, VI: 251-60.

Miller, J. Maxwell, and John H. Hayes

1986   *A History of Ancient Israel and Judah* (Louisville, KY: Westminster John Knox Press).

Moriarty, John

1999   *Dreamtime* (Dublin: Lilliput, rev. edn).

Müller, P.

1988   *Anfänge der Paulusschule. Dargestellt am zweiten Thessalonischerbrief und am Kolosserbrief* (Abhandlungen zur Theologie des Alten und Neuen Testaments, 74; Zurich: Theologischer Verlag).

Murphy-O'Connor, Jerome

1995   *Paul the Letter-Writer: His World, his Options, his Skills* (A Michael Glazier Book; Collegeville, MN: Liturgical Press).

1996   *Paul: A Critical Life* (Oxford: Oxford University Press).

Murray, Paul

1991   *T.S. Eliot and Mysticism: The Secret History of Four Quartets* (London: Macmillan).

Neill, Stephen, and Tom Wright

1988   *The Interpretation of the New Testament, 1861–1986* (Oxford: Oxford University Press).

Nelligan, Thomas P.

2012   'The Quest for Mark's Sources: An Exploration of the Case for Mark's Use of First Corinthians' (PhD diss., University of Limerick).

Nodet, E., and J. Taylor

1998   *The Origins of Christianity: An Exploration* (Collegeville, MN: Liturgical Press).

North, Robert

1968   'Biblical Archaeology', in *JBC*: 74.

O'Leary, Anne M.

2004   'John's Use of Matthew as a Source in the Context of the Use of Sources in Greco-Roman Antiquity' (PhD diss., University of Limerick). (The first half of this dissertation was published in 2006—see the following entry under O'Leary.)

2006   *Matthew's Judaization of Mark: Examined in the Context of the Use of Sources in Greco-Roman Antiquity* (LNTS, 323; London: T. & T. Clark) (see preceding entry under O'Leary).

Orton, D.E.

1989   *The Understanding Scribe: Matthew and the Apocalyptic Ideal* (JSNTSup, 25; Sheffield: JSOT Press).

Palmer Bonz, Marianne

2000   *The Past as Legacy: Luke–Acts and Ancient Epic* (Minneapolis: Fortress Press).

Pfeiffer, R.H.
    1963   *History of New Testament Times* (London: A. & C. Black).
Polzin, Robert
    1980   *Moses and the Deuteronomist: A Literary Study of the Deuteronomic History, Part I* (Bloomington, IN: Indiana University Press).
Pope Pius XII
    1943   'Divino Afflante Spiritu', in *RSS*: 80-107.
Porter, Stanley E.
    1997   'The Use of the Old Testament in the New Testament: A Brief Comment on Method and Terminology', in C.A. Evans and J.A. Sanders (eds.), *Early Christian Interpretation of the Scriptures of Israel: Investigations and Proposals* (JSNTSup, 14; Sheffield: Sheffield Academic Press): 79-96.
    2006   'Further Comments on the Use of the Old Testament in the New Testament', in Brodie, MacDonald and Porter (eds.) 2006: 98-110.
Praeder, Susan M.
    1980   'The Narrative Voyage: An Analysis and Interpretation of Acts 27–28' (PhD diss., Berkeley, CA: Graduate Theological Union).
Propp, William H.C.
    2000   'Moses', in *EDB*: 919-22.
Puech, E.
    1988   'Les écoles dans l'Israël préexilique: données épigraphiques', in J.A. Emerton (ed.), *Congress Volume: Jerusalem, 1986* (VTSup, 40; Leiden: E.J. Brill): 189-203.
    1988a   'Un hymne essénien en partie retrouvé et les Béatitudes: 1QH V 12–VI 18 (= col. XIII-XIV 7) et 4Q Béat', *Review de Qumran* 13: 59-88.
    1991   '4Q525 et les péricopes des Béatitudes en Ben Sira et Matthieu', *RB* 98: 80-106.
Radcliffe, Timothy
    1999   *Sing a New Song: The Christian Vocation* (Springfield, IL: Templegate Publishers).
Rahner, Karl
    1978   *Foundations of Christian Faith: An Introduction to the Idea of Christianity* (London: Darton, Longman & Todd).
    1979   'Towards a Fundamental Theological Interpretation of Vatican II', *Theological Studies* 40: 716-27.
    1981   *Theological Investigations XX* (trans. Edward Quinn; London: Darton, Longman & Todd).
Reynolds, F.E., and C. Hallisley
    2005   'Buddha', in *Encyclopedia of Religion*, II (Detroit, MI: Thomson–Gale, 2nd edn): 1059-71.
Richards, E.R.
    2004   *Paul and First-Century Letter Writing* (Downers Grove, IL: InterVarsity Press).
Robbins, Vernon K.
    2010   *Sea Voyages and Beyond: Emerging Strategies in Socio-rhetorical Interpretation* (Emory Studies in Early Christianity; Dorset: Deo).

Robinson, Marilynne
    2010   'The Strange History of Altruism', in *Absence of Mind: The Dispelling of Inwardness from the Modern Myth of the Self* (New Haven, CT: Yale University Press): 31-75.

Rogerson, J.W.
    2006   'Israel to the End of the Persian Period', in J.W. Rogerson and Judith M. Lieu (eds.), *The Oxford Handbook of Biblical Studies* (Oxford: Oxford University Press): 268-84.

Roudiez, Leon S.
    1980   *Desire in Language: A Semiotic Approach to Literature and Art* (New York: Columbia University Press).

Ruiten, J.T.A.G.M. van
    1992   'The Intertextual Relationship Between Isa 11,6-9 and Isa 65,25', in F. García Martínez *et al.* (eds.), *The Scriptures and the Scrolls* (VTSup, 49; Festschrift A.S. Van der Woude; Leiden: E.J. Brill): 31-42.

Sarason, R.S.
    1981   'Towards a New Agendum for the Study of Rabbinic Midrashic Literature', in E. Fleischer and J.J. Petuchowski (eds.), *Studies in Aggadah, Targum and Jewish Liturgy in Memory of Joseph Heinemann* (Jerusalem: Magnes Press).

Sawyer, John
    1993   *Prophecy and Biblical Prophets* (New York: Oxford University Press).

Scheid, John, and Jesper Svenbro
    1966   *The Craft of Zeus: Myths of Weaving and Fabric* (Cambridge, MA: Harvard University Press).

Schoot, Henk J.M.
    2000   'Aquinas and de León', in T. Merrigan and J. Haers (eds.), *The Myriad Christ: Plurality and the Quest for Unity in Contemporary Christology* (BETL, 152; Leuven: Peeters): 331-47.

Schneiders, Sandra S.
    1998   'The Study of Christian Spirituality: Contours and Dynamics of a Discipline', *Christian Spirituality Bulletin* 8: 38-57.

Schweitzer, Albert
    1910   *The Quest of the Historical Jesus: A Critical Study of its Progress from Reimarus to Wrede* (London: A. & C. Black, 1910; German original, 1906).

Segbroeck, F. van *et al.* (eds.)
    1992   *The Four Gospels 1992* (Festschrift Frans Neirynck; BETL, 100; 3 vols.; Leuven: Leuven University Press/Peeters).

Sevenster, Albert
    1961   *Paul and Seneca* (Leiden: E.J. Brill).

Shelton, John
    2012   'The Puzzle of the Centurion (Luke 7, Matthew 8) and the Royal Official (John 4)' (PhD diss., University of Limerick).

Smith, Dennis E.
    2002   *From Symposium to Eucharist: The Banquet in the Early Christian World* (Minneapolis: Fortress Press).

Sobel, Dava
    2000   *Galileo's Daughter* (New York: Penguin Books).
Spencer, Richard A.
    2000   'Stoics', in *EDB*: 1252-53.
Stackert, Jeffrey
    2007   *Rewriting the Torah* (FAT, 52; Tübingen: Mohr Siebeck).
Stanley, C.D.
    1992   *Paul and the Language of Scripture: Citation Technique in the Pauline Epistles and Contemporary Literature* (Cambridge: Cambridge University Press).
    2004   *Arguing with Scripture: The Rhetoric of Quotations in the Letters of Paul* (London: T. & T. Clark).
Steiner, G.
    1975   *After Babel: Aspects of Language and Translation* (New York: Oxford University Press).
Stendahl, K.
    1954   *The School of St Matthew and its Use of the Old Testament* (Acta seminarii neotestamentici upsaliensis, 20; Lund: Gleerup).
Sterling, Gregory E.
    1992   *Historiography and Self-Definition: Josephus, Luke–Acts and Apologetic Historiography* (Novum Testamentum Supplement, 44; Leiden: E.J. Brill).
Stockhausen, Carol K.
    1989   *Moses' Veil and the Story of the New Covenant: The Exegetical Substructure of II Cor. 3.1–4.6* (AnBib, 116; Rome: Pontifical Biblical Institute).
    1993   '2 Corinthians 3 and the Principles of Pauline Exegesis', in C.A. Evans and J.A. Sanders (eds.), *Paul and the Scriptures of Israel* (JSNTSup, 83; Sheffield: Sheffield Academic Press): 143-64.
Stott, Katherine M.
    2008   *Why Did They Write This Way? Reflections on References to Written Documents in the Hebrew Bible and Ancient Literature* (JSOTSup, 492; New York: T. & T. Clark).
Stroumsa, Guy G.
    1998   'The Christian Hermeneutical Revolution and its Double Helix', in L.V. Rutgers *et al.* (eds.), *The Use of Sacred Books in the Ancient World* (Contributions to Biblical Theology and Exegesis, 22; Leuven: Peeters): 9-28.
    2009   *The End of Sacrifice: Religious Transformations in Late Antiquity* (Chicago, IL: University of Chicago Press).
Svebakken, Hans
    2010   'Exegetical Traditions in Alexandria: Philo's Reworking of the *Letter of Aristeas 145-149* as a Case Study', in Patricia Walters (ed.), *From Judaism to Christianity: Tradition and Transition: A Festschrift for Thomas H. Tobin, S.J.* (Novum Testamentum Supplements; Leiden: E.J. Brill): 93-112.
Talbert, C.H. (ed.)
    1984   *Luke–Acts: New Perspectives from the Society of Biblical Literature Seminar* (New York: Crossroad).

Tatum, Gregory
    2006   *New Chapters in the Life of Paul: The Relative Chronology of his Career* (CBQMS, 41; Washington, DC: Catholic Biblical Association).

Thatcher, Tom (ed.)
    2007   *What We Have Heard from the Beginning*: *The Past, Present and Future of Johannine Studies* (Waco, TX: Baylor University Press).

Thompson, Michael B.
    1998   'The Holy Internet: Communications Between Churches in the First Century Generation', in Bauckham (ed.) 1998: 49-70.

Thompson, Thomas L.
    1974   *The Historicity of the Patriarchal Narratives: The Quest for the Historical Abraham* (Berlin: W. de Gruyter).

Tobin, Thomas H.
    1983   *The Creation of Man. Philo and the History of Interpretation* (CBQMS, 14; Washington, DC: Catholic Biblical Association).

Treacy, Bernard, with Frances M. Young, J. Cecil McCullough and Thomas Brodie (eds.)
    2009   *Reading Scripture for Living the Christian Life* (A Doctrine and Life Special; Dublin: Dominican Publications).

Ulrich, Eugene
    2000   'Dead Sea Scrolls', in *EDB*: 326-29.

Underhill, Evelyn
    1930   *Mysticism: A Study of the Nature and Development of Man's Spiritual Consciousness* (London: Methuen, 12th edn).

Utzschneider, H.
    1989   *Künder oder Schreiber? Eine These zum Problem der 'Schriftprophetie' auf Grund von Malachi 1,6–2,9* (Beiträge zur Erforschung des Alten Testaments und des antiken Judentums, 19; Frankfurt: Peter Lang).

Van Hoozer, K.J.
    2002   *First Theology: God, Scripture and Hermeneutics* (Downers Grove, IL: InterVarsity Press).

Van Seters, John
    1975   *Abraham in History and Tradition* (New Haven, CT: Yale University Press).
    2006   *The Edited Bible: The Curious History of the 'Editor' in Biblical Criticism* (Winona Lake, IN: Eisenbrauns).

Volkmar, Gustav
    1876   *Marcus und die Synopse der Evangelien nach dem urkundlichen Text und das Geschichtliche vom Leben Jesu* (Zurich: Schmidt).

Young, Frances
    2000   'Christology and Creation', in T. Merrigan and J. Haers (eds.), *The Myriad Christ: Plurality and the Quest for Unity in Contemporary Christology* (BETL, 152; Leuven: Peeters): 191-205.

Walsh, J.T.
    1996   *1 Kings* (Berit Olam. Studies in Hebrew Narrative and Poetry; A Michael Glazier Book; Collegeville, MN: Liturgical Press).

Walsh, P.G.
    1961   *Livy: His Historical Aims and Methods* (Cambridge: Cambridge University Press).

Wang, Stephen
    2010   'God and Nothingness: Sartre Revisited', *Tablet* (20 February): 8-9.
Wansbrough, Henry
    2010   'Relighting the Fire of Scripture', *The Tablet* (11 December): 6-7.
Weigend, G.G. *et al.*
    2003   'Mediterranean Sea', in *Encyclopaedia Britannica, Macropaedia* (Chicago, IL: Encyclopaedia Britannica), XIV: 307-10.
Weinfeld, M.
    1972   *Deuteronomy and the Deuteronomic School* (Oxford: Clarendon Press).
Wellhausen, J.
    1876   *Die Composition des Hexateuchs und der historischen Bücher des Alten Testaments* (Berlin: Georg Reimer).
Wesselius, Jan-Wim
    2001   'The Writing of Daniel', in J.J. Collins and P.W. Flint (eds.), *The Book of Daniel: Composition and Reception* (VTSup, 83/2; Leiden: E.J. Brill): 291-310.
Wilson, A.N.
    2009a   'Why I Believe Again', *New Statesman* (2 April).
    2009b   'Religion of Hatred', *Daily Mail* (11 April).
Wikipedia
    2010   'Joseph Barber Lightfoot' (accessed 30 April).
Winn, Adam
    2010   *Mark and the Elijah–Elisha Narrative* (Eugene, OR: Wipf & Stock).
Wright, David P.
    2009   *Inventing God's Law: How the Covenant Code of the Bible Used and Revised the Laws of Hammurabi* (Oxford: Oxford University Press).
Wright, N.T.
    2005   *Paul: In Fresh Perspective* (Minneapolis: Fortress Press).
Yarbro Collins, Adela
    2007   *Mark: A Commentary* (Hermeneia; Minneapolis: Augsburg Fortress).
Young, Frances
    2000   'Christology and Creation', in T. Merrigan and J. Haers (eds.), *The Myriad Christ: Plurality and the Quest for Unity in Contemporary Christology* (BETL, 152; Leuven: Peeters): 191-205.

INDEX OF REFERENCES

INDEX OF AUTHORS

INDEX OF SUBJECTS

Lightning Source UK Ltd.
Milton Keynes UK
UKHW022020040620
364445UK00006B/1257